THE
TRIUMPH

GLEN ALLSHOUSE

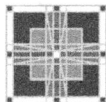

Letcetera
PUBLISHING
CHICAGO

ISBN: 979-8-396486-84-3

DESIGNED & PRODUCED BY
Letcetera, Ltd.
www.letcetarapublishing.com

"There is only Christ, He is everything." — Colossians 3:11

ACKNOWLEDGEMENTS

I am very grateful to two of my friends,
Laurel Anderson and David Cook, who spent
many hours proofreading and correcting numerous errors
as well as providing very good suggestions for changes to
certain phrases. I am also indebted to Kathryn McBride
for helping me publish this novel, creating the
book cover and completing finishing touches.

I also want to thank my wife, Elaine, for her
encouragement and excitement in what I do.

PROLOGUE

This story is about a sweet old man who puts his trust in God in all that he endeavors from helping a little boy who was erroneously taken from his mother and then rejoined with her, to saving the life of his great-grandson who was in immediate danger of death by abortion.

In life, Christians think, pray, and try to act in accordance with God's word which this story reflects that so clearly.

Some of the events of this book are very similar to my own experiences. I have personally felt the hurt and dilemmas of Doug Wisp. I have personally heard confessions similar to that of Kelly. So much of this story brings back delightful memories of my life in the mountains and working with Christian Service Brigade.

There is romance, humor, adventure, and drama throughout this story. It has been 25 years in the making and I feel the time I spent writing this story was well worth it. But read it and see for yourself. Enjoy!

At the end of this book is a list of names of characters and a description of who they are. I found this list helpful to me in writing this novel. As a name comes up, many chapters after it was introduced, the list will help clue you in as to who that person was.

Glen Allshouse
February 2023

CONTENTS

CHAPTER 1

THE BEGINNING
of the MEMORIES

There was standing room only at Washington Park, as Pastor Tim Weber asked Thomas Atkins to come on stage for his presentation of "Every Life, Priceless" as part of the celebration of Sanctity of Life Sunday. It was only fitting to have this young man lead the long list of speakers. Tommy turned the tide of human emotion against abortion. This eventually led to last year's renowned U.S. Supreme Court decision to make illegal, by federal law, the horror and absurdity of the abortion of infants for any reason other than the life of the mother and to shut down Planned Parenthood and other abortion operations. According to the outcome of the decision, for an abortion to be approved, the danger of the woman's life must be proven to, and accepted by, a specialized panel of doctors directly under the authority of the US Surgeon General. Tommy's life being spared was not in vain. The purpose of this gathering was to celebrate this decision, give God glory for the accomplishments of the Pro-Life movement, and ask for divine guidance and additional miraculous events that would lead to the sparing of other innocent lives.

Cheers and gestures of gladness permeated throughout this great crowd as Tommy came to the microphone. His voice was soft and timid as he spoke. All were silent and eager to hear his message. This young man, an honor graduate of the class of 2024 of the CSU Medical School, had lobbied for and made many successful achievements for the Pro-Life movement. He debated and crushed every proponent of Euthanasia, and enabled California to take the leading role in eliminating state laws (one by one) that condoned and even promoted suicide and assisted suicide.

Not far into his speech, his eyes watered as he made an introduction of his most trusted mentor, his friend and loving great-grandfather, Tom

Wisp. Not a soul was left sitting, not a face was without a smile or look of joy, as the old gentleman approached the stage. His cane wobbled as he slowly made his way to the steps. This was no ordinary man. Yes, his stature was small, but his character was that of a giant. His love was so evident, his faith so strong, and his stand so steadfast. He was unknown to some, but to this flock of Pro-Life supporters and to Christian congregations across America, he was a hero. He would never attribute his endeavors to his own ability, but as proof of the power of Christ and the grace of God.

In his thoughts, Tom was remembering. Remembering his great-grandson, the events before and after Tommy's birth, and the ordeal that led to this very moment. Wasn't it yesterday? Could it be true that so many years had passed? But the years were good to Tom, his memory intact. Even now he recalled every detail of what led to that fateful day and how it all started.

· · · · · ·

Ring, Ring, Ring!!! Normally during his early morning-prayer time, Tom would have the telephone volume down low, so his ever important talk with the Lord would be uninterrupted. As the ringing persisted, he finished his prayer, and stood from his knees to reach for the telephone.

"Good morning and bless you, my friend!" This was often Tom's greeting to early callers. "Good morning, Grandaddy, please may I come to visit you next month?" Kelly's voice was cheerful and giggly as she continued her conversation, not waiting for an immediate answer. "It has been more than a month since I've seen you, and I have so much to talk about with you, I mean about me and my friends and so many things happening this very month. It is nearing the end of the school year, and I just have two more years left in high school. Have you started dying your hair yet? Maybe I could help! I've dyed my hair three times this year so I am really getting to be quite an expert at it. I even chose the hair color for several of my friends and helped them. So you see......"

Her message was cut short by a deep resonant chuckle. "My child, whatever in the Lord's creation gave you the idea that I would even think of changing my hair color. I thought you liked my natural color of gray!" Tom pretended to be a little put out at her change in attitude about his hair.

Kelly was eager to explain, "Oh yes, but last week I saw this elderly man who worked at the CD shop, and he had the coolest silvery gray head of hair, even finer than yours. I just had to ask him about it. He told me the exact brand and color he used to get it that way." The humor of the topic was starting to turn, and Tom knew if he did not control the conversation it could continue for hours. He loved listening to his grandchildren, especially Kelly, his oldest and most precious, but not on the telephone this early in the morning. As she continued to talk and talk, Tom was completing his entries in his planner for the busy day ahead, all the while listening with sincerity and interest.

It was time he made his move. "In regard to your request for the weekend sleepover, it is a joy having you here anytime. Each morning the birds sing your song, hoping for your return to join them with your operatic soprano supreme. And the squirrels miss you too. Munchi and Dusty knock on the windows continuously in your room like playmates seeking out their best friend."

The guest room was designed specifically for Kelly, since she was the first grandchild. The forest green color wallpaper and carpet and a forest scene mural on one of the walls contained various mountain birds and, off to the side, a small flock of mourning doves in the background. Most teenagers would have considered the room too childish, but not Kelly. She loved animals and that room displayed such a beauty of the woodlands with animal figurines all about and a window view of the lake and forest. The flagstone fireplace was a special attraction. Tom built it himself and created little stone shelves with each displaying a little stuffed animal.

"Oh Grandaddy, you are so funny! How is Grandma? I have been praying for her every night." At this point she expressed concern because her grandmother had been ill for a few weeks.

"She is doing very well, Kelly-Joy. Yesterday she was up and about, almost back to her old spry self. I tried to tell her that I could handle the dishes just fine, but don't you know she insisted on completing her work in the kitchen and even restacked the dishes in the cupboard. It seems that you are the only one that can put things away how she likes. Thank you for your prayers! I know they played a big role in her recovery."

Even though her grandfather was retired from a southern California engineering firm, he kept busy counseling those in the church with troubled marriages, giving seminars on financial budgeting, and monitoring court hearings for the California Children's Defense League (CCDL). Then there were those many hours on his knees before God. He was always encouraging and non-judgmental. His Christ-like love for everyone just seemed to flow from him in every remark and gesture. Kelly thought that the romance he and her grandmother had with each other was so cute. Even after all these years, they would often hug and flirt with each other, write poetry of love to each other, and take long walks, hand in hand. How often she had hoped her own mother and father would have that kind of lasting love. However, their divorce became final last month and it seemed hopeless. But still, she kept praying for them.

Kelly remarked, "Oh, did you finish my painting yet? I can't wait to hang it in my room! After I have it here in my bedroom, whenever I look at the stream, the log bridge, and the waterfall, I'll think of you there at Fernview Cottage." Excited about the prospects of bringing the painting home for her newly decorated room, she danced about with the telephone in her hand, tangling the cord around her body.

Tom responded, "Yes, yes, and I have it all framed and ready for you. Of course, you know this painting does not give proper justice to the real thing, so you make sure you're able to come next month. The irises in Shelby's Court are in full bloom and the dogwood blossoms provide a white canopy wherever you go. Look, we better say goodbye now. Give your mother a big hug for me and tell her that I don't think it will be long before I see some mourning doves in the meadow here at Woodridge Falls." Tom always ended a message to Mary in that way. He tried his best to encourage Doug and Mary to work out their problems, and they both appreciated his efforts, but Mary was certain the love she felt for Doug was gone, gone forever. During the last session he had with them before the divorce, she told Tom that "mourning doves would flock to Woodridge Falls before I have any feelings for your son again!"

The altitude of this region prevents the many doves in the valley below from making any visits to the meadows and hills of the mountains. Decades ago there used to be flocks here but no longer. This expression was common to people there, but Tom continued to believe, as did Kelly.

Kelly smiled at her grandfather's gesture of hope and at the same time a tear made its way from the corner of her eye to the edge of her lips. "Bye, Grandaddy. I love you!" then she whispered, "I love you very much!"

"Goodbye, my Kelly-Joy. I love you too." He slowly dropped the receiver to its place and said a silent prayer for her.

During that month, Tom made his weekly trips to Vale Road to join the small group of abortion protesters. Dr. Willis lived a block from their meeting place, and the Pro-Life activists met there to pray and hold up signs along the road in an attempt to reach the calloused conscience of the abortionist. It was now the last week of April and it was especially important to be there. Another abortionist from the distant city of Cortez was visiting Dr. Willis for the weekend. As the younger doctor drove up the road with the senior Dr. Willis at his side, his facial nerves tightened with anger at the sight of the gathering ahead. The passenger smiled at the young doctor and touched his shoulder.

Dr. Willis spoke candidly, "Bob, they're just a few local yokels. Don't let them get you riled. Just smile and wave. After all, you know they have our best interest at heart!" This last comment had more than just a hint of sarcasm. "They want to convert us, save our souls, and help us get right with God!"

Bob Logan spoke harshly, "Yeah! Right! Look at them! Faces of angels but hearts of stone. They don't fool me. If they had their way they would string us up right here and now. Where are the police? If this was Cortez, the riot squad would not put up with this. Why do you take this? You don't have to, you know!"

With a smile still on his face, Dr. Willis replied, "Why make waves? These are my neighbors."

Bob quickly returned, "Some neighbors they are. Look at that sign over there! Hey, there's one with my name on it! How did they know I was here?"

The elder doctor grunted, "Woodridge Falls is a small town. We're big news around here. These old timers and losers have nothing else to do but hassle us 'well to do' doctors. They're partially just jealous, I guess. A few might be sincere to the cause, being so pious and self-righteous."

Bob quickly hit the brakes of the car, "That does it! That little boy has a sign that calls us murderers."

Dr. Willis reached for Bob's shirt, "What are you going to do? He's just a boy, with parents who are probably making him carry that."

"We'll see!" Bob shouted as he opened the door. "You people get out of here, or I'll call the police right now and have you all arrested. Especially you, you little brat!"

He was pointing at Jimmy Silvers and started towards him with fists clenched. Positioned in front of the boy, Bob's foot was high in the air as he made his stance to kick through the sign. Suddenly Bob found himself on the ground looking up at the boy who was now smiling at him and extending out his arm to help the doctor from his awkward position on the street. He quickly pushed the little arm away as his anger turned to fury. He lifted himself from the roadside and turned to look for the intruder. Tom was just re-positioning his cane as Bob thrust his face, with cold deep eyes, nose to nose with the elderly gentleman.

Tom stood confident and strong. His eyes, rather than full of fear or anger, were twinkling with joy, as he started to brush the dirt from the young doctor's coat.

"What are you doing?" Bob asked, pushing the large rough palms away from his coat.

Tom ignored his question and with a very serious expression whispered, "Do you really think you would have walked away from here if you had harmed that child." Bob looked at the boy, and then back at Tom. He was taken by surprise at the old gentleman's calmness.

"You see," Tom went on whispering, "Jimmy is a miracle child to us! Oh, he still has scars on his back and arms from the salt solution, but he survived the horror of an abortion. As you know, seldom is a child so fortunate. His thinking is just a mite slow from his initial lack of oxygen, but he has a heart of gold that more than makes up for it."

Bob glanced back at the small arm that was once extended to him in friendship and noticed the skin which showed burn scars from the elbow up.

Tom went on, "Then there's Maggie, there in the blue blouse. Pretty isn't she! She has great despair since she will never bear children due to errors performed during an abortion."

Bob blasted out, "Every surgical procedure has its risks, even the minor ones!"

"Yes!" Tom's head was tilted to one side as he looked at the young man from the corner of his eyes. "But that was an unnecessary 'surgical procedure' as are all abortions, and it took the life of her child. Neither she nor her mother wanted the abortion, but a school teacher talked her into it without even notifying her parents."

It was becoming evident to Bob that this group of protesters was not there out of jealousy or to find some sort of perverse entertainment, but were really committed to what they were doing and for good reasons. But he could not afford to let himself get concerned about the aftermath of abortion. This was his profession and it was a well paying one. He worked hard to get where he was. With money pouring in the way it had been, in just a short time he would have the largest abortion clinic in the Inland Empire, as this portion of southern California was commonly referred to. Especially now, with the presidential veto of the Partial Birth Abortion ban, he would continue receiving those exorbitant funds from research corporations. He could not let his emotions ruin all that he had attained. He liked the prestige he was getting. He liked not having to worry about finances. He was raised in a poverty stricken neighborhood and during his whole childhood he saw the depression of being poor. When he left home for medical school on a government grant, he was determined to be a millionaire by the age of 35, and it seemed evident that this dream was secure. These protestors would be gone in an instant and things would be 'business as usual'. He just needed to get away from these people, and especially this old man who was just trying to make him feel guilty.

Bob reassured himself, "After all, I am doing a great service to the community and the world. I donate twice the time most doctors do for free service to those who are not eligible for government funding for their abortions. Just last year the President of the United States personally presented me with Planned Parenthood's, Good Samaritan Award for the many articles I submitted to medical journals to improve abortion techniques, especially partial birth abortions by making them safer and faster. This community should be grateful for my efforts. But no, what do I get, jeers and threats. There are actually fewer Maggies because of me. And if the law enforcers would do their jobs, there would be fewer Jimmys too!" As he thought this, he turned to look at Jimmy once more. Then he slowly bowed his head. Internally there was a fierce struggle going on. Quickly he jerked his stature to its full upright position and thought, "I just need to get away from here!"

Bob did not dare look back at the gray haired gentleman, but quickly made his way to the Town Car waiting for him. He could hear the sounds of the crowd asking him to repent. Their shouts, "Seek the Lord!" "Stop the killings!" "You were trained to save lives, not take them!" "Abortion kills children!" echoed through the chambers of his conscience.

He pushed the buttons that would electrically close all of the car windows and hoped this would drown out the messages he was hearing. He said nothing to Dr. Willis, but looked straight ahead and drove as fast as he could. Soon they were all in his dust, as he prepared for the turn ahead. All this time, Dr. Willis was studying Bob intently. "What happened back there? I saw you fall. Are you OK?"

Bob gave a short response, "Yea, I'm OK! I'm just fine."

CHAPTER 2

The COURT HEARING

Kelly's grandmother had spent the day preparing the guest room. She was excited about the upcoming weekend. Humming and then singing Christian hymns, she went about her work dusting, sweeping and cleaning. She did not notice the lean figure standing in the shadow of the doorway. Tom's height was average, but it towered over the short five foot, four inch angel who pranced about the room. His hands were rather large and his shoulders square as he stood. With a delightful little grin, he watched the lady in her graceful moves of toil before him. He placed his cane against the wall outside the doorway. Most of the time he did not really need his cane, but at times, his leg wound from the war would flare and cause him to buckle and fall. There were no warnings when this occurred, so he used the cane as a precaution. He now placed his attention on his lovely wife. As she was dancing with the sweeper, she turned to complete the umbrella walk around the vacuum cleaner. Just then the large palms reached from the doorway and swiftly caught her waist, not missing a move of the fox-trot step.

In mid-turn, Tom glanced at the vacuum cleaner, which continued to hiss and roar, "Sorry Chap, this is our dance, so I just had to cut in."

After completing the last bar she was humming, just as her gentle-natured husband was about to end with a grandeur dip, she stepped back to catch her breath. Giggling, she lightly tapped Tom on the chest. "You nearly startled me out of my wits. Sneaking up on a lady like that, I may have...."

Tom interrupted, "What, bopped me with your broom, feathered me with your duster, or perhaps that 'fate worse than death', blasted me with your 409 cleaning solution!" Tom dramatically continued, "I don't care. It would have been worth it, even to have touched your fair delicate hand, my Sweets."

As he bowed to gently kiss the hand of Janet, she quickly pulled herself from his grasp, "Enough of this! I've got things to do and so do you, young Sir Gallahad. If you turn those gallant eyes to the dining room table, you will find a list I've written for you."

"Hmm", Tom gestured, "I must be losing my charm. It seemed like I could always distract you before. And these lists! Why resort to these frivolous scraps of ink and paper when I have an excellent memory?"

Janet responded, "Well, what about those 'frivolous scraps of ink and paper' I find in the car, in your pockets and on the bathroom mirror?"

"Those aren't lists, not lists at all." Tom remarked. "They are part of a technique I'm using to aid in my memory of Scripture."

Janet smiled that irresistible smile that made her spouse internally quiver from head to toe, "So just apply that 'technique' to those items on the list and I will feel assured that Kelly's visit will be well prepared for."

"All right." Tom surrendered, as he walked to the other room. Then he shouted as he glanced at the Honey Do List, "But these are no menial tasks for a man of my age, engaged in such hardships of labor."

Janet responded, "I'm sure, holding the garden hose over the patio umbrella and using your air blower to clean the driveway and..."

"OK. OK. I'm just kidding." Tom walked to the bedroom to give his wife a long hug and kiss. He then tipped his hat and said, "I will not return until the dragon is slain, the blouse is bagged, and ..."

This time Janet cut him off, "You just get those chores done by noon, and I'll have lunch all ready for you, including your favorite dessert, pumpkin pie."

Tom's eyes, which normally are squinted deep in the socket, suddenly widened as he hopefully questioned, "With whipped cream?"

"Yes, with 'homemade' whipped cream!" came the response.

"Yahoo!" Tom said as he quickly grabbed a cup of coffee. Out the door he went with a list in hand. "TA-TA Duckie!" Of all his pet names for Janet, Tom liked this the best. They had met in a park as she was feeding ducks with the class of second grade girls that she taught as an intern teacher. Each time he used this pet name, he would instantly see her in his memory with sheer delight. Her dress was aqua-green with a matching silk scarf around her neck.

He remembered thinking when he first saw her, "What a lucky scarf indeed, to be hugging such an ivory tower of beauty!" Tom stopped in his tracks as he recalled that moment. He still found it hard to understand what she saw in him. She could have been the governor's wife, living high on Capitol Hill. She believed in him like no one else could, and she chose him. Then he thought of Jesus Christ choosing him and dying on the cross for his sins. Jesus! That name that changed his life, forever. He did not like the Vietnam war. But if it were not for the war, he may not have ever come to know his Savior. As these thoughts penetrated his heart, he took off his hat and said a silent prayer with a lump in his throat, as emotion overwhelmed him.

"Lord, Lord, I don't understand why you chose me. I don't know why you encouraged Janet to choose me. I seem to fail at so many things, yet you are always there, helping me, pulling me out of one mess or another. Thank you so much! Father, with you by my side I can say, as did Paul in Philippians 1:20—*I eagerly expect and hope that I will in no way be ashamed, but will have sufficient courage so that now, as always Christ will be exalted in my body, whether by life or death.*"

Then Tom quickly prayed: "Lord, please be with that doctor I talked to last week. Remove the scales from his eyes that he might see the truth of Christ and that you may be glorified from it. In Christ's name, Amen."

Tom and Janet spent their Sunday visiting friends after church. But Monday had come quickly and caught Tom off guard. Reviewing his planner, he realized he had a court hearing to go to for the CCDL that morning. He had been up for two hours, yet it seemed his quiet time with God had been just a few minutes. Tom bowed his head for one last request. He did not know the little boy he was to represent that morning, but he remembered reviewing the case and the problems associated with it. Reggie was only six years old. His father died suddenly three years ago. Relatives were all back East and Betty, the boy's mother, had no one to help her. Reggie's legs were paralyzed at birth from Muscular Dystrophy. Betty could not read and did not qualify for support from welfare because she owned the small trailer home they lived in. She had tried several places for financial help but was frustrated and confused at the mounds of paperwork she was handed. Of course the courts would not have completely understood her frustrations. They thought she was just lazy and apathetic. They would only see the facts before them in black and white. The court records showed reports of the boy being left alone several times to fend for himself while his mother worked at a local bar. In addition, the home was completely unsafe for the boy and often therapy sessions were skipped.

The information that Tom had in the California Children's Defense League folder was archived by another League member from telephone discussions with neighbors and friends of the McCoy family and from much follow up research. Jack's Bar and Grill was really more of a diner, and Betty was a cook there. Of course the small trailer was not wheelchair accessible, which meant the doorways were not wide enough to pass a wheelchair through and there was no ramp to the pavement below the trailer. Betty would have to carry Reggie down the steps to the car whenever they would go anywhere. She would also carry Reggie when moving him from one room to another. The courts would not view this as an acceptable home environment for the boy. The reports were untrue of her leaving Reggie alone while she worked, but there were a couple times she made a quick trip to the corner convenience store while her son was sleeping. The other problem was therapy. Betty would take the boy to the clinic once a week, but that would not be sufficient in the eyes of Children's Welfare. Research by the League found Betty to be a very good mother.

Reggie's therapy treatments were not neglected because his mother knew exactly how to perform them with Reggie and did so daily. Tom would recommend that the boy stay with her. It would not be an easy case though. Thinking it would be good for Reggie to have a few weeks of a new specialized therapy treatment, Betty signed papers to temporarily turn custody of Reggie over to the state. The welfare worker lied to her, and the papers she signed gave permanent custody to the state. Tom had seen similar cases go either way. His responsibility was just to monitor the hearings and make recommendations as a representative of the CCDL. There were times though, when he did just a little more. Well, actually a lot more, but Tom knew his limitations and whatever good came from his efforts was truly that of God's grace. Now on his knees before his Maker, Tom finished his morning visit lifting Reggie and Betty up before the Lord.

As Tom made his way through the corridor of the county seat, Reggie was not hard to spot. He was sitting in his wheelchair near the courtroom entrance and watching the traffic of people whisk by. The little boy was expressionless as Tom sat next to him on an old oak bench. Immediately the elderly man reached into his briefcase and pulled out a string puppet. He found out, many years ago, while in this ministry that this was one thing a child could not resist. Tom had whittled each piece of the puppet himself and the end of each string was tied to a finger of a large rubber glove, which made it very easy to slip on and off. The boy did not even look at Tom and had no idea what was taking place. Within seconds the small dragon was dancing before Reggie, and his reaction was instantaneous.

A grin shot across his face from ear to ear, and his troubled dark blue eyes widened and began to twinkle as he giggled ever so faintly. Even his freckles seemed to burst to life as his eyes were fixed on the dancing little figure. The puppeteer started his story. Although he must have told that same story a hundred times, it became better than the one told before. In the briefcase was a whole set of puppets, each portraying a lively character in the delightful story. Traffic started to slow and then stopped as an audience formed in a circle around the man and boy. But the eyes of the crowd were not fixed on the puppets as much as they were on the child as he joyfully watched the tale come to life and bounced to the movements of the little figures. Just as Tom finished his story, a shout was heard from the end of the corridor.

"What's all this! Come on! Break it up! Keep on moving!" The bailiff's voice was authoritative but not harsh.

As the crowd dispersed, the bailiff walked to the center of the attraction. Tom was showing Reggie how to make the dragon move about as the uniformed man towered over them, tapping his foot to get their attention. Tom took a hard swallow and stood face to face with the bailiff. Reggie placed the puppet in his lap as he moved back to make room for the skirmish which seemed about to take place. He thought to himself, "If only my feet were normal, I'd kick that mean officer!"

As the two men glared at each other, they could keep the stern expressions no longer. In a burst of laughter they shook hands, as the two old friends greeted each other.

Tom started the conversation, "Well, Sam, your timing is as impeccable as ever. I didn't even get a chance to pull a collection from the crowd."

"Yea, but I did let you finish that tale. I must have seen you perform this show to the kiddos a dozen times, and this is the first time I got to see the ending," bellowed the bailiff as he rocked back and forth from heel to toe. His pot belly wiggled with each movement.

"And who is this young lad?" the bailiff asked as he turned his head to one side and squinted at Tom. His black beard was neatly trimmed and the brim of his police hat shadowed his eyes.

The answer came from behind them, "His name is Reginald McCoy, and if you gentlemen are quite through with this nonsense, I would like to get him into the courtroom!"

This was obviously his case worker. As she stepped near them, the sound from her high heels echoed down the hallway. The men parted to allow her to pass. She glanced at neither of them, but went directly to Reggie and stood behind his wheelchair, preparing to push it into the next room. When Reggie tried to reach across to place the puppet on the bench, Tom's hand stopped him and guided his hand and puppet back into the lad's lap.

"I do hope you will accept this as a gift. I can tell you have great potential as a puppeteer." Tom spoke sincerely as he looked gently at the boy.

Reggie looked pleadingly up at the lady and waited for an expression of approval.

After a short while, she slightly nodded, yet her feeling of uncertainty was obvious.

Reggie exploded in gratitude, "Thank you so much. I will take good care of him and treasure him always."

Just then Reggie's mother entered the hallway and quickly ran to the boy, engulfing him in her arms. "I surely missed you, Pumpkin! How are you?"

She spoke excitedly, although deep within, concern over the outcome of this court hearing wrenched her heart with anxiety.

"I was feeling very sad until this nice man performed a puppet show and then gave me one of his puppets. I can even make him dance!" Reggie held the little dragon high over his lap and moved his fingers as the puppet danced about.

Sam excused himself. "See you later, Tom. I'd better get in there before the judge puts a warrant out on me."

Betty cordially greeted the case worker and then turned to talk to Tom. As she glanced back, she noticed Reggie being pushed into the courtroom. She whispered to Reggie, "I'll be there in a moment, Sweetie."

She was curious about the distinguished looking gentleman standing next to her as she spoke to him, "I'm Betty McCoy, Reggie's mother. Thank you for cheering up my little boy. He has had a very difficult month. Child Welfare would only let me see him on weekends and ..."

The lump in her throat prevented her from saying another word. She stepped away from the doorway as she burst into tears. After the sleepless night of weeping, she thought there were no tears left within her, and her emotions caught her off guard.

As Tom handed her his neatly pressed handkerchief, he gently said, "It's OK. I'm sure this month has not been easy for you either. You do not need to explain any further about Reggie. My name is Thomas Wisp. You see, I'm here from the California Children's Defense League and I want to help you and Reggie."

She could hardly believe her ears and thought, "Help Me! Someone really wants to help me? Lord, you do answer prayers! Through all of this, no one, I mean no one has ever considered me or even what was really best for Reggie. They seemed only concerned about policies and procedures. And now as I entered this building and stopped just for a moment, I prayed for help. And here is someone who wants to help, right out of the blue. Thank you, Father!"

Betty spoke rapidly with excitement, "So, you are a lawyer. Oh, just what I needed! I cannot afford to pay you much, but just the fact that you are here is such a relief. No one would take me as a client because I have so little money. But I will pay you, whatever the cost."

Tom was prepared for this reaction, which was quite typical. The assumption that he was a lawyer is nearly always the first thought from the parents. "Unfortunately I am not a lawyer, but the Children's Defense League does have a certain amount of clout, and I will do my best to persuade Child Welfare to return Reggie to you."

For an instant there was a look of disappointment on Betty's face, but then she realized that she should not be ungrateful for whatever help God provided. Besides, although she had never heard of the Children's Defense League, it did sound pretty impressive. She thanked Mr. Wisp and handed his slightly soaked handkerchief back to him.

Betty expressed her gratitude again, "Whatever you can do, Mr. Wisp, will be so much appreciated. It's just so nice to have someone on my side. Again, thank you so much!"

She then entered the courtroom. Her hopes were raised, and she held her head high as she walked down and sat behind her son. Tom followed her and sat in a seat fairly close to Sam. Although Sam could not officially do anything to help, in the past his gestures and motions were helpful at determining the judge's mood and willingness to bargain. Sam had been working for Judge Crawford for nearly seven years and was very familiar with his ways.

Sam asked everyone to stand as the judge entered the courtroom. Once the hearing started, the county attorney and judge conducted the bulk of the conversation regarding the reason for the hearing and the recommendations provided by Reggie's county case worker, Mrs. Parks. Betty kept waiting for her turn to talk, but the discussions were carried out as though neither she nor Reggie were present. In a way she was glad they didn't call on her because she had no idea what to say or what to ask except "Please let me take my son home!" But that, she knew, would be a mistake without more of a defense for herself. She closed her eyes and again prayed for help. Tom was not surprised at the court's conduct and quickly took a cassette recorder from his briefcase and walked over and handed it to Betty. He motioned for her to turn it on and went back to his seat. All this time Mrs. Parks was completely caught up in the dialogue between the judge and attorney and didn't even notice what Tom was doing.

Betty was puzzled at first but then placed the earphone in her right ear. She turned it on and, at the same time, was struggling to understand what the judge and lawyer were saying. The voice on the cassette was obviously that of Mr. Wisp. He was giving her instructions to somehow make her presence known. She was to then play the tape for instructions on what to say, turn off the tape, repeat the provided monologue, wait for the response from the court, answer the court, then turn the tape back on for additional instructions.

Betty handled the situation like a pro. The right side of her face was turned away from the judge and lawyer so they could not see the recorder and her right hand covered the control keys of the device. She memorized the keys and their positions.

She then stood, slightly raised her hand, and said in a nervous but matter of fact tone, "Excuse me gentlemen but I would like to say something on behalf of myself and my son."

Every eye was suddenly on her, but she was determined not to be intimidated. She then repeated the messages of the cassette tape flawlessly and the entire courtroom, which up to this point was bored to slumber, was suddenly refreshed by Betty's remarks of both humor and wisdom. The county lawyer and judge marveled at her legal knowledge and were speechless as she called Mr. Wisp as a witness. Before Tom reached the witness stand though, an unusual series of events took place which he and Sam would talk about for years to come.

Mrs. Parks was sitting next to the right side of the aisle with Reggie in his wheelchair next to her on her right. Reggie's mother was sitting directly behind Mrs. Parks. Just to the left of Mrs. Parks was a very young lawyer, nervously reviewing his notes for the next case before the judge. He was sitting in on this case to familiarize himself with Judge Crawford's ways of handling cases.

The case worker was so shocked at the eloquence of the language she was hearing from someone who she perceived to be an illiterate bar girl, that her glasses dropped to the edge of her nose as she quickly turned her head to be sure it was really Mrs. McCoy speaking. In the process of the turn, her glasses flew over the stack of papers on the young lawyer's lap and onto the floor. Reggie was amused at Mrs. Parks' expression as she quickly leaned forward, over the young man to fetch the spectacles. Unfortunately, a bald elderly gentleman sitting on the other side of the lawyer, instinctively reached to retrieve the flying object at the same instant.

The head of this man and that of Mrs. Parks collided. Mrs. Parks, temporarily numbed by the collision, was thrown off balance. She frantically waved her arms in an attempt to grab anything to stabilize her body. In the process she knocked the mound of paperwork from the lawyer's grasp, causing a rainfall of white sheets all around the area. Her fall ended with her embarrassingly in the lap of the lawyer. The lawyer's face turned bright red. Reggie was tickled by the whole ordeal, once he realized Mrs. Parks was OK.

The judge, who had been watching Mr. Wisp approach the bench and knowing nothing of the events leading to the free-fall of paper, jumped to his feet. As he pounded his gavel on its sound block, the head of the gavel broke off and went rolling across his desk as he called the court to order. The expression of the judge as he watched the wooden cylinder slowly roll off the edge of his desk was just too much. Even Sam, who was normally serious and formal in the courtroom, had to turn completely around and cover his mouth in an attempt to stifle his expression of laughter. The judge kept pounding the block with the broken end of the gavel, sending a faint tapping sound across the courtroom. Reggie was now giggling and slapping his knees in delight. Judge Crawford was still tapping with the headless gavel. Reggie was laughing all the more. He had expected to have a very boring day in court, but even the best performance of circus clowns could not top this. The judge gave a look of disapproval at Mrs. Parks as he ordered her to her seat. Sam rushed across the front of the desk to retrieve the wooden cylinder and then waved his arms in a motion for everyone to sit down as Mrs. Parks went rushing to the ladies room. Judge Crawford then wisely called for a thirty minute recess.

As the room was clearing, Tom and Sam walked near one of the corners and had a little chuckle about the whole thing. Then Tom explained to Sam his anger at the social worker for deceiving Betty into signing papers which turned Reggie permanently over as a ward of the state. Then Sam raised his forefinger and placed it near his temple.

He then asked Tom, "Wait a minute! Did you say that Mrs. McCoy cannot read or write?"

Tom responded promptly, "Yes, that is exactly what I said. What Mrs. Parks did was unethical and should be illegal as well!"

Sam asked, "Were there any signatures of witnesses on the paper as well?"

"Of course not," Tom answered.

"Then it is illegal, Tom!" Sam spoke matter of factly. "Three months ago a state law was passed making it illegal for someone to coax a second party to sign a document if, indeed, the second party could not read the document. A third party must sign the document to witness that the entire content was read to the second party with the second party completely agreeing to the conditions of the document. Judge Crawford is also very careful to ensure this law is enforced. Yesterday an American Hispanic was providing a defense that he was not informed of the content of a sales contract. When the judge found out that he could not read English and a third party did not sign the document, he was outraged and immediately rejected the document and ruled it as not legally binding. As a result the salesman was issued a heavy fine for violating this law."

Tom closed his eyes to offer a silent prayer of thanksgiving to the Lord. This was just the break he needed. He knew he could now easily win this case, and Reggie could at least for the time being return home with Betty. But it was clear that she could not continue carrying Reggie from room to room. The county has no problem taking a child from his mother and spending a large sum of money from the state budget to help a caretaker provide for the child, but will do nothing to help the mother do the same thing. It doesn't make sense.

Then it occurred to him that maybe, just maybe, something could be done.

He then spoke, really just thinking out loud, "I sure wish I had a copy of that law right now."

Sam responded, "My office is right here in the next room and I can pull off a copy from my computer in just a moment."

Tom smiled as he left his friend and said, "Thanks, Sam, I'll see you soon."

Tom left to search for Mrs. Parks. He was glad for the delay in the court proceedings enabling him to present a set of circumstances to the social services department that may help Mrs. McCoy to keep her son. This might also spare Mrs. Parks further embarrassment in the court hearing.

Mrs. Parks was just leaving the lavatory as Tom approached her. Seeing Tom, she turned to walk away, but Tom gently touched her with his cane. Her head quickly turned around. "What is it you want!" she whispered, expressing her anger with each movement of her mouth as she formed the words.

The gentleman smiled as he gently spoke, "Hello, Mrs. Parks! I'm sorry I did not take the opportunity to introduce myself earlier. My name is Thomas Wisp and I represent the California Charter of the Children's Defense League. May I speak with you for a few minutes concerning this case? I have tried to contact you several times in the past two weeks, but with no success."

Mrs. Parks remembered the messages left on her phone mail. She deliberately ignored them and deleted each one promptly after skimming through the introduction. The last people she wanted to talk to about anything were these pesky, persistent, busy bodies, trying to tell her how to do her job. The department head discouraged all social workers from communicating with members of the CCDL.

"Oh yes," she replied cordially, "I have just been too busy with this and other cases, to get back to you. I appreciate your concern, Mr. Wisp, but I assure you I have ample information of Reggie's situation and I doubt you could enlighten me in any way regarding his circumstances."

Tom did not take offense but responded with his natural gift of charm. "I know you work very hard and are careful to be well informed on every case, but please hear me out on this. What could it hurt, and we both have thirty minutes to spare. I'll even buy you a cup of cappuccino from the corner coffee shop. The owner is a friend of mine and always adds a little extra cream for my guests. What do you say?"

Tom then gave a little harmless wink that put even his toughest counterparts at ease.

"Well," Mrs. Parks responded with just a slight grin as she sighed, "After that ordeal, I sure could use a good cup of cappuccino, and we do have a little time. All right, Mr. Wisp, I'll 'hear you out.'"

Sam was just closing the court doors as Tom and Mrs. Parks approached.

"How about joining us for some cappuccino, Sam?" Tom hopefully asked.

Sam knew Tom felt uncomfortable about being alone with a woman other than his own wife and suspected that the couple had planned a chat

about the case. Of course, he knew it would be totally inappropriate for
him to comment on anything about the discussion, but he also knew that
Tom would not involve him, so he felt very much at ease in accepting
the invitation. As he turned to accept, he carefully slipped a folded sheet
of paper into Tom's hand who immediately tucked it away in his inside
jacket pocket.

Roger was just finishing with a customer as the trio walked into the
restaurant. "Tom! Gosh, it's good to see you. What are you doing with
that bearded scalawag?" Roger smiled and waved at Sam as he leaned over
the cash register and said, "I'll be right with you folks. Just take any open
table, Tom."

As Tom pulled a chair out for Mrs. Parks, a waiter hurried to
accommodate the three. But before the waiter spoke, Roger motioned for
him to attend to the other customers in the shop.

He turned to Tom and slapped him lightly on the shoulder as he
spoke, "Well, how are you doing, buddy!" Before waiting for an answer,
he reached over to shake Sam's hand and glanced at Mrs. Parks, who
patiently waited for an introduction.

Tom motioned with his right hand in Mrs. Park's direction and said,
"Roger, this is Mrs. Parks of the Child Welfare Department. Mrs. Parks,
meet my good friend, Roger Miller."

Roger smiled as he spoke to the lady, "Nice to meet you. I know what
these gentlemen want, but what about you, Mrs. Parks? Could I interest
you in a great cup of cappuccino?"

She responded affirmatively, and Roger then rushed off to begin his
creations. She then looked intently at Tom and asked, "OK, Mr. Wisp, just
what is it you would like to suggest?"

Tom paused for a few moments to get his thoughts together. He
then glanced at Sam, who slightly leaned back in his chair, cupped both
of his palms around the back of his neck and stretched his elbows out in
opposite directions as he looked back into Tom's eyes.

Tom looked back at Mrs. Parks and spoke with concern, "I know you
don't feel it is acceptable for Mrs. McCoy to take care of Reggie, considering
the problems associated with the home not being wheelchair accessible."

Mrs. Parks added, "Not to mention her missing Reggie's therapy
appointments, working nights as a barmaid, leaving him unattended, and ..."

Tom broke in, "Well, I have some documents here that you might be
interested in." He pulled a sheet of paper from his planner and handed it
to the lady. "This is a certificate indicating that Mrs. McCoy has completed

extensive training on physical therapy. And this is a statement from her employer that she works strictly as a short order cook, and not a barmaid, as you believe. I also have letters from some of her neighbors stating that Mrs. McCoy is a very competent mother. All she needs is a little help! We are going to get her into a reading program and help her get a better job. There is also a group of boys at my church, in an organization called Christian Service Brigade, and they are planning to build a ramp to the front door for Reggie. But you must understand that entryways in a mobile home cannot easily be widened. I know of cases where the county has helped caretakers of handicapped children by building an additional room onto their home for the child. Yet nothing is ever done to help the mother to keep her handicapped child. There are motorized wheelchairs that are narrow enough to fit through a mobile home doorway. If the county could provide her with one of these, it would make life so much easier for Mrs. McCoy and Reggie and would save the county so much money for the expenses of a private caretaker."

The lady at the other end of the table raised her brow as she spoke, "She has already signed a release form making Reggie a ward of the state. This hearing is just a formality, and a needless one at that."

The conversation was interrupted by Roger placing a large decorative cup of heaping cappuccino in front of each person at the table. Detecting an air of intensity concerning the conversation that was interrupted, Roger quickly left the group as he tipped his head toward Tom.

Tom then reached in his jacket and pulled out the paper provided by Sam and commented, "Yes, about that release form. I too, believe this hearing is needless. Once you read this state ordinance you will see why."

After skimming the page, Mrs. Parks bowed her head. Tom had hoped he could convince Mrs. Parks to support returning Reggie to his mother without resorting to this.

Mrs. Parks then lifted her head to speak with stern cold eyes, "I see what this is all leading up to!" Her teeth were clenched as she moved her lips, "Really, Mr. Wisp! Do you honestly think you can get away with extortion! I didn't even know about this law."

Tom quickly responded, "But you did lie to Mrs. McCoy about the contents of that form and you knew she could not read. Anyway, I have no intentions of using extortion. I did not have to show you this law. Judge Crawford is quite aware of it and would have asked about a witness signature point blank, as soon as the release form was presented. You would have been fined, and once your unethical conduct was reported, you would lose your job as well. Reggie would also be immediately returned to his mother. I came to you in good faith to spare you all of this trouble. Yes, I did hope as a gesture of thanksgiving on your part and that of your department that you would try to do something to help Mrs. McCoy, but there are no conditions here. Go ahead and continue with this hearing if you think the judge will not ask about a witness signature. I assure you, I will not present this law against you and Mrs. McCoy has no knowledge of this. You have my word on that."

The expression on Mrs. Parks' face changed. She slowly stood and walked away, without a word. She stopped at the cash register to pay, but Roger smiled at her and told her that the bill had already been covered. Tom did not know how this would all end.

He thought, "Lord, I guess I messed up again. I may have just made things worse for Reggie and his mother. I'm so sorry! Maybe the judge won't confront her about the signature and I would just have to sit there and watch the injustice take place without saying a word. This may stir even a greater hostility of Mrs. Parks towards Mrs. McCoy. If only I hadn't been so persistent about Child Welfare helping Mrs. McCoy, maybe this misunderstanding could have been prevented. I should have had faith that you would do the providing. In spite of whatever may happen, I love you, Lord. I only ask that you forgive me and help Reggie be returned to his mother. Amen!"

Sam could see that Tom's eyes were watering as the silence persisted. He could only guess what Tom was thinking. Whatever it was, he knew Tom needed encouragement at that moment. Then he spoke softly, "Tom, you did your best. I couldn't have approached her better about this. No one could have. It's now in God's hands. Let's get together with Roger in his office and pray about this."

As Sam went to talk to Roger, Tom stood there with a lump in his throat, thanking God for Sam and Roger. He knew if Sam had not spoken with such gentleness, he would, at this moment, be asking the Lord to take him out of this work. Self-pity and bitterness would have entered his heart. But now there was hope. Wherever two or three come together in the name of Christ, there is great hope.

Roger's office was just to the side of the café entrance. Sam was quietly explaining the situation to Roger as they entered the room. When they left the office, they were laughing and joking. It was Roger who bore the brunt of the laughter, but he took no offense because he loved these men as brothers, and he himself saw the humor in it all. It so happened that, just as they finished praying, they started to sing the Doxology. Roger's wonderful tenor voice hit a resonating tone that echoed throughout the room when they heard some glasses in the kitchen fall and break at that instant. Sam jokingly said that Roger had better get his voice insured for glass damage. This set off a series of other humorous remarks.

As the two men left, Roger peeked around the corner into the kitchen, where the dishwasher was sweeping the glass he had dropped into a pile. As the boy looked up, Roger tilted his head to one side, raised his eyebrows and said, "I hear money."

He only charged the boys 20% of the cost of items they broke. It helped them to be cautious without taking too much from their paychecks when accidents did happen.

The boy just looked down at the pile and said, "Yes, Sir".

Just before leaving the restaurant, Tom heard a vaguely familiar voice coming from a booth behind a divider. He then asked Sam, "Do you mind if I take just a moment to talk to an acquaintance?"

Sam looked at his watch and answered, "OK, but you'll need to really make it short, Tom."

Dr. Bob Logan was enjoying his lunch with his lawyer sitting across the table. He was at the county court house for a trial involving an abortion protester at his clinic. Hearing the tapping of a cane on the hardwood floor reminded him of the elderly gentleman from Woodridge Falls. He did not want to think of that ordeal at this time but it just popped into his head. The sound was getting louder when it suddenly stopped as a shadow was cast across the table. Bob looked up in surprise to see that same man with that same smile.

Tom spoke first, "How are you doing Dr. Logan? I don't know if you remember me, but we met in Woodridge Falls last week."

Stuttering a bit, Bob responded, "Y-Yes I do remember you, but I seem to have forgotten your name."

"Oh, we were never actually introduced. My name is Tom Wisp."

Bob could not believe he would actually volunteer his name. He looked at Tom's cane intently and said, "You aren't planning on tripping me again, are you?"

Tom chuckled and said, "Not if you're not planning on kicking around little children."

Bob's face turned red, and now he was clenching his fist, "Is there something you wanted?"

With the smile still on his face, Tom said, "I just wanted you to know I was praying for you. I don't think you really like what you are doing. But it probably won't be for long. God has great plans for you, Bob."

This time Bob's lawyer spoke, "If you intend on hounding my client, we will take legal action, immediately."

Bob now was more reserved and reached across the table to calm the attorney. "It's OK Bill, he means no harm." A peace seemed to come over Bob as Tom's last words swirled in his mind. Those words! He heard them before, but where? Where?

Tom was now aware that he had to go right away. He could hear Sam tapping his foot from the other side of the divider, so he ended the conversation abruptly. "Well, Dr. Logan, nice seeing you again. I really must go. Goodbye."

With that, he lifted his cane from the center of the staff about chest high and tipped his head. He then turned and quickly walked to rendezvous with Sam.

As Sam and Tom walked down the hall toward the courtroom, Tom broke the silence, "What do you think she will do?"

Sam thought for a moment and responded, "I think she went directly to the county attorney to get his opinion about what to do. Even with the document in hand, county letterhead and all, I think she doubted the validity of it."

Though he didn't say it, Sam was also thinking that she may just plead ignorance of the law and assure the judge that she had notified Mrs. McCoy of the total contents of the document. Then it would be just her word against Mrs. McCoy's. Mrs. Parks seemed like she could be a very able actress.

They were now in front of the courtroom. "I must get to my post, Tom. Remember, this is in the able hands of God." Sam waved as he went to the front to prepare for the entrance of the judge.

Tom lowered his head as he slowly took his seat.

Sam gave his short monologue and everyone stood as Judge Crawford entered from his chambers. The attorney for the county and Mrs. Parks were having a quiet little conversation prior to the judge entering the room. Once the court was called to order, the attorney approached the bench and presented the judge with a note. The judge was silent a few moments as he skimmed through the contents of the note and then peered intently at the attorney over the top of his glasses.

The judge then spoke to the attorney, "I don't quite understand this."

The lawyer looked back at Mrs. Parks and then asked the judge if the three of them could have a short discussion in his chambers. The judge excused himself from the court and announced an additional 5 minute recess.

Once the three returned, the judge gave a short dissertation, announcing that the charges had been dismissed and that additional research had indicated that Mrs. McCoy was indeed competent to raise her child. He looked at Mrs. McCoy and told her Reggie was released as a ward of the state and as of that moment, fully under her custody.

Reggie, confused by all of the legal talk, burst out, "Sir, does that mean I can go home now?"

The judge for the first time smiled and said to the child, "Yes son, you may now go home where you belong."

There was a lot of excitement and celebration about the courtroom. Mrs. Parks and the county attorney rushed into the hallway to avoid any further embarrassment. After hugging her son, Betty went searching for Mr. Wisp.

Tom had just finished silently thanking God, when he felt a hand on his shoulder. It was Mrs. McCoy. She looked so happy and Tom stood to congratulate her.

As she was thanking Tom, Reggie pulled up and held his puppet high as he spoke, "Mr. Wisp, this is my new good luck charm."

Then Betty asked, "Mr. Wisp, do you know what is going on? I mean, I know your tape helped me make a good impression on the judge, but it had to be more than that!"

A little red in the face, Tom responded, "Well, they must have unexpectedly received some information about how competent you are as a mother."

Betty smiled, "I saw you walking away from the court with Mrs. Parks earlier. I think you had more to do with this than you are letting on. I don't know how to thank you."

Tom responded, "Just keep on doing the great job you're doing with Reggie. He's a fine little boy!"

"A fine boy, indeed." Sam said as he joined the group.

Tom introduced Sam to Betty and then turned back to Sam who he knew was about to say something, but Tom beat him to the punch, "I know, Sam! God's able hands. He surely is good to me."

"Me, too!" Betty agreed.

Then Reggie shouted, "Me three!" which started a burst of chuckles.

Tom then asked, "Are you a Christian, Mrs. McCoy?"

She returned, "Yes! A year before my husband died, we attended one of Greg Laurie's Summer Harvest outreaches and accepted Christ as our Savior. Both of us! And last year at Calvary Chapel, Reggie went forward and asked Jesus into his heart. I know Jim is in heaven right now. It's the Lord that enabled me to get through the ordeal of Jim's death and continue raising Reggie. As we have seen today, God is Goo-oood, to all who trust in him."

Sam commented, "That's quite a testimony, Mrs. McCoy."

He then lightly slapped Tom on the back and said goodbye to his good friend. He then turned to Betty, "Nice to meet you. And congratulations on the outcome of the hearing."

He then shook Reggie's hand, tipped his police hat, and slightly lifted his palm to meet the boy's for a symbolic 'High Five' in bidding goodbye to him. He then walked up to the judge's desk to tidy the area up.

At this point with his hand grasping his cane just below the curvature of the top, Tom lifted it a little above his chest to bid farewell to his new found friends. He then picked up his briefcase and walked from the courtroom. Betty watched him leave, feeling a fondness toward the old gentleman, like that of a granddaughter. Reggie shouted as he moved the strings of the puppet's right front leg, "Goodbye, Mr. Wisp! Benny, my dragon, says goodbye too!"

With tears in her eyes, Betty smiled at her son and joyfully pushed him from the courtroom.

CHAPTER 3

KELLY'S TRIP *to*
FERNVIEW COTTAGE

The rest of the month went by very quickly for Tom and Janet. Friday was a day of excitement in anticipation of Kelly's visit. They received a letter from her earlier in the week telling them that she would be arriving in San Ricardo on the afternoon Metro-Link train.

Tom had already finished his quiet time and was in the kitchen making coffee as Janet came racing down the stairs and calling her beloved, "Tom! Tom! Where are you?"

Tom responded, "I'm in the kitchen, Duckie." He was pouring her a cup of coffee as she entered the room a little out of breath.

She gave him a quick kiss on the cheek and exclaimed, "You really shouldn't have let me sleep so late, Honey! You know we will need to get down the hill early to pick Kelly-Joy up. I don't want her to be in that depot alone!"

Tom reassured her as he smiled and softly spoke, "Relax, Janet. Our Kelly-Joy is a big girl now. We have plenty of time! She is arriving on the afternoon train. Remember? We will get there quite early. "

Then he added with a bit of humor and sarcasm, "Besides, the Boogie Man won't snatch her up in the middle of the day!"

"You stop patronizing me, Thomas Wisp!" Janet had her hands on her waist and her eyes were widened, complimenting her smile which allowed her perfectly shaped teeth to gleam between her lips. "I know I often think of her as still a little girl and sometimes overreact, but you must admit there are many dangers lurking about in that depot. OK, we do have plenty of time but I do have some finishing touches to do in her room and fix my hair and ..."

Before she was able to continue, Tom wrinkled his brow, stepped back, lifted his cane about a foot from the brim of his nose and squinted one eye over the top of his cane as he spoke, "Now Janet, how can you possibly improve on those waves, curls, and shimmering beauty of that remarkable bundle of sheer delight that resembles a cluster of gold on the head of a queen."

Janet blushed and grinned so that identical dimples showed on each side of her face. In spite of the passing years, her complexion was as fresh as a child's. At least it seemed so, in Tom's eyes. This man, whom she loved dearly, could always make her blush. No one else could do so as easily. Even though they were best of friends, he still had his mysterious ways about him. Sometimes he would look at her as though seeing her beauty for the first time. She never considered herself very attractive, but Tom was so convincing and sincere in his compliments. At times she thought that he must be blind. Indeed he was blind. Blind with so much love for her that there was nothing she could do that would detract from her beauty as he saw her. In her mind the real mystery was his love for her. Why? She knew she was often selfish. Everything had to go her way. Yet he was always so patient and tender. Then her thoughts turned to Jesus. Yes, in a way like Jesus.

She prayed in that very short instant of time, "Thank you, Lord, for Tom and his love for me. Seeing his even greater love for Jesus, helped me come to know you and love you as well. Where would I be if it were not for Tom? Even more frightening is where would I be without Jesus? I praise you. I thank you! I love you!"

She then wrapped her arms around her husband's neck and stood up on her tiptoes to passionately kiss him. After a moment she spoke, "You always know how to sidestep the issue don't you? You are very sweet, but I do need to do more with my hair and other things. But first I want to make a wonderful breakfast for you. Now, what's your fancy, sir? Hot cakes with strawberry syrup or French toast?"

Tom asked her, "Strawberry syrup with real strawberries?"

"Yes, with real, wild, sweet, strawberries from the strawberry patch along the crest!" she responded with enticement, raising her eyebrows up and down as she pronounced each adjective.

"I'm sold!" Tom mentioned with excitement. "Hotcakes it is, and I'll pour the orange juice and set the table."

It was a rainy day. Tom did not like the rain much, but Janet did. She liked the way mist hung through the trees during the light rainstorms they occasionally had. She especially loved the way everything looked fresh and clean during the light drizzle of rain.

Tom and Janet walked hand in hand up the steps to the train depot, Tom with his cane and Janet with her umbrella. They arrived a half hour before the train carrying Kelly. They were reminiscing of previous trips to the depot.

With a smile on her face, Janet continued her conversation with Tom. "I remember the last time I rode on the Metro-Link with you. It was my birthday and we decided to ride the train to Los Angeles to visit the art museum. It was raining, just like it is now." A grin and quiet sigh came over her as she recalled the outing. Then with a little chuckle said, "Do you remember what you did right here in front of the depot?" She didn't wait for him to answer. "You knew my favorite movie was 'Singing in the Rain', so right here, with people scurrying from the train and waiting to cross the street, you took my umbrella and sang the theme song, dancing all the while, just like Gene Kelly. You were really good and sang wonderfully with that great baritone voice of yours. The women looked at me with envy, and I blushed so much I had to hide my face. You were so romantic! Even though I was embarrassed, I kept wishing you would dance all night. And then when you suddenly took my hand, Thomas Wisp, and made me dance with you in the middle of all that rain and all those people, I could have died!"

Tom turned his head and raised his eyebrows, "Made you dance with me, Ha! I merely held out my hand and you flowed into my arms. After all, it was your birthday, and I knew how you enjoyed dancing. You loved it all and you know it!"

He was right. She did love it. It was a memory she had always treasured and would treasure for a lifetime. Then she remembered more of the trip to the museum.

Her beautiful blue eyes sparkled as she started the conversation again, "I remember that you were not too impressed with the modern art exhibits."

"Hmm!" Tom responded, "The way I remember it, I was outright offended that they could actually call some of that stuff art."

Janet suddenly started to laugh as she remembered an incident from that trip, "Oh yes, and that stack of cardboard boxes glued together near the end of the exhibit. It was just near the exit door and you ..." she was now laughing so hard she had to stop speaking for a moment to catch her breath, "you started to push the stack out the door, thinking they were actually trash that the janitor forgot to remove from the floor."

Tom smiled as he spoke, "Now Janet, I just moved that stack a few inches. Once I realized they were glued together, I stopped and that was it. It was the only exhibit with a description on the other side of the item, so I didn't see it. What else was I to think?"

"There was more to it than that and you know it!" She was now giggling like a schoolgirl, and then stopped to continue. "The guard saw you looking at the exit as you pushed the exhibit and thought you intended to steal the artwork. The way he grabbed you, I thought he was going to haul you off to the police station right then and there."

Tom was now shaking his head. "Janet, he did not grab me. He just asked me to keep my hands off of the exhibit."

Her eyebrows were raised near the top of her forehead in reprisal, "Do you mean to tell me that you don't remember that he pulled on your jacket, taking you away from the pile of boxes?"

Tom spoke again, "Yes, I remember that, but he didn't grab me. He was trying to help me."

She then turned directly to Tom and put one of her hands on her waist and said, "He was trying to help you alright! Help you out the door."

"No!" Tom reassured her, "Remember I used to carry that ring of keys hanging from my belt? Well, the ring got caught on the exhibit and the guard thought my jacket was somehow stuck, so he was pulling my jacket as I was trying to get the ring untangled. Now that I think about it, the sight must have been pretty comical at that." Tom chuckled a little, then added, "But at the time, I just wanted to get out of there. Everyone was looking at me like I was a criminal or something."

Janet laughed a little with Tom, and then suddenly stopped, "Oh no! Why didn't you let me know that at the time?"

Tom said as a matter of fact. "I told you I just wanted to get out of there and at the time I didn't want to talk about it. I guess the subject just never came up again after that. And you actually thought the guard was roughing me up?"

She covered her face as the memory came back to her, "That is why he looked so strange when I hit him with my umbrella. That poor man. I feel so bad."

"I didn't see that! I was walking far ahead of you to get away from the crowd. You actually hit the guard with your umbrella!" Now it was Tom who was laughing, "It's a wonder we both didn't get arrested!"

The time passed very quickly, as it always did during their conversations, and the train was now entering the depot. As Tom saw the train approaching through the large depot window, he tipped his head toward the dock and said, "Here she comes. We better get out there pretty quick. You know how Kelly-Joy likes to see us there waiting for her."

Kelly was standing near the railcar doorway and waving joyfully at the couple as the train came to a stop. She was the first off the train and went running into the arms of her grandparents. Her cheeks were rosy as she hugged them both and they exchanged kisses. Tom lifted Kelly slightly off of the ground with delight and swung her around as she was laughing all the while. Tom kept his cane in a position to reclaim his balance should it stray as he was spinning her around.

Through her laughter she spoke, "Oh Grandaddy, I'm so glad to see you. So glad to see you both!"

It was Janet who now spoke, "Let's all hurry home. I've got your favorite dish in the oven, Sweetie!"

Tom rushed off to get Kelly's luggage as she and Janet walked together to the car. Kelly, of course, dominated the conversation as her face quickly transformed through a variety of expressions, each complemented by a change in the pitch of her voice which echoed through the depot with excitement. Tom looked back as the silhouette of the two faded into the crowd.

It was not until they were home and sitting at the table that Tom first noticed a change in Kelly. It was their custom for Tom to start the prayer and then each member of the family at the table would add something, providing a specific praise, request, or thanksgiving.

When Kelly's turn came, she just bowed her head and said quietly, "Amen."

This caused everyone at the table to feel very uneasy. Janet was thinking that perhaps she was just tired from the trip or depressed a little about her parents' divorce. But Tom knew Kelly a little better. He knew there was more to it than that. No matter how exhausted or depressed Kelly had been, with her respect for her grandparents, she would never deny giving God praise or thanksgiving unless... unless there was something separating her from a relationship with Him. But what could it be? They both knew Kelly had not yet asked Jesus to be her Savior, but she seemed to be on her way. After dinner, Janet hurried about, clearing the table. Kelly usually helped her, but Janet suggested that she play a board game with her grandfather. She knew Tom was looking forward to playing games with Kelly, and she thought that if something else was bothering

Kelly, she might discuss it during the game. Tom was a great listener and Kelly always confided in him. Once the game started, she did perk up a bit, but was careful to keep the discussion focused on the game. Once the game ended, she hugged her grandparents and quietly went to her room.

CHAPTER 4

WHAT'S WRONG
with KELLY?

Before bedtime Tom knocked on her door to have a little talk with her. "Come in—Grandaddy." Kelly's voice was low and weak.

Tom opened the door and with his cane preceding his every step, he approached the bed where Kelly was sitting. She was admiring the wonderful painting that Tom had completed and framed for her. The painting was leaning against the window there near the bed. Kelly was lightly running her fingers along the strokes that formed the river's edge as though it was real water.

As she turned she had a smile on her face, "Thank you so much for this masterpiece. I will treasure it always." She then hugged her grandfather and squeezed him with affection. They were then both silent for a while before Tom finally spoke.

He chose his words carefully because he knew if he forced the probe, she would just be silent. "You mentioned on the telephone last month that you had a lot to talk to me about. How about us talking about some of that now?"

Kelly's mind was racing as she searched for some innocent topic to discuss. She tried to remember exactly what she spoke of in that telephone call so many weeks ago. She remembered saying something about his hair. As she gazed on it now, she thought how silly it was for her to even suggest he dye his hair. The hair of the man in the CD shop could not hold a candle to her grandfather's elegant gray hair with waves that shimmered in the firelight. Her room had a fireplace in it, and Tom had started a fire to warm the room for Kelly early that evening. The rain continued to pour. Kelly loved the sound of the rain on the trees and bushes outside her window. That sound so wonderfully complemented that of the crackling fire, refreshing her heart with a bit of peace.

"Well!" as Kelly stared at her grandfather, a smile made its way across her face, "I am doing very well in school and soccer season is almost over. I haven't made any goals yet, but sometimes the coach still lets me play as a forward. I think he keeps hoping I'll somehow make a goal and prove that height is not a limitation in this game."

Like her grandmother, Kelly's stature was small and her energy level high. She knew her grandfather was expecting more out of her than she was willing to share at this time. She also knew exactly how to get out of this precarious situation.

"Grandaddy, I know you want to hear more about me, but we do have all weekend for that and what I would really enjoy right now is one of your fabulous stories. And then, to top the evening off, a puppet show."

Tom grinned and slightly shook his head, "Do you mean to tell me Kelly-Joy, that you are not tired of that same old puppet fable. You must have seen it more than thirty or forty times."

Kelly shot back, "I kno...ow", her voice was sweet and almost childlike. "But each time you tell it, you always change it. It just gets better and better!"

Now Kelly started to giggle for the first time as she spotted a familiar dark object that protruded from one corner of her closet. "Grandaddy, you knew I'd be asking for that puppet show, didn't you?"

Tom jokingly responded, "Now why would you say that? I know that you are quite a young lady now and childish things are left behind. Your box of Barbie dolls are stuffed in the attic, along with your collection of 'My Little Ponies', and....."

Kelly jumped into the middle of his sentence, "And your puppet case is sitting right there in my closet where you conveniently placed it for this very moment!"

Her grandfather turned his head and realized that his plot had been uncovered.

"OK, OK! I was just hoping that a small portion of the little girl still lurked about your chambers."

Kelly added, "And now you know she does! And I'm glad she hasn't left me completely yet. But it gets scary sometimes thinking I'm almost an adult. I feel like there is so much I need to know, and the only way to find out is by making mistakes. Mistakes that......"

She suddenly stopped, noticing that her grandfather was looking at her with great intensity. She couldn't say more of this. She had to change the subject. "Grandaddy, it's getting late, and you haven't even started your story yet."

Just then at the doorway of her room, her grandmother stood, with a tray of hot chocolate and sweet rolls for dessert. The aroma reached Kelly's nostrils with such delight. She suddenly felt like a little girl again, and she liked that feeling. Things were so simple then.

She was thinking, "Why do things have to change? Back then her faith in God seemed so much greater and He seemed so much more real. Whenever thoughts that were bad entered her mind she would just recite Scripture, and it would go away. But now she scarcely remembered the verses her father and grandfather diligently helped her memorize. She used to have such a feeling of peace. Could it ever be that way again? Could it ...?"

Her grandmother broke the moment of silence, "Tom, would you set up that card table near the fireplace for this tray?"

Tom reached over next to the fireplace and pulled out the card table, setting it up for the three of them. He then unfolded two of the chairs and placed them on opposite sides. Kelly would sit on the bed, as was her custom.

Now Kelly looked at her grandfather with 'puppy dog eyes' and said, "A story would go very well with these snacks."

Tom looked at Janet, waiting for her approval.

"Tom, don't you know that one of the best things about a visit from a grandchild is that I get to hear those stories you come up with."

Tom replied, "I don't ever remember you sitting in during storytime."

Janet smiled as she looked at her imaginative husband, "Well, I never told you this before, but often I would stand at the doorway and listen in. I'm surprised you never heard me chuckle during some of the humorous parts of the tales."

Tom dipped his chin, looked up at Janet in a quizzical way, and spoke in a deep tone, "You're a sly one, Duckie!"

He then slapped his knees and said, "OK then. This story is called 'Debbie and the lost ancient arctic city of Crystal Valley.'"

Janet poured the hot chocolate and divvied up the sweet rolls as Tom began the story. Kelly listened with great interest.

An hour later, the hot chocolate was gone, the sweet rolls consumed, and Tom was just completing the adventurous tale. The ladies clapped their hands at the conclusion and cheered as Debbie completed her ordeal. Kelly hugged her grandfather and walked over to the briefcase containing the puppets. She grasped it and set it next to the gentleman's seat. Tom opened the container and passed a puppet to Kelly and then one to Janet.

Janet protested, "No Tom, really. I can't work one of these!"

Tom reminded her, "You're the one that volunteered me for the children's fair at church, and one of the conditions of my acceptance was that you be my assistant. Remember? This is an excellent time to learn. Kelly can show you how easy it is."

Then Kelly shouted, "Yes, see Grandma! It's really easy."

Kelly moved her fingers very rapidly, causing the hands and feet of the puppet to appear so animated. As Janet tried, she was surprised how quickly she caught on.

Tom had not created a new dragon puppet yet, so he made up a new story for the King, Queen, and little boy puppets that were left. The little ladies had a great time trying to match the movements of the characters with the events of the tale being created. Tom made the story short so that there would be time for a quick Bible reading session and prayer.

When the puppet story was completed and the Bible study started, Kelly suddenly got very quiet and seemed disinterested. Tom did not say anything to Kelly. He was certain something was wrong but knew that this was not the time to talk about it. He wisely finished the study, said a prayer, and kissed his granddaughter good night.

It was Janet who first brought up Kelly's change in attitude at both the dinner table and just before bedtime. Just as she and Tom were preparing to pray together, as they often did just before retiring, Janet mentioned, "The divorce has surely caused that child so much pain. Did you notice the way she acted tonight at the table?"

Of course, she knew Tom noticed Kelly's behavior, but she presented her comment in the form of a question to probe Tom for his thoughts on the matter.

Tom looked seriously at Janet. "There's more to it than the divorce. Something has severed her relationship with God. There is some sin in her life that she is not willing to share right now, but it's eating her insides with guilt and shame. We must be patient with her and wait until she is ready. I must say though, she really has me worried."

Janet knew her husband had a special gift to see deeper into an expression or attitude. But this time, she hoped more than ever he was wrong.

She tried to convince herself of it. "Oh Tom, you just worry too much! Kelly-Joy would never do anything wrong. Not something really wrong like drugs or anything. Has Mary said anything to you about her keeping bad company?"

Tom shook his head, "No. Mary did not say much about Kelly. She mentioned that Kelly was initially upset upon learning that the divorce was finalized. But after some discussion, she seemed quite content with the situation. She is doing very well in school and she has been especially helpful around the house. But I wonder!"

Janet tenderly took her husband's hand and they both knelt in front of the bed.

Janet started the prayer, quietly and sincerely, "Lord, again we come before you with heavy hearts. Indeed we are thankful for your blessings, and it is wonderful having Kelly-Joy here, but there seems to be something really bothering her. Oh, we know you love that sweet child, even more than we do, but we also know that you allow us to choose sin, even though it is so harmful. I pray it is something minor and temporary. Perhaps it is a passing thought or feeling of sorrow about her parents. Speaking of Mary and Doug, please Father! You know the tears we have shed for this lovely couple. Doug is trying so hard! His love for her is nothing short of Tom's wonderful love for me which I treasure. Please help Mary come to treasure Doug again. I still don't understand how the breakdown in their relationship started. We know that with prayer before You, our marvelous Creator, miracles happen. We love you, Father. We have faith in you and trust you. This is why we can say, even under the most tragic situations: "Let Your will be done!"

She was clenching Tom's hand very tightly and held it close to her. Tom felt her tear land ever so faintly on his hand. He could feel her pain and shared that pain. Tom knew Doug still loved Mary, and deep down he knew she still loved him. But there was a lot to forgive. Doug was a great pastor of a small church in San Pedro, but dedicated himself so much to serving in the church, he lost sight of his foremost ministry, his very home. Oh, he was a very good father and always set aside time to spend with Kelly and do devotionals at home with her and Mary. But he did not set aside time in his busy schedule for intimate talks with Mary. They practically never ate out alone. There were many times that Mary wanted to talk to Doug to express her concern about his workaholic attitude, however she could not get time alone with him long enough to bring the subject up and discuss it. Whenever she did hint about his spending too many long evenings handling one problem or another in the congregation, he would defend his position by saying that he was called by God to do this work.

She would always think to herself, "What about your promise to God to love and cherish me!"

Then there were those numerous occasions when Doug would volunteer her for one committee or another without even asking her consent. She also didn't want to play the organ for church every week, but

Doug felt the church couldn't afford to pay an organist just then. It was just planned to be temporary but continued for years. She kept those unexpressed concerns inside for years until they overshadowed her love for him. She was determined she would never again be taken for granted. The only way, she felt, to ensure herself of this was to divorce Doug.

After a hard swallow, Tom spoke to the Lord. He added a little extra to Janet's request and also prayed for their other children, Gretchen and Don and Don's wife, Maggie. He then thanked God for each of their grandchildren, as he mentioned them by name and then closed in prayer with additional thanksgiving. After being settled in bed, he and Janet embraced for a long while. As he was relaxing, his thoughts turned to Betty and Reggie, and he wondered how they were doing as he quickly fell into slumber.

CHAPTER 5

REGGIE'S RAMP

During the morning the next day, the rain subsided temporarily. Tom had made arrangements for the Christian Service Brigade to complete the ramp for Reggie today so he was happy to see a break in the weather. He didn't like rushing to a project during Kelly's visit, but he only needed to introduce the boys and leaders to Betty, and be there to see that everything started off well. Then he could leave right away and hopefully get back before Janet and Kelly were even up. Usually Janet liked to get up early on Saturdays, but he knew that after rainy nights her sleep was deeper and she would be getting up later in the morning. The same was true for Kelly. After a cup of coffee and a few telephone calls to ensure the Brigade rangers were ready, Tom started out the door for the rendezvous. They were all to meet at the church and head down the hill from there.

Tom drove near the church parking lot in his old truck. For projects like this he used his oldest vehicle. As was the custom, Tom stopped at the edge of the drive where all the boys jumped from the large boulders of granite near the parking lot entrance into the bed of the truck. The unspoken rule was: Mr. Wisp would not move until all the boys were sitting in the truck bed. All the boys were seated. Of course, some squeezed in tightly against others, but as long as tempers didn't flare and blood wasn't spilled, the adventure would start. Tom moved the shifting lever to four wheel drive and pressed heavily on the gas as he drove up the rocky hill next to the lot and hit a few dips and holes on the way. With each bump the boys would yell in excitement and laughter would spew from the back of that truck. As he re-entered onto the blacktop and moved down from the small hill, the boys gave each other 'high fives' and said 'Yahoo' at their successful completion of the wild ride and bumpy ordeal.

They all loved Mr. Wisp. He was like a grandfather to them all and they treated him with great respect. They especially liked his cane and imagined special things about it. Billy thought the handle could be pulled from the lower part which was like a sheath, exposing a fine sharp blade of pure silver. Of course, Mr. Wisp would only use it in self-defense. Andy imagined the cane to be partially hollow and full of small gold nuggets. Mr. Wisp would often tell the boys stories of the old days of the gold rush and, as old as Mr. Wisp was, surely he must have taken part in the whole thing. Andy thought Mr. Wisp knew so much about gold that he just had to have some, somewhere. Jack was the most innovative of all. He knew Mr. Wisp loved the Lord greatly. He imagined the cane to be full of ancient, valuable, Biblical manuscripts, all rolled very carefully and safely sealed in that wonderful cane.

Tom always wore his safari hat on projects with the boys. He looked just like an English colonel in India or Africa, so the boys respectfully nicknamed him The Colonel, and often addressed him as Sir. Decades ago Tom started the Christian Service Brigade unit in that church with a handful of boys. Many of those boys were now Brigade leaders in many churches. Several of the rangers leading this group of boys started as boys in Tom's Brigade unit.

Just as the truck came to a stop, the boys hurriedly jumped from the vehicle and rushed to get into formation to impress The Colonel. Tom knew exactly what was going on so he took a little extra time preparing to leave the driver's seat, allowing the boys more time to position themselves. Jack was the squad leader and took the responsibility very seriously as he personally checked each boy for the correctness of their stance.

Once Tom saw Jack at attention in front of the rest of the squad, he took his cue and stepped down from the cab of the truck. Just like a band responds immediately in unison to the lifting of the baton, these boys watched Jack very carefully to likewise respond simultaneously as one. As Tom turned to face the boys, Jack's hand was moved quickly to his forehead to salute The Colonel, as did each of the boys. Tom stopped in front of Jack and, without moving his head, pretended to carefully inspect the boy. He then slowly walked in front of each of the others looking them straight in the eyes as he passed. Upon returning to the front of the line, he carefully moved his hand to about the middle of the cane, lifted the curvature of the cane to the brim of his hat, lightly touching it as he tilted it forward, essentially returning the boys' salute. They were all waiting for this moment, because once the salute was returned, they rushed forward to mob The Colonel, patting him on the shoulder and exchanging the special handshake they secretly had with smiles and shouts.

By now the leaders were approaching the group. One by one each of the rangers extended his hand forward to greet their guest.

With a smile the chief ranger spoke. "It's great to see you, Colonel! No one can handle the boys as well as you. Are you sure you don't want to come out of retirement?"

Tom was quick to respond, "You men show a fine example of Christian leadership to these boys. Don't kid yourself. No way could I do a better job than any of you. Besides, they need someone like you who can lead them to blaze the trails, traverse the cliffs, and race to the finish lines. Not an old codger wobbling on a cane."

This caused the boys to rebuke that last statement with shouts of protest, "Don't talk like that!" "You're the best, Colonel!" "You're not an old codger!"

Tom smiled and raised his hands to quiet the boys. "All right boys, we need to thank God for this opportunity and pray for a safe work day. Then we will need to load that equipment into the back of my truck."

Tom winked at one of the rangers. Once everyone's hat was off and heads bowed, the ranger spoke a wonderful prayer of praise and thanksgiving, adding requests for members of the congregation in need, along with a request for helping Reggie and his mother. This time of prayer was special to everyone.

Once the prayer was over, the rangers quickly took charge and organized the boys in groups to handle the lifting and moving. Soon the truck was full, and the boys scurried to their assigned vehicles for the trip. Jack had luckily picked the short straw, enabling him to ride with The Colonel. As he was entering the cab of the truck, he couldn't wait for the trip down the hill to start. Whatever story The Colonel chose, it would surely be a memorable one. The caravan started with The Colonel in the lead.

It was a long trip, but to Jack it seemed only like moments as The Colonel came to the conclusion of the story. Reggie was waiting outside with his mother as the vehicles pulled into their driveway. Jack thanked The Colonel and then rushed from the truck to help take charge of the other boys.

As Tom walked over to greet Betty and Reggie, the rangers and boys headed in the same direction to meet the McCoy family. Reggie wanted to be outside when everyone arrived so he could meet them right away and watch as the ramp was being built. Some of the boys initially thought they were going to feel uneasy being around a boy in a wheelchair, but once they saw how cute and cheerful the little boy was, they felt quite comfortable being around him. Reggie had a small decorative chest on his lap with a gold chain and lock. Everyone seemed curious as to what was in the box.

After all introductions were completed, Andy's curiosity got the best of him, so he inquired, "Hey Reggie, what's in the box?"

Just as with Tom's cane, the box stirred up the boys' imagination. It looked like a small treasure chest and each boy had his own idea as to what was in the chest. Still they wondered what kind of treasure could a small boy like that have, since he lived in a place like this.

Reggie didn't say a word, but proudly unlocked the chest and opened it. The inside of the chest was lined with blue velvet. Reggie did not open it wide enough for the spectators to view inside. Instead he placed his right hand in the box with the lid partially closed. The boys were waiting but getting impatient. Suddenly Reggie jerked his hand out so quickly that everyone was startled and jumped back. To their surprise, a little dragon danced about before them. Reggie had been practicing and he could even make the puppet's mouth move. As Andy tried to pet the dragon, Reggie pulled the strings nimbly, causing the wooden figure to appear to be biting Andy's finger.

Andy played along and quickly pulled his hand away yelling with a grin, "Ouch! You little stinker."

Reggie had created his own cute, short story about the dragon and eagerly told it to the boys. Reggie was so funny and cute and dramatically set the story to life with the movements of the puppet. When it was over, the boys clapped their hands. Of course, it was nothing compared to the stories The Colonel told, but for a boy of only seven years old, it was not bad.

At this, one of the rangers, Bill Blake, raised his right hand and as he moved it in a small circular motion, shouted, "OK boys, we've got a lot of work to do, so let's get started."

Jack stood out front and called some of the boys' names, dividing them into teams. He and the rangers had already discussed the duties and the boys that would be needed in each team. At first Reggie felt deserted, but it was not long before Andy came running over and pushed Reggie's wheelchair up to the truck. He then threw a small blanket over Reggie's lap and part of the chair and loaded a few small boards across the armrests. Reggie was giggling with excitement as Andy pushed him toward the worksite. Reggie felt he was actually helping the other boys.

They all made him feel so much like a part of the team, and he was. He would tell 'knock, knock' jokes to keep the boys laughing as they worked. Then he would make up other stories. The rangers had never seen the boys work so well together. Each of them had a turn at wheeling Reggie to the truck for more light supplies and loved every minute of it.

Tom looked up toward the mountains and noticed clouds forming over the tree line. He looked at Betty and said, "I'm sorry about leaving so soon, but my granddaughter is visiting and I really ought to get back home."

Betty also peered at the clouds over the mountains and spoke with concern, "You should be leaving now! Those clouds look as though they are about to burst at the seams. I've heard of the many rock slides on that main road up to Woodridge Falls during storms like the one that seems to be brewing. Please, be careful Mr. Wisp."

Tom took one last look at Reggie and the boys.

Betty spoke again, "Don't worry about Reggie. I have never seen him have so much fun. There aren't many children around that will play with him here, so he is really having a field day with your boys. I just hope they don't get tired of his corny jokes and stories."

Ranger Bill had just walked over from the worksite and overheard the conversation. He laughed as he broke in, "Are you kidding! These boys adore Reggie. It's because of him that they are all working so well. I have not heard a single complaint about the work being boring or hard or dirty, and that is very unusual. We may have to commandeer Reggie for other work projects!"

Bill and Tom shook hands. As Tom was getting into his truck, Bill shouted, "Tom, say hi to Kelly for me. We'll look forward to seeing her in church."

Tom responded, "I will Bill. And thanks for what you are all doing here."

Betty and Bill waved and Tom drove over to the worksite. He beeped his horn and all of the boys waved goodbye to him with smiles and cheers.

CHAPTER 6

THE MAGIC *of the* MOUNTAIN

As Tom reached about the half-way point up the mountain road, the rain came pouring down. He looked towards the valley below and could see bright sunshine there, but under this canopy of thunderclouds, darkness prevailed over the mountainous area in front of him. He was hoping that Janet would have a nice fire waiting for him with hot chocolate and a warm breakfast. He peered at the dash of the truck and noticed a piece of paper stuck to it with writings of the latest Bible verses he was in the process of memorizing. He quickly looked away from the paper and attempted to recite the verses. As he looked back at the paper, he realized he was off by just a couple of prepositions. Again he went over each verse, then turned his head away and tried to visualize the words as they were written. As he recited the verses again, this time he was sure he was correct. Indeed he was. The last verse on the paper was a milestone because it marked the end of the chapter that he had finally memorized. A chapter a year. That was his goal, and since he started five years ago, he had met that goal each year. It was getting progressively harder though, because with each new chapter, he was committed to have all of the previous chapters fresh in his mind as well. Soon the whole book of Ephesians would be hidden in his heart for eternity.

With each few hundred feet, the road had twists and turns. Some of the turns were over three hundred degrees, while others varied greatly. He cautiously made his way up the highway. As he entered his driveway, he couldn't believe his eyes. It was Kelly-Joy, dancing in the rain! How so much like her grandmother she was. Had it not been for her age, Janet would foolishly be right out there with her, laughing and jumping for joy. But Kelly did not have any rain gear on, and her clothes were soaked. She stopped near the edge of the woods to pick some bright irises. Then she ran across the bridge over the stream and up the hill toward the lake before Tom could get his door open to yell for her to get into the house. With a quick turn he pulled his poncho over his torso and snatched up the spare from behind the seat. He then ran up the steps towards the bridge in hopes of an upcoming rendezvous with the child. He could see her in the distance, standing near the lake. She was barefoot and wore a tee shirt with shorts. By the time he reached the lake, her hair was wet and stringy and her chin was quivering from the cold. She didn't move as he covered her with the poncho.

She grasped the railing around that part of the lake as she spoke, "I wish I could stay here forever, Grandaddy! I feel so strong and confident up on this mountain. I feel as though I could tackle anything up here. The wind, the storm, lightning, thunder... anything. But when I leave, I feel so small and helpless, unable to face anyone or anything. Is it magic or my imagination? Is it the aroma from the foliage or the sight of that eagle there in flight? Look at him, Grandaddy!"

For a long while the two of them stood there watching the eagle in flight. He would pose himself with wings angled up and legs down in a forceful position under his plumage as though he was holding back the power of the mighty wind. The wind was strong, but in that position, the eagle maintained his ground, not gaining or losing distance. He would then calmly tuck his feet under the plumage of his belly and move his feathers to make a complete 360 degree loop to return to that same position where he previously made his stand. It was awesome to watch and completely captivated the two who were forgetting the potential danger of the cold and rain to their bodies! As they looked about, there were no other birds to be seen. During such a storm, no other bird than the eagle would dare to attempt such a feat.

Tom suddenly was taken back in time to the same spot. And during a storm just like today where a mighty eagle struggled in the wind. But instead of his granddaughter, he was holding the hand of his little boy, Dougie.

"Look at him Daddy!" Dougie was Tom and Janet's oldest son.

The boy's sister, Gretchen, was three years younger than he, and his brother, Donny, was five years younger. Dougie was a daddy's boy from day one, though. Tom worked second shift for a defense contractor, and was able to spend most of the day with the children he loved so much. Whatever Tom was doing, Dougie had to be there right with him.

He would ask his dad things like, "Where does the water in our faucet come from?" and "Why does the light turn on when we turn the switch?" and "Why is the moon sometimes orange, and sometimes white?"

Some parents would tire of such questions but not Tom. He liked his son's inquisitiveness. He would usually stop what he was doing and draw some pictures to help his explanation. Tom was a great artist, and his pictures in their simple ways would do wonders in answering the questions at hand.

And there they were in front of the lake when Tom felt compelled to talk to his son. Sometimes this little boy understood him better than anyone else. The simple faith and common sense of this child were often more successful at understanding Tom than a dozen of his friends. Tom's focus was transferred to the sky where the quality of strength shining from that wonderful bird was a message Tom very much needed at this point in time. But how would he explain this to anyone? How would he explain this to Dougie?

Tom stooped down, putting his left arm around the shoulder of the young boy, he pointed with his right hand to the small whirlwind above the struggling eagle. "You see that funny looking cloud, Dougie? I don't think that he is an ordinary eagle. I think he is a special bird from God. He must have flown down from heaven through the center of that whirlwind just above him!"

Dougie's eyes were very wide as he whispered, thinking anything above a whisper might cause the eagle to return to his heavenly home. "But why, Daddy? Why would he come here during this wind and rain?"

Tom looked serious as he spoke, wondering if he could actually explain his situation to such a small child. "Well, I've been having some trouble at work and other things have been making me feel afraid. Remember last year when you kept thinking there was a wild bear in your closet? We looked and looked and could not find him, but you were still afraid. Remember?"

Dougie smiled as he remembered the incident, "Yea, and then a few nights later, we found that when you closed my door part-way, the air from the heater vent would bounce from the door to the fringes on my poster, and they would shake in front of the small night light, causing a shadow that looked like a bear near my closet."

"That's right!" Tom stopped speaking for a moment to gather his thoughts, then continued, "Well, sometimes adults get afraid over something we think is very frightening, but really isn't. God wants us to be brave, just like we wanted you to be brave after not finding a bear, but you were still afraid. It was only after we showed you what caused the image to appear on the wall that you could laugh about the whole thing and sleep. Even though in the Bible God tells mommies and daddies not to worry about the future, we still worry and get scared. But just now, seeing the endurance of that beautiful eagle has given me courage to continue and just do my best and give the rest to God."

"Does that mean you aren't scared anymore, Daddy?" Dougie asked just to ensure he was on track with what his father was saying.

Oh, Tom did not really believe that eagle was from heaven, but he did believe God used that eagle to speak to him and calm his fears.

Tom squeezed his son, thrilled that the message came through. "Yes, Son, I'm not frightened anymore."

Then Dougie shouted, "Daddy let's pray and thank God for His eagle, and ask Him to help the eagle get back home safely."

Dougie was always wanting Tom to pray. Even at times when Tom didn't feel much like praying, that little boy would encourage him, and he would sometimes pray the best prayers ever. After the simple prayer Tom squeezed Dougie again, affectionately. Dougie giggled and giggled, but it soon faded as Tom returned from this memory.

After a long silence, Kelly spoke again, "I get so much excitement from just looking at the eagle's beauty and courage. The wind tears at his feathers, yet he steadily defies it, not ever giving in. Now look! As the wind tosses him about, he maintains complete control, so calm and unconcerned about the possible danger to him. Wow! It gives me goosebumps! I wish I could do that!"

Tom asked, "What? Fly?"

Kelly looked deep into Tom's eyes as tears flooded hers. Tears she thought would not be seen with the rain pouring so heavily upon her face. But Tom could see them. He could feel her pain, not knowing the facts, just feeling the pain.

"No," she sighed, "Not giving in. Not giving in to the wind that tries to push you in its own direction rather than the right direction. Do you know who that eagle reminds me of?"

Tom was beginning to understand. He hugged his granddaughter as he answered, "Jesus!"

For the first time in the conversation she smiled, "Yes. Jesus! I remember a verse from Jesus's own lips, Matthew 7:25,

The rain came down, the streams rose, and the winds blew and beat against that house; yet it did not fall, because it had its foundation on the rock.

You know that tee shirt you have which displays a school of fierce looking fish, all going one way, and right in the middle, the fish symbol for Christianity traveling in the opposite direction? Well, that little symbol is similar to this eagle to me. What verse does that tee shirt have on it, right under the picture?"

Tom answered, "Matthew 7:13,

Enter through the narrow gate. For wide is the gate and broad is the road that leads to destruction, and many enter through it. "

Now Tom spoke again, "Hey cutie, let's get back into Fernview Cottage before we catch pneumonia."

Years ago, Tom coined the name for the old place and it stuck. Fernview Cottage was a lovely home, and often neighbors would drive by slowly, just to take in the beauty of it. It was a little white house with dark green trim. Ferns with a variety of shapes and dark patterned colors of green surrounded the little place. Tom's cane led the way as they walked arm in arm toward the bridge.

They stopped just for a moment to watch the waterfall in the stream. Then they took one last glance at the eagle, waved, and made their way toward the cedar framed house that stood before them. Smoke rose from the chimney of Fernview Cottage, and they looked forward to the wonderful heat that would be permeating from the fireplace. They imagined the warmth and could almost feel it as they neared the doorway.

CHAPTER 7

THE LONG NIGHT *of* SICKNESS

By now, Janet had the door open and was motioning for them to hurry inside. Once they were in the house, she helped them remove the dripping wet ponchos from their bodies, while speaking to them: "Land sakes, you two! What were you doing out there for so long? And you, Kelly! Running about in that rain and cold without even so much as a jacket or shoes on!"

Tom chuckled a little as he spoke, "Now Duckie, this girl is definitely her grandmother's granddaughter! You know yourself, if this had been a few decades ago, you would be right out there with her, barefoot and all."

She responded, "Thomas Wisp! Well I never....."

Tom tilted his head and dropped his mouth open as he spoke, "Ah, ah, ah! I distinctly remember our first night in this old shack. You were so happy with this isolated little cottage. It was drizzling with the first spring rain. You were so excited looking out the bathroom window at the drops of falling rain as they painted different shades of green across the foliage, that you felt you just had to be a part of it." He then stopped and grinned, "Even though you had just stepped from the shower and ..."

On hearing this, Janet immediately stuffed a towel into his mouth as she was laughing, "Now you just stop right there, you old tattle tale! Don't say another word about this to anyone, you hear? You exaggerate so much that someone is liable to take you seriously!"

Kelly's eyes were opened wide as her smiling face expressed both surprise and humor at what her grandfather was saying. "Grandma, really! You!"

Janet was quick to respond, "Kelly. You know how your grandfather goes on! He likes a good tale and ..."

Her conversation was interrupted by the sound of the oven timer. Janet was so thankful for that ugly sounding buzzer. It not only reminded her about the meal being ready to take from the oven, but saved her from further embarrassment.

She was thinking, "That man is so unpredictable at the things that will jar that memory of his. And, of course, he has to say it without even thinking about how embarrassed I might feel. It's a good thing this wasn't during one of my Bunco gatherings with the ladies from the church."

Then she smiled at the thought of Tom doing just that. Then she was thinking, "He would do it, too! My, I do love that man! Not only in spite of his funny ways, but also because of them. There's surely never a dull moment around this household!"

Then Janet rushed to the kitchen to finish preparing the meal as Tom took Kelly's hand and walked with her towards the fireplace. Right away he noticed how cold her hands were and how pale she looked.

He spoke with concern, "Kelly-Joy, you are still freezing. You had better get out of those wet clothes and take a nice hot bath, pronto!"

With chattering speech, Kelly answered, "I think that is a good idea. I do...do feel a bit of a chill about me. If you will excuse me, Grandaddy, I'll try to be done in time for breakfast."

Kelly then scurried off to her room. Tom's clothes were fairly dry, thanks to that great poncho of his. He sat in the rocking chair next to the fireplace and picked up the newspaper to catch up on events about the town. The front page covered the main event of the spring for Woodridge Falls, the fishing contest. The lake was stocked with the tagged fish. There were many prizes but the grand prize was the talk of the town, a new Jeep pickup. Tom looked at the picture, admiring the nice features of the automobile. He hadn't fished in a couple years, but he used to be one of the finest in the area. One year he did win first prize. Of course, back then, first prize was a meal for two at The Eagle's Nest restaurant. Just then he looked at the medallion that hung above the fireplace. Janet placed it around his neck at the festival celebrating the winners of the contest. Later that week, at The Eagle's Nest restaurant, they danced so wonderfully together. He remembered holding her soft hand and floating about the room to the rhythm of the music. It was a weeknight, so not many people were there and they were the only two on the floor. With a twitch of his hand, Janet took each cue and flowed through the series of maneuvers that they so often did. The two moved as one, just like their spirits moved as one towards Christ, their Lord and Savior. Sometimes they would go out with other couples to dance, and some of the ladies would love to dance with Tom. But he would have nothing to do with that. Dancing with Janet, he felt so intimate with her, and he did not want even the possibility of experiencing that with someone else. Of course, there was no threat of that happening, but it was just too personal to him. The ladies would not really feel offended though. They understood and mostly felt envious of and glad for Janet. Tom was still staring at the medallion when Janet called for him and Kelly to be ready to sit at the table for breakfast.

The meal looked marvelous. After they were all seated, Tom said grace. Table talk then began, with Kelly-Joy, of course, dominating the conversation. The French toast was delicious. Partway through the meal Kelly became silent again, and Tom used the opportunity to tell of his morning activities. Janet and Kelly listened with interest and expressed that they were happy that Reggie fit right in with the Brigade boys. Tom told about the events of the whole morning, from meeting the boys at the church, to Reggie's wheelchair being used as a wheelbarrow. His expressions were very comical as he told the story. As a result, much laughter from the two ladies filled the room along with Tom's timely chuckles.

Tom was glad that the rain was still falling. This gave him the opportunity to play some board games with Kelly and Janet. They played games the rest of the morning. After lunch, Tom set up the slide projector for some fun, looking at family slides from yesteryear.

To most people, the slides would have been boring and unmeaningful, but to the trio who were comfortably positioned in front of the projector, these pictures were precious and very exciting to watch. They brought back a flood of memories to Tom and Janet. Some of them were memorable to Kelly, but others were before her time. Kelly loved seeing her dad as a child. Many of the shots of him were comical and in each his expressions were priceless. She had seen some of them before, but others were either new or ones she had forgotten. From the pictures it was obvious to her that he had not changed much since a child. In one of the slides the Wisp family was all piled upon each other. Doug was caught in midair like a Boeing 747 in the process of landing. Everyone looked hilarious as they expressed an expected jolt from the forthcoming addition to their stack. The next slide showed the aftermath of the event. Kelly remembered a family picture very similar with her, her mother, and, of course, her father right on top, with the same gleam in his eyes, and the same smile on his face.

Kelly laughed at one of the slides of Aunt Gretchen. A series of the slides showed the events of a 'whip cream war' between her aunt, uncles, and father. Each of the children had home-made holsters for two cans of whip cream, one on each side of the belt. And each child held a can, with a finger pressing against the tip causing a spray of cream like a shotgun blast upon the victim. Then the last slide in the series was a treasure. There was Grandaddy in the middle of the three little munchkins. It was unbelievable! He had two belts criss-crossed over his chest with three holsters on each belt, a total of six cans in all, and with two additional cans of whip cream, one in each hand. He had a patch over one eye and an old western hat on his head. He looked like John Wayne in *True Grit*. All he needed was a horse rein in his mouth to really look the part. Kelly couldn't tell who was getting sprayed the worst, but it was obvious that they all had a great time, absolutely forever memorable. She remembered her father telling her of this very battle and how he loved it. The time went by fast as they were all enjoying viewing slides from the past.

As Tom was putting away the projector, Kelly candidly questioned, "Is Aunt Gretch ever going to marry?"

Janet quickly came to Gretchen's defense. "What do you mean by that statement Kelly-Joy? She is only 33. It's not like she is, as you would put it, 'over the hill'. There are a few men she is interested in, but she is being very wise and cautious. Marriage is forever, you know. In fact, we just got a letter from her. As you know, she is in Brazil at the orphanage. It's quite a commitment, but she loves it. She speaks Portuguese fluently now and enjoys communicating with the children and teenagers there. The letter is there on the table if you would like to read it."

Kelly picked up the letter and took a long gaze at the envelope. She so admired her aunt's handwriting. It looked nearly like calligraphy with quick even strokes to every letter. She opened the letter and read its contents. She loved her aunt dearly. Kelly felt cheated because she did not inherit her grandmother's dimples, yet her aunt did.

"Oh, Aunt Gretch is so beautiful!" she thought.

Kelly wondered if she would ever even possess half the beauty that her aunt was graced with. Yet talking to her, you would never even guess that she considered herself lovely. She just sort of felt content about the way she looked and considered it an average yet acceptable appearance. Information from the letter indicated that she would be back home in time for Christmas. Kelly always had so much fun with her aunt that she considered her more of a sister at times. But other times she would be very direct and confronting to the teenager. It was a good relationship, though.

It was now early afternoon, and Kelly was starting to feel really sick. The shock of the cold rain on her body earlier that morning, and the thin mountain air had taken its toll. Kelly ran to the bathroom to make an oral deposit into the bowl. She always hated vomiting and hated being sick, especially while here at Fernview Cottage. There were too many fun events planned for her to be stuck in bed with a thermometer in her mouth. Her grandparents were right. She should not have gone out into that rain. But how could she have resisted? The sound of that rainfall and the dancing of the little drops upon the large ivy leaves outside her window were a calling she just had to yield to. And weren't those ice cold droplets stimulating to the tongue and so tasty as she danced about with her head stretched far back, to take in as much of the rain as she could? But now she regretted the whole ordeal.

Janet had a little homemade brew in the refrigerator for just such an occasion. She heated it quickly in the microwave oven and carried it to the bathroom where Kelly lay moaning on the floor, waiting for the next upheaval. It was finally over, and there was her grandmother, cleaning her face and helping her to the vanity stool next to the shower. That special drink her grandmother had provided was so refreshing. It rinsed away the horrible taste along with chunks of debris that had remained in her throat, which would otherwise have been a torment trying to swallow.

Janet spoke with authority and concern, "Just a sip or two more now!"

As she supported Kelly's shoulders and neck for her to take another small drink, she could feel the enormous heat from her granddaughter's body. She knew she must remain calm, but the intensity of the fever that Kelly had frightened her.

As the loving grandmother helped the teenager to her room, she called for Tom, hoping not to sound too alarmed, "Tom, please bring me the thermometer and some ice for cold compresses!"

As soon as the ice was in hand, Janet busied herself placing the ice in several light towels that she had taken from the linen closet. She stopped just a moment to place the thermometer into Kelly's mouth. The ice compresses were placed on Kelly's face and around her neck. A few minutes later, Tom watched Janet's face closely as she read the thermometer that she removed from the lips of the teenager. Most people would not have even noticed the slight change in Janet's expression, but Tom knew by the slight rise in her brow and paleness of Janet's face that the fever was very serious. He left the room to call their doctor. Janet joined him just as the doctor picked up the receiver. Tom immediately handed the telephone to Janet.

The discussion was brief. Janet told the doctor that Kelly's temperature was 105 degrees, her throat was very sore, she had been vomiting, and that she had severe pains in the left side of her abdomen. The doctor without reservations suggested they call an ambulance to take her to the hospital, just to be on the safe side. As soon as the conversation was completed, Janet dialed an ambulance service. The response from the service to her request to have a vehicle dispatched immediately alarmed her even more. She slowly hung up the receiver and looked at Tom as she wrinkled her forehead in concern over the situation.

"Tom, the highway up the hill is closed because of rockslides. They don't expect to have it cleared until morning. With the heavy rain still in process, the dispatcher apologetically said that it would also be too dangerous to send up the flight for life helicopter. What do we do?"

Tom walked over to her and placed his arm around her shoulders. As he firmly held her, his tone was low and gentle, "We will do what we've always done in these situations. We will pray, do our best to keep her fever down, encourage her to drink fluids, and trust in our Lord. I'm sure she'll be just fine once the fever breaks. What we need to do right now is call Mary and Doug. We don't need to worry them, but they should know she is sick. I was going to call Doug tonight anyway to find out what time we could expect him to be here Monday. I'll tell you what, you phone Mary and I'll go and see how Kelly-Joy is doing. Then later tonight, I'll contact Doug."

They were silent for awhile just holding one another. After a few moments the silence was broken by a call from Kelly for water. As Tom entered her room, Kelly could only see the silhouette of her grandfather approaching her. Perspiration covered her face and from the tears and the deposit of droplets flowing into her eyes from her forehead her vision was very blurred. She breathed in large gasps between the surges of pain in her side. Tom lifted the small frame of Kelly's upper body to help her get into position to take a few sips of water.

The water was refreshing to Kelly's mouth, but as it entered her throat to be swallowed, it took a great effort to get the water past what felt like a gigantic boulder blocking the passageway. Her throat felt so sore, her body so hot, and now sleep was overcoming her, although it would not be a sound sleep, but rather one continually interrupted with tossing and turning. As evening and then night approached, her continual high fever caused Kelly to become almost delirious. Throughout the evening, her grandmother and grandfather were there at her bedside, changing cold sets of a wet cloth from her forehead, holding her hand, repositioning pillows, and doing everything they could to lessen her discomfort.

Whenever she woke, Tom or Janet would convince her to drink more water. Her grandparents knew that they had to keep her from dehydrating. She was losing so much water through her pores. The water was ice cold and helped temporarily numb her throat. Then she would fall back to sleep.

Janet was exhausted and Tom convinced her to get some sleep. She gently kissed her granddaughter as she went up to bed. She left one message for Tom before she went up to bed, "Tom, now you make sure you let me know if her condition changes, for better or worse!"

Tom reassured her, "Dear, I'll wake you as soon as the fever breaks. Everything will be fine. I telephoned John Cast during the last trip I made to the kitchen for coffee. He has a crew working on the rockslide and told me he would let me know as soon as they make a breakthrough. At that time, if Kelly-Joy hasn't improved, we'll take her to the hospital."

Janet walked over to Tom to kiss him goodnight. After doing this she fell to her knees, as did Tom, and they held hands as they asked the Lord for help. They thanked God for His many blessings and praised Him. There were many things they prayed about, but none had near the emphasis that had been placed on the request for Kelly's recovery. Janet felt much more confident that all would be well. A peace had come over her which would enable her to fall asleep quickly. As Janet made her way up the stairway, Kelly continued to be unsettled.

Tom placed Kelly's hand, sandwiched between his two rough palms. The heat emitted from her hand was intense. Tom felt compelled to express his adoration for her.

He spoke to Kelly as though she was fully conscious, "I sure love you, Sweetie! You are the best and kindest girl. I'm sorry you have to go through all of this."

To his surprise she, with eyes still closed, shook her head violently from one side to the other as she spoke, "No! No, Grandaddy! I'm no good! Don't love me, please, don't love me. I'm no good, no good to anyone!"

He did not want to hear those words. He knew that in her delirious condition he could easily probe for more information as to what was bothering her. He was certain it was more than just low self-esteem. So much more, but what?

But no! It would not be right to invade her privacy under these circumstances. He must only, and in the best way he could, assure her of his love for her. Assure her of Jesus' love for her and convince her that no matter what she did or thought, that love for her was unconditional.

Throughout the rest of the night, every so often, Kelly would wake and loudly cry out, "Grandaddy, don't love me! I don't deserve your love! No one can love me now!"

And Tom would always respond, "Kelly-Joy, I will always love you! Always!"

Tom knew, whatever danger Kelly was in as a result of this illness, it had no comparison to the danger that her spiritual welfare was facing. As stated in Romans 8:13,

For if you live according to the sinful nature, you will die, but if by the Spirit and put to death the misdeeds of the body, you will live.

With a small reading light next to his chair, Tom held the Bible in his hands. He slowly stroked the ridges of the leather cover of the Bible, looking at it like an old trusted friend. Indeed it was. Not so much the book, but what was written in it. The Word of God. How often he opened this wonderful book, seeking God's counsel. He knew very well many of the passages that would console him at this time. But the book marker was in Psalms 4.

Tom thought, "That's strange! I don't remember placing a bookmark here. Could Janet have...?"

His thoughts were interrupted by the words which he read at the beginning of that passage. Tom had been praying for Kelly every day. He somehow thought this would protect her from any wrong-doing that she might be tempted to do. In a way, Tom felt it was God's responsibility to ensure Kelly would not falter in temptation. After all, Tom had fasted one day a week for the last ten years for family members, especially for Kelly. Didn't God hear his requests? Couldn't God see how serious he was about this hope? Wouldn't God honor this?

His eyes went directly to the words of the passage as though they were being guided by a little beam.

How long, O men, will you turn my glory into shame?
How long will you love delusions and seek false gods?
Know that the Lord has set apart the godly for himself, the Lord will
*   hear when I call to Him.*

*In your anger do not sin; when you are on your beds, search your
     hearts and be silent.*
Offer right sacrifices and trust in the Lord.
*Many are asking, 'Who can show us any good?' Let the light of your
     face shine upon us, O Lord.*
*You have filled my heart with greater joy than when their grain and
     new wine abound.*

Those words written so many years ago were for him right here and
now. Yes! It is time to be silent and trust in the Lord! His heart was so
touched by that visual representation of God's own voice. Tears flowed
down his face, and he thanked God for this message of confrontation and
reassurance.

He gave a slight laugh at himself in frustration as he looked up
shaking his head. "Will I ever learn, Lord? Will I ever stop trying to put
You in a box? Having the delusion that You should be a God that fulfills
my every wish list? Will I ever stop insisting that You do everything my
way? My way! How arrogant of me. You are so much wiser than I, Father!
No matter how painful, how shameful, and how horrible it all might look
to me, please Lord, let Your will be done in my life, Kelly's life, Janet's life
and in the lives of all those I hold so dear. No matter how horrible the
ordeal may seem to be to accomplish this, I trust You so much more than
myself; at least I want to."

At this, his eyes were weary. He closed them, intending it to be just a
moment, but sleep overcame him. To his surprise, when he opened them,
it was morning and Kelly was sleeping in peace. He quickly pressed his
hand against her forehead. Praise God! The fever was gone. There was no
perspiration on her face. The fever must have broken hours ago.

CHAPTER 8

TOM'S VIETNAM HISTORY
Part 1

The moment of joy, suddenly turned to sorrow as he remembered the events of the night. Kelly's constant denial of any love from him, from anyone. As he remembered her shouts, he felt her shame, but not understanding why. What was it she had done? What could that sweet child possibly have gotten involved with to cause her so much rejection of herself? Tom walked up the stairs to inform Janet of the good news of Kelly's recovery. From the looks of the condition of the coverings on the bed, Janet didn't sleep well last night. As he stood over the bed, he looked at Janet with great tenderness.

He gently spoke to her, "Honey, Honey!"

As he softly shook her, Janet suddenly opened her eyes and quickly sat up, "Tom, how is she!"

Waiting for an answer, looking at Tom, her first thought was that Kelly was in grave danger. Tom's expression was serious and showed that he was in deep thought.

Again she asked, "Tom, please?"

This quickly drew Tom out of his thoughts and he immediately answered, "Oh, Dear, she's just fine! See, I told you the fever would break and she would be OK."

"Yes, you did. I guess I should have had more faith. I worried so much last night, I got very little sleep. You look tired, too. Why don't you come to bed, and after all of us are rested, we can enjoy this day together and celebrate. Look outside! The rain has stopped, and everything is fresh and clean."

Tom glanced out the window but the sunshine brought no relief to his sorrow. He had to know. Know what was going on in Kelly's life, what was driving her to plunge into depression. So much had changed in her life with the divorce. The separation from her dad, the move to a new area, the separation from her friends, and the move from the Christian school she had loved and attended since Junior High to a public high school near her old elementary school. What toll did all of this take on her confidence, on her self-esteem? ...On her faith? He didn't want to alarm Janet until he knew for sure the facts about Kelly.

He managed a smile as he spoke, "No, dear. It's Sunday and I need to go to church. But you go ahead and sleep in today. Of course, I'll miss you at my side, and your lovely voice lifted in praise to our Lord. When I get home, we'll all have a wonderful time celebrating Kelly's recovery, just as you say."

"You are a stubborn man, Thomas Wisp. It'll take more than a little loss of sleep to keep you from God's house, won't it? You're the Tough Stuff!" Janet's dimples glowed as she smiled at her aged husband.

It's been awhile since that expression was used. He sheepishly remembered during their courtship how often he jokingly talked about himself as 'The Tough Stuff'. Now he didn't feel very tough. In fact, he felt very vulnerable. No pride. Just concern.

He chuckled a little as he responded, "Not the Tough Stuff, just a simple man with a simple request of God. I think with all of those voices in praise and prayers being uplifted, it might help me draw close to Him and help me with the request I need to make."

Now Janet was serious, "It's Kelly-Joy isn't it? She really is in some sort of trouble!"

Tom spoke honestly, "I don't know for sure, I only suspect. But God knows. If Jesus is going to use me to help her, I must have a long talk with Him. I don't feel much like prayer right now, but that has never stopped me before, and it won't stop me now. Even so, you know I usually have special time with God here at home in solitude, but perhaps something will happen at church to encourage me and help me. Anyway, I have planned a special teaching and treat for those kiddos in Sunday school. I don't want to let them down. I'll be OK, although I might need a short nap when I get home before celebrating."

Janet gave her husband a warm hug and then snuggled comfortably under the blankets, "Say hi to everyone for me. Oh, today is little Katelyn's birthday. I have a gift in the closet for her, all wrapped and ready for delivery. Would you do the honors? I wish I could deliver it myself to see her face light up. She may already suspect what it is. Ever since the craft fair, she has been hoping for one of my hair bows with Noah's Ark animals embroidered on it. I will look forward to seeing her wear it next week. Good night, Honey!"

These last few words were spoken softly as she fell into slumber. Tom presented a short prayer to God and then cleaned and dressed himself for church. He still had almost an hour before church started but thought maybe getting there early for a change might be nice. He went to Kelly's room to give her a quick kiss goodbye.

He was surprised to find her awake and dressed for church. "Hey, where's that sick young lady I saw in here last night?"

Kelly was sparkling. "Grandaddy, you didn't think I would miss church and all of my friends there did you? I honestly feel great now. Please! I really want to go."

She looked so grown up. Quite the lady, she was. He pulled up a chair and turned it completely around. He then sat on it. With his hands cushioning his chin, he rested his head on the back of the chair and watched as she brushed her long reddish-brown hair. Kelly looked through the mirror at her grandfather and smiled at him. Then she gave him a wink.

"OK! OK! You know just how to get your way with me, don't you?" Tom noticed her fresh pink color had returned, and she did look quite healthy.

Tom had some hot rolls and hot chocolate made, so he went to the kitchen to get them in order to eat them with Kelly in her room next to the fireplace. When he returned, he quickly said grace after setting up the table. Immediately afterwards, Kelly got up from her bed and walked away from her grandfather to the fireplace to warm her hands. As she turned around to face him, she looked deep into his eyes and he looked deep into hers. She wanted to turn away quickly, but his blue eyes looked somewhat like dark blue waves upon a sandy beach and captivated her for the moment.

Tom spoke softly and was very direct and to the point, "Kelly, you need to tell me what is going on."

She took a deep sigh and sat there silently, not knowing how to explain it all.

Tom continued to keep eye contact with Kelly and said, "Several times during the night you kept telling me not to love you. Do you remember that at all?"

Kelly was expressionless as she whispered, "No, I don't."

"Kelly-Joy! Kelly-Joy! This is Grandaddy. You can tell me. You can tell me anything!" Tom had his arms extended with his hands on Kelly's shoulders.

"I can't!" Tears were now starting to flow like two narrow rivers down her face.

"You're so good. How could you understand? How could you ever understand? You only watch "G" rated movies for heaven's sake. You spend your life helping others, never thinking of yourself. You not only know the Word of God, you live it. You have never had an evil thought in your mind your whole life. What could I say that would bring anything but your condemnation on me? Not that I don't deserve it!"

Tom was calmer than he thought he could be in this situation, "Is that what you think of me? Tell me what do you think of God?"

Kelly's head slowly dropped as she looked at the floor and quietly spoke, "The same way. Jesus never had an evil thought either. Isn't that right?"

Her grandfather dropped his arms to his side. "Yes, Jesus never had an evil thought in His life. But He was tempted for forty days. He knows what it is like to be tempted. He also knows what it is like to be rejected and spat upon, and betrayed by a loved one, and humiliated. All because He spoke the truth. Truth that men did not want to hear. Because of that experience, He can identify with you, with all of us sinners. The difference is, He was able to maintain a pure and sinless mind and heart through it all. He is the Son of God, but he also is the Son of Man. He understands so much more than you could ever realize. God created you. He loves you!"

Another period of silence went by before Tom spoke again, "As for myself, I can say as Paul often did, 'I am the chief of sinners.'"

Kelly looked up, puzzled and confused, "I don't understand! Paul was responsible for many Christians going to prison, and some being put to death. I know you're humble, Grandaddy, but I also know you would never do anything wrong."

Tom quickly responded, "Christ changes people. He changed Paul and He changed me. That is why I love Him so dearly!" A lump was forming in Tom's throat, and his eyes were starting to water. Kelly didn't know what to make of it. She knew her grandfather's love for God could easily draw him to tears. Often in church, a certain song would be sung and he would suddenly stop singing and tears would overcome him. But what was all of this talk about his being the 'chief of sinners'. She patiently waited for him to continue.

"You know, Kelly, I have heard many testimonies from people who have been converted and, through the hand of God, taken out of a life of horror and wrongdoing. At one time my heart was full of only guilt and shame. I do not like talking about it, but it might help you understand me better, and hopefully help you see how forgiving God really is. Do you know the story behind what happened to my leg?"

Kelly had a puzzled look on her face as she responded, "My daddy said you were wounded while trying to save children in a village in VietNam. You received the Congressional Medal of Honor for your bravery and heroic action. Isn't that true?"

The memory was painful to Tom. He spoke slowly as though still feeling the pain, "I said nothing upon receiving the award. Later I threw it away."

Tom moved to reposition himself on the chair before continuing. "When I was just getting out of high school, I felt the Vietnam War came at an opportune time for me. I was not a Christian at that time, though I'm sure I thought I was. Up to that point, I had never accepted Christ, but I did believe in God and thought that it very well was possible that Jesus was His son. I knew with the war on, I could enter college, and through the officer training program (ROTC), my last two years of tuition would be paid for, and I would be commissioned as an officer upon graduation. (Indeed, I was). As an electrical engineer, I was assigned to a communication unit. Although I wasn't a Christian, I had high moral standards, at least initially."

"I found myself on my way to Vietnam to be stationed at a communication site there. Air support played a vital role in the war, and the success of the air strikes depended heavily on the communication relay sites between Vietnam and Thailand. I knew no one in Vung Tau. All the guys I was with in training were transferred to different places. I missed them very much. Many of them were Christians and kept me accountable during leave time while we were stateside. Without them I felt so alone and somewhat afraid. Of course, on my way to war I felt afraid of being wounded or killed, but little did I know that there was greater danger to my morality and integrity? Like everything else, I decided to just do my best and try not to think about it."

"Most of the guys I worked with at the communication site had little concern for morality. They felt like it was their duty to 'make a man out of me'. That meant convincing me to go with them on their regular trips to the whore houses, getting drunk, and getting high on drugs. When I refused, they called me every name in the book. Our commanding officer, Major Steven Canter, was a devout Christian. The guys thought of me as 'brown-nosing' the CO. They thought by not going with them, I was just trying to make myself look good for a promotion. Needless to say, I had few friends there. I liked the Major, but I felt a little uncomfortable around him. Every morning he was up early to spend time alone in praying to God. Often during lunch, he would read the Bible. I never knew anyone that close to God and so to me it seemed unnatural."

"The first few months while on leave I did OK. The bell boys at the hotel would consistently try to sell me drugs or fix me with a girl, but I would decline. I was morally in a dangerous condition, being alone, on leave and with no accountability. But it was even more dangerous being with some of my fellow officers who gave bad advice. One weekend I did drink a little with them, but I didn't get drunk. I had convinced them to go bowling with me. Well, on the way to the bowling alley, they stopped at a bar, which was really a whore house. I was naive and went in with them. Internally I struggled, but eventually gave in and slept with one of the girls. I was literally sick upon leaving that place. We went to a restaurant, but all I did was lay my head on the table. They thought I was drunk, but I was actually silently weeping. I felt like a traitor to myself and my future wife, whoever she might be."

"I never went with those guys again, but there were a few times when I ventured on my own to a place where I would find a girl to sleep with. I never let anyone know about these little outings though. After giving in to myself the first time, it was just easier to do it again."

Kelly knew this was going to be one of Grandaddy's long stories and she listened with great interest. She was always so intrigued about her grandfather as a hero, she often wanted to hear the whole story, but her father would not go into details about the matter.

From her grandfather's last statement she thought, "I do know what he means about it being easier to continue doing wrong once you take that first step away from what is right and good."

Tom poured himself and Kelly another cup of hot chocolate from the thermos.

He then continued. "The CO was very kind to me and thought I was this really great guy. He heard about what happened and knew that if it were not for the bad influences of some of his other officers, I would not have done what I did. There were a few Vietnamese officers on the compound being trained on the radio equipment. They spoke English fairly well, but for the most part, kept to themselves. To encourage a greater exchange of ideas and a closer working relationship, a 'buddy system' was set up between the Vietnamese officers and American officers on the compound. The CO assigned me to one Lieutenant Chi Nguyen. We were to bunk in the same tent, eat together, and perform many of the routine duties together as part of the information exchange. I thought I was the one to do the teaching and he was to do the learning. What could a boy from a small village in Vietnam possibly know about technology or anything important? Boy was I wrong. As a child, Chi was led to Christ by a Church of the Nazarene missionary from the United States who once lived in his village. The missionary also taught him English which he spoke fluently and gave him many scientific periodicals to read and learn from."

"It didn't take long for us to become good friends. He had a great sense of humor, and honor was of the utmost importance to him. We laughed and joked about so many things. He was proud, yet humble. He would quote things from the Bible that fit perfectly with the subject at hand. He learned troubleshooting on the electronic equipment very quickly. In fact, when his turn came to insert problems in the equipment for me to isolate and correct, I found myself often at his mercy. Chi was about ten years older than I, but he was so small and looked so young. I found it hard to believe he had four children. His oldest was Kim and she was eleven."

"After a few weeks of knowing him, he invited me to visit his village. It was Easter weekend, and we both had a few days off. We took a bus to a town near his village. It was quite a walk from there, but when we arrived, we were welcomed by a whole group of kids. When Kim heard her dad was returning, she personally arranged a welcoming committee with her friends. She was a little eleven year old bundle of energy and had been in a tree since dawn, waiting on the path a few hundred yards from the village gate. Once she saw us in the distance from her perch at the top of the tree, she started pounding on the tree with a hollow bamboo stick. Immediately children, mostly small thin girls, came running after us. These children were much different from those in the little villages around the army post. They were curious and friendly but reserved. I was waiting for their hands to be thrust in my face for money, but no one took such an opportunity. They just wanted to help carry my bags and touch my hands and arms.

They all had smiles and were very glad to see us. Kim gave her dad a big hug and then asked for my name. She could speak English well, but some of her pronunciations were a little coarse. She pronounced my name Tum. Soon all of the children joined in and said; 'Hi, Mr. Tum.' Kim was at my side the rest of the way to the village, asking me questions about my family and a variety of other subjects.

As we walked, she suddenly turned and said to me, 'Are you going to be our new teacher?'

I looked over at Chi wondering why she would ask such a question.

My inquisitive expression brought an immediate response from Chi: 'You see Tom, last year, Mr. Greg Larison was a missionary here. He and his wife taught the children. He was their Sunday school teacher, and he also played many games with them. Every few years the Church of the Nazarene in the United States would send a couple here to preach the gospel. That is how I came to know Christ as a child. As the fighting came closer to this area, it was mandated that all missionaries be sent away for their own protection and that of the villagers. Christianity is a western religion, and the Viet Cong would destroy any village associated with Christ. Mr. Larison was to baptize Kim, but had to leave quite abruptly. Of course, our village minister could baptize her, but she wants to wait for a new missionary. She was hoping maybe you were that missionary.'

I smiled at Kim and said, 'Sorry to disappoint you little one, but I'm a soldier.'

At first she looked sad, then she perked up and said, 'Mr. Tum, I think the war will be over soon, and then you won't need to be a soldier. Maybe then you could be our teacher. I believe it!'

I put the topic completely to rest by just saying, 'Maybe.'

To change the subject, which I really wanted to do, I looked at her sweet smiling face which was complemented by a matched set of dimples, and said, 'Do you mind if I call you Dimples?'

Without moving her head, her eyes focused on mine.

With a sort of puppy-dog pout on her face she asked, 'Why? Don't you like my name?'

I then explained to her that in my country we sometimes have special names for special friends.

This cheered her up and then she said, 'OK, but I must have a special name for you then, Mr. Tum.'

I was almost afraid to ask, 'And what might that be, Dimples?'

She lifted her shoulders above her neck and placed her small hands momentarily over her mouth to cover a little laugh and then said, 'Whiskers!'

With reservations I responded, 'Well, Whiskers it is then.'

I had not shaved that morning, and with it nearing the end of the day, a five o'clock shadow was forming on my face. I chuckled as did Chi. We waited a moment as Kim stooped to pick some wild flowers.

Now Chi was quietly laughing as he looked up at me and whispered, 'Whiskers! It sounds like the name of a cat.'

Then I said, 'Yea, and you know what I think of cats.'"

"As we reached the gate of the village, the rest of the community were there to greet us. The village leader, who was also the church minister, was first to greet Chi and me. Like all of the other men there, Chem Lee was very old. Chi explained to me that the younger men were either like himself, in the South Vietnamese Army, or in larger towns, working to finance provisions for this little village."

"That whole weekend was a memorable one for me. There was a small storage shack behind Chi's little house which he and his wife, Kep, quickly set up as a guest room for me. Kim had to add the finishing touches: some flowers in a vase and a mosquito net over the bedding to protect me from the numerous insects.

Then Kim asked, 'Mr. Tum, I mean Whiskers, may I read to you? Mr. Greg used to let me read to him to improve my English reading skills.'

I told her that I would like that and in a flash she was back with a book. It was several moments before I realized she was reading from the Bible and did so quite well. I complimented her and asked what part of the Bible she was reading.

She looked surprised and said, 'Don't you know, Mr. Tum? That is Psalm 23. It is my favorite Psalm.'

She then asked what mine was. I stuttered a little and out of the blue mentioned, 'Psalm 1.' Of course, I had no idea what was in those verses.

She immediately turned to it and read, 'Blessed is the man who does not walk in the counsel of the wicked or stand in the way of sinners or sit in the seat of mockers.'

I was startled to hear these words. I had just been thinking about those men at the post who led me astray and how fortunate I was to have a friend like Chi. It was as though God was speaking to me, warning me to have nothing more to do with those wicked fellows. In fact, I asked to see the verse, just to be sure.

After reading the whole chapter, Kim said, 'That is a wonderful Psalm. I especially like the part where it says,

For the Lord watches over the way of the righteous.

Do you think that verse is true?'

Without waiting for a response, she shouted, 'I believe it!'

Her enthusiasm really impressed me.

I remember thinking, 'Why would a few words like that excite this child so? If these people were truly righteous (which they were), why would they not doubt this verse with all of the turmoil about them? One would expect this small group of simple people, caught in the middle of a messy war, to be depressed and sorrowful. To see their land in flames and hear the echoes of explosions from one hillside to the other and see their soil drenched in blood. How could they be so cheerful with so much tragedy about? What was their secret? Who was this Jesus that I thought I knew so much about, but was now just beginning to discover?'

Seeing me look so serious, Kim reached over to tickle me. Being very ticklish, I laughed and laughed. I bellowed in fact. It felt so good to laugh. It seemed like such a long time since laughter had made its way from my innermost being. There seemed so little to laugh about here. But to Kim, every moment was eventful and full of excitement. To her, each day brought the mystery of the unknown and the hope of God's goodness. It brought tears to my eyes. I was crying and laughing at the same time. Laughing from being tickled and crying because I had missed it so much!

Seeing my tears, she suddenly stopped and asked, 'Mr. Tum, I'm sorry! Was I hurting you?'

I just hugged her and said, 'Dimples, don't be sorry. These are not tears of pain, but tears of joy. Thank you!'"

CHAPTER 9

TOM'S VIETNAM HISTORY
Part 2

Tom continued with his story to Kelly. "It was then dark and time to retire. In the village, when darkness came, so did sleep, at least until the gunfire and explosions started. The fearsome sounds would always bring Kim, shaking and running to her father. Chi was a great dad. He would hold her, stroke her hair and sing Christian songs. Soon she would join in and then the noise of war that surrounded us would stop.

I could hear them singing from my bunk. I remember thinking, 'Maybe God does watch over the way of the righteous. With the sound of children's voices, he calms the fighting spirit of men, silences the mortars, and puts to rest the sputtering blast of gunfire.'

At this I fell into slumber and awoke to a group of curious eyes who were anxiously waiting for me to rise.

I smiled and said, 'Good morning.'

In unison, as though in a classroom they all responded, 'Good morning, Mr. Tum'.

They all followed me as I walked to a basin of water to wash my face and brush my teeth. Chi came in, looking stern and clapped his hands several times at the children, chasing them out of the room. Once outside, they stopped to wait for my exit.

Chi smiled as he watched the children line up outside, and as he chuckled he said, 'I'm sorry your privacy was imposed upon, my friend, but you see last night you made quite a hit with these kiddos and the rest of the people here.'

I looked a bit dismayed, so Chi went on to explain.

'They heard you laughing so, all over the village. Many of the parents have told me that your joyful laughter caused these kids to gradually burst in a series of giggles. Watching the children, many of the parents started laughing too, but none held a candle to the bellowing sound of Mr. Tum.'

He went on, 'They miss Mr. Greg and you hold quite a resemblance to him.'

As I dried my face with a towel, I said, 'Maybe in appearance, but not in spirit, for sure.'

Chi looked a little surprised.

I continued, 'Oh, I thought I was a Christian. I suppose most Americans do. But after being around Major Canter and you and hearing about Mr. Greg and seeing the faith of the people here, especially the children, I know my faith isn't real. I don't know Christ. Not like you do. I've heard of him most of my life. But I've never witnessed him. Not like this. It's powerful. Almost frightful! I've never accepted Christ into my life. I guess I, more or less, took God's love for granted. I was never excited about it or anxious to read His Word. Kim keeps saying that she believes it. I know you do too.'

Chi had a look of hope in his eyes as he spoke, 'Tomorrow is Easter. There is no time like the present to be a part of the wonderful Spirit of Christ. Will you ask Jesus in your life now? Here? I would love to be a part of this great beginning of eternal life for you, Tom.'

It was tempting, but I was not ready to completely surrender myself to the Lord. There were times I felt so evil and thought evil thoughts. Although I knew they were wrong, I somewhat enjoyed them. I didn't realize Jesus could conquer them; I thought I had to do that myself before calling on Him, to be worthy. First I had to first be righteous like these lovely people.

I thought 'Maybe I could learn from them and perhaps then I would ask Christ into my life once and for all.'

My face hardened, 'No Chi.'

Apologetically, I forced myself into a smile and said, 'I mean, I'm just not ready yet.'

He smiled too. Then he said, 'In God's time, He will choose you. And that will be a joyful time for us all.'

I was confused and asked, 'What do you mean, God will choose me? I am the one that must do the choosing. Isn't that right?'

His answer was even more confusing, 'Yes and no.'

My brow wrinkled as I pondered over his words.

Then he quoted Scripture right from memory, 'John 6:29

Jesus answered, "The work of God is this, to believe in the one He has sent.
In John 6:44 Jesus said,
No one can come to me unless the Father who sent me draws him.'
Again I looked puzzled.

He laughed a little and threw up his arms, 'It's a miracle. There is no other way to explain it. We are chosen by God. Yet at the same time, we must choose Him. There are those God chooses and draws them to Him. Simultaneously the human spirit must accept Christ.'

I still did not quite understand. It was obvious to him just from the look on my face.

'Tom, it's like the mystery that Christ was 100 percent man, yet 100 percent God. To us this does not make sense. Everything must add up to 100 percent, no more. But to God it is different. As it says in Matthew 19:26

Jesus looked at them and said, "With man this is impossible, but with God all things are possible."'

Well, I decided to let it go at this point. I thought that if Scripture is to be believed, it must be understandable. This is not understandable! As I think on it now, it reminds me how some of Jesus' disciples felt after the teachings of John 6:60

On hearing it many of His disciples said, 'This is a hard teaching. Who can accept it?'

I just couldn't accept it at that point. It seemed contradictory and surely God must not be that. I went outside to greet the children. Kim was right in front. Her dimples were beaming as she smiled.

I asked them, 'Is there a game you would like to play?'

Boy was that a mistake.

Right away they all shouted, 'Buck Buck'.

Then again and again, 'Buck Buck'.

I had never heard of this game before and immediately thought it had something to do with money.

I thought, 'Maybe these kids aren't so sweet and innocent after all.'

But I played along. I said, 'OK, show me what to do.'

They led me to a tree and instructed me to bend over. Then they took my arms and wrapped them around the tree. It was an ideal spot for them because there was a little mound right behind me. I was waiting for one of them to grab for my wallet, at which point I was going to reach for that munchkin and throw him or her into a small puddle of water just to my right. I heard much giggling behind me, but I patiently waited. I heard the piddle paddle of little feet, and before I knew it a tiny body had pounced on my back. Then another. And another. I grasped the tree tighter and tighter to hold up the progressive weight as the children were challenged to jump higher and higher on the ever growing pile of human flesh. Those on the stack were frantically trying to push other children that were beneath and over them off of my back. I then became alive and part of the action. I swayed my body about like a human earthquake. Then the laughter really began, not only from them but also from me. From my peripheral vision I could see children falling the two foot distance to the soft ground on my left and right. Each child had a unique composure as they tumbled to the ground. Within minutes it was all over. Not a child was harmed. The rest of the village stood about smiling, clapping, and gesturing excitement over the fun of it all. Except for Chi, the other men were all too old for that kind of game and it had been so long since they saw the children so happy. Mr. Greg taught them that game and was obviously responsible for that impressive man-made mound from which the children leaped. I had no pain in my back from the ordeal. At least not at that point, but boy would I feel the folly of it all the next day. But oh, it was worth it.

I asked, 'How many other games do you know?'

That game was fun, but I was looking for something with a little more structure and a little less activity. They named a few that I was not familiar with. Obviously, this Mr. Greg came from a different part of the USA than me.

After hearing shouts of one mysterious game after another, I finally raised my arms and said, 'Does anyone know how to play baseball?'

The crowd became very quiet as they looked for someone who might know this game.

Kim said, 'Mr. Tum, I read about it once in a book that Mr. Greg had, but I have never played it.'

I said, 'Well Kim, obviously you know more about this game than the rest, so how about you being one of the captains?'

She shook her head affirmatively, and I picked a boy from the group to be the other captain, who happened to be her cousin, Sal. I had with me a small black exercise ball that I used for strengthening my wrist and hand muscles. I pulled it out and searched for a stick to be used as a bat. They were all anxious to learn this new game. They followed me as I went from tree to tree in my search.

Finally Kim shouted, 'Mr. Tum! Here is the perfect bat.'

Indeed it was, at least for the time being. I stepped off the distance between bases and established the baseball diamond. The little ones followed me, each marching in very large steps, trying their best to mimic my activity. I motioned for each child to pass me, and as they did I called out a position for each. After the last had gone by me, I asked each to repeat his or her position, just to see if they were listening. They did. I then did my best to explain the function of each position. The ball was soft, so they would not need mitts to catch it. I divided the teams and positioned the infield and outfield players. I instructed the pitcher to stand next to me to watch and learn. Kim was my interpreter and passed information on to those who did not understand English well. Kim was the first batter and had a vague idea of what to do. I pitched and she hit the ball right down the center. Kim ran like a pro, and as the ball passed me all of the players left their positions to scurry for the ball. They pushed each other in an attempt to be the one to get the ball. Needless to say, there was not much teamwork established. I stopped the play and again explained what they were supposed to do. Most of the morning we worked on this. We returned after lunch, and by then their progress was encouraging. They were finally really enjoying the game and its structure.` `

"The next day was Easter Sunday, and everyone in the village turned out for the church service. They all had special clothing for this celebration, and Chem's vestment would have drawn the Chancellor of Canterbury to envy. The children's choir sang beautifully and though most of the songs were sung in Vietnamese, the sincerity and obvious love for Christ was expressed so clearly. I felt a little empty because I did not feel the same way about what happened at Calvary. During the service, Chi often glanced my way to see if a change of heart had taken place. I felt sorry for disappointing him, but I could not pretend to be something other than what I was. It did, though, cause me to question myself and what and who I really was. I never thought much about it before.

The whole day was festive and many of the families met together for song, prayer, and praise to God.

The next day Chi and I left for the long trip back to the post. I was surprised that there were no children outside my door.

I imagined that the novelty of my being there had worn off. I would miss them, but I thought, 'Maybe it was better this way. Good-byes are always hard.'

Well, just as we left the village gate, there they were. A whole string of children along the path leading away from the village. They were singing a special goodbye song that nearly caused me to cry. Chi told me that it was the same song they had sung for Mr. Greg and his wife as they left. I remember thinking how hard it must have been for them to leave. As we passed each child, they hugged me and fell in line behind us to follow us part way to the top of the hill. I don't ever remember feeling so loved. The last child was Kim. Tears flowed down her face and she started to sob. She gave her father a long and lingering hug. Her whole body trembled and her hands were so tightly clutched that they were turning red. I'm sure she was thinking that this may be the last time she would see him alive. Many of the village men were dead from the war. With her head on his shoulder, her gaze was fixed on the cross at the top of the hill which marked the entrance to the village graveyard. After a while she regained her composure and walked over to me. She handed me a small gift. As I unwrapped it, I saw that it was a brightly beaded chain with a cross made of beads attached to it. Chi told me that all of the children participated in making it. Each child had a special prayer for me as they carefully added their beads in creating the chain and cross. Kim then hugged me so tight that my head was throbbing. As she released her grip to look into my eyes, her chin was quivering.

With hesitation she slowly said, 'Will we ever see you again, Whiskers?'

I pulled the black ball from my pocket and handed it to her. The kiddos surrounded us. I thanked them for the necklace and pointed to the ball, assuring them that I would be back to play baseball and Buck Buck with them. Then Kim reached forward to tickle me and soon all of the children were piled on me, tickling my sides and neck. As before, I bellowed in laughter. This time so loudly that it echoed down the valley. Then the children gave one last wave and turned to run down the hill. Only Kim lingered. She smiled as she waved with dimples that twinkled as sunbeams reflected from tears deposited there. When we reached the top of the hill, we looked back to see the village with hands waving in the distance. Soon that was all behind us and we were on our way."

CHAPTER 10

TOM'S VIETNAM HISTORY
Part 3

After a hard breath of air, Tom returned to his story, "Several times we did go back together. Then, one time, Chi could not go because of conflicting assignments. He urged me to go alone. Hesitantly I went. I would live to regret that for the rest of my life. I usually brought back some special snacks for all of the children. This time I wanted to give a few of the kids something really special. Some of them had especially enjoyed baseball, so I ordered six baseball caps through a catalog. They arrived just before my return date to the village. Not being directly involved in fighting there I was very naive. I was warned not to give American items to villagers, but I thought it was because they did not want the items placed in the Black Market. I knew the kids would never part with these caps, but I did not realize the danger the caps would cause the whole village.

When I arrived, I passed out the snacks to the children. Then later, after one of our baseball games, I awarded some of the especially good players the caps. Kim, of course, was one of the recipients. The others were all boys, including Sal. They were so excited, especially Kim. I explained to the other kids that once they worked as hard on the game, I would get them one as well. I could tell that some of them were a little disappointed but it was generally accepted that the ones I chose worked the hardest and were the best players. Chim Lolw, one of Kim's friends, though, was more than just a little disappointed. She stomped off wearing a frown with her arms crossed. She seemed to get over it and later came back to play. She was more determined than ever to win herself a hat.

Then that evening, late at night, the shelling and gunfire started over the ridge and Kim became terrified. With her father not there, she came to the shack where I stayed. To her it was very innocent. I was Mr.

Tum, like Mr. Greg, like her very own father. I didn't sing the Christian songs like her father or Mr. Greg would have done. I wish I had. Oh how I wish I had! I did stroke her hair but before the night was over I…. ," Tom placed his face in his hands as he sobbed slightly and then continued, "I molested her."

Kelly stared at him in disbelief. Impossible! No Way! She could not believe that of her grandfather. He could never hurt a child like that. He could never be that selfish. He loved children more than anyone she knew. Practically every kid at church thought of him as Uncle Tom. She was at a loss for words. Kelly just sat there, waiting for him to continue.

After having a few sips from his cup of hot chocolate, Tom proceeded with the story. "I tried to justify my actions, but the guilt remained. When I returned to camp I tried to avoid Chi. He could tell something was wrong. He kept asking what was happening to our friendship. I couldn't tell him the truth. I just couldn't. Instead, I told him a partial truth. I said that he suddenly made me feel very uncomfortable because I was not a Christian, and I felt very dirty and sinful whenever I was around him.

He smiled and said, 'This is good. The Holy Spirit is convicting you.'

Then he looked very serious and said, 'It's OK. It is part of the process. But Tom, don't shut me out. I haven't changed. We are still good friends and nothing you could do would change that.'

My stomach was quickly in knots. I wanted to say, 'Oh really, well try this on for size!', and then tell him what I did to his daughter. But I couldn't. I didn't have the courage. I appreciated Chi too much to hurt him like that. I guess I knew the truth would come out sooner or later, but like everything else, I also thought that maybe I would get away with the sins I committed, just this, one more time.

After weeks, Chi finally convinced me to return to his village with him for a weekend. I was glad to return because I had missed the children. When Chi saw Kim and others with their baseball hats, he became very angry and wanted to talk to me. I did not understand his concern, but walked to the far side of the village to hear what he had to say. He paced a few minutes and was in deep thought before he spoke. Then he stopped and looked me straight in the eyes.

After a few moments of silence he really let me have it, 'I realize you have not been here long and are not directly on the battle lines, to see the destruction and danger first hand. But this is not Denver or Kansas City or Boston! Many of my people are being killed for so much as a hint that they condone what your country is doing here. Surely you remember the hiding place we have for you here, should the Viet Cong or North Vietnamese forces enter this village. This village is in constant threat of that. We have scouts around this parameter so we will know if the enemy approaches. But the children are very loyal to you, maybe too loyal. The hats that you gave them could cost them their lives! They wear them like a trophy. They even sleep with them. They can wear them while you are here, but when you go, you must take the hats with you!'

I hadn't really thought of the danger I had placed the children in. I apologized and assured him that I would take the hats with me when we left. Later I explained this to Kim, Sal, and the rest of the children. Hesitantly, they accepted this although I could tell they did not fully understand.

Since my return, Kim acted as though nothing had changed. Even though I hadn't even asked, she had already forgiven me. Internally, I was blaming others for what I did to her: Chi, for convincing me to go there alone, Kim, for coming to me for comfort, and even God, for allowing it to happen.

Sunday morning came and I planned to sleep in instead of going to church. Chi knocked on my door an hour before church. I told him I was not feeling well and was not going to church. To my surprise though, I could not sleep and ended up getting dressed and reading the Bible. Chi came to my room to check on how I was feeling before leaving. After talking with him a little about God, I decided to go to church after all.

We prayed and sang songs. I was only half-hearted through it all. The children sang beautifully. Chem came forward to give the sermon. I heard many sermons before but none like this. Chi interpreted for me as Chem spoke. This message was for me, straight from Jesus, from God's word in Matthew chapter 18:

At that time the disciples came to Jesus and asked, "Who is the greatest in the kingdom of heaven?"

He called a little child and had him stand among them.

And he said: "I tell you the truth, unless you change and become like little children, you will never enter the kingdom of heaven.

Therefore, whoever humbles himself like this child is the greatest in the kingdom of heaven.

And whoever welcomes a little child like this in my name welcomes me.

But if anyone causes one of these little ones who believe in me to sin, it would be better for him to have a large millstone hung around his neck and to be drowned in the depths of the sea.

Woe to the world because of the things that cause people to sin! Such things must come, but woe to the man through whom they come!

If your hand or your foot causes you to sin, cut it off and throw it away. It is better for you to enter life maimed or crippled than to have two hands or two feet and be thrown into eternal fire.

And if your eye causes you to sin, gouge it out and throw it away. It is better for you to enter life with one eye than to have two eyes and be thrown into the fire of hell.

See that you do not look down on one of these little ones. For I tell you that their angels in heaven always see the face of my Father in heaven."

I suddenly felt the millstone on my neck. The weight crushing my body. I looked and it appeared I had no hands. But it was not my hands that had sinned, but my heart. I thought, 'Shall my heart leave me also!'

Before me flashed all of my past sins. I don't understand it all, even to this day. As each sin was brought to my vision, so was the consequence to others. Their hurt! Their pain! I felt great sorrow over what I had done. There was no one else to blame but me alone. That was crystal clear. I thought, 'God! Jesus! I will repay each restitution for what I have done. Please just forgive me!'

But it also became clear that the debt from my sins was so great, the hurt from each so deep that a lifetime of servitude would not significantly reduce the debt, not even one iota.

My whole body was damp with sweat. My breathing shallow. I could feel my heartbeat echo throughout my whole inner being. I thought I was going to die right there.

While I was having this experience with God, I was oblivious to what was happening in the church service.

Suddenly though, I opened my eyes and saw Kim in front of the congregation. She then began to sing the most beautiful song of God's grace and forgiveness that I have ever heard. The song was one that I had never heard before and have never heard since. I cannot remember the words, but it was about how we expect condemnation when we confess our sins, yet it is then that God provides his greatest kindness to us with words that lead us to repentance and change our hearts, forever!

After that song, I staggered to the front of the congregation and openly confessed my sins, asking for God's forgiveness. With my greatest sin spoken, I looked up at Kim, who had been praising God throughout my confession and now had tears streaming across her face and down her chin as did I. A goose egg was forming in my throat as I asked for her forgiveness.

Before she could answer, Chi had come between us. His eyes were cold with hate. Chi was indeed a Christian, but he was a proud man. He was Kim's father and I had betrayed him and caused much dishonor to him and his family. His right hand was on his knife which had been a part of his everyday attire since the war began. He had no reservations of killing an enemy on the battlefield and he saw me, now as a traitor, one of his greatest enemies. But I would make no defense. I had asked Jesus into my heart and there was for the first time in my life, a great feeling of peace and joy. So great was this feeling, that I could never explain it. So great, that I would even accept this ending to my life with full compliance to God's will.

The congregation was shocked at the words they had heard from my lips. Those who did not understand English well were having my words interpreted to them in whispers in their own language. Even Chem, standing to the side, had an expression of disgust, disappointment and disbelief. It seemed only Kim understood the full significance of this moment in my life.

Before Chi could pull the knife from its sheath, Kim had her little hand on his. At first he was stunned at her insolence, but soon her words tore through his hatred.

Her voice was gentle as she spoke but quick and to the point. 'Father, would you dare curse God in this way rather than praise him for answering your prayers? How often have you prayed for Mr. Tum's salvation? Ten times? A hundred times? A thousand? I remember hearing you from my bed, your weeping, as you sincerely asked the Lord to draw him to Christ. Is it for you or God to decide the sin to finally bring this man to his knees? Does it not say in Luke, chapter 15 verse 10:

I tell you, there is rejoicing in the presence of the angels of God over one sinner who repents?

Father, would you dare turn this rejoicing of the heavenly host into sorrow?'

Kim was silent for just a moment before continuing. She bowed her head as she spoke,

'Though I wish it were by some other way, I am still joyful that God used me to bring Mr. Tum to Christ.'

She then turned to me and looked deep into my eyes.

'Yes! Yes, Mr. Tum! I do forgive you!'

Chi looked lovingly at Kim. She had brought God's truth to him.

The hatred left him and a smile appeared on both Chi's and Kim's faces. Chi dropped to his knees to come face to face with me. His eyes were flooding with tears of happiness. A new aura had occurred over the whole congregation. Even their disgust had turned to joy. The children surrounded me. Hugging me! Happy for me! I will never forget that moment and God's miracle that occurred there. I had been transformed into a new person. The old man was, indeed, dead and a new man arose. Reborn in Christ Jesus. I finally knew how it felt to be a Christian and the exceeding joy of being chosen by God. I closed my eyes to relish the moment. I breathed in a deep breath to take in the new breath of life that I felt and knew to be true. I was forgiven. I was as white as snow, though my sins were as red as scarlet. Nothing would ever be the same again. Praise God! Praise God! That was all I could think or say.

When I opened my eyes again I could see Kim and the rest of the children grasping for my legs. Soon I was lifted on their shoulders and the men of the village were laying hands on me, praising God. They were all literally lifting me up before God in thanksgiving. This was truly the greatest day of my life. Never again would I ever even think of harming a child the way I did Kim."

Now Kelly was crying as she leaned forward to hug her grandfather. So hard she hugged him. So tightly. She had forgotten the discussion that had brought her grandfather to this story. She had never heard such a testimony. Now she understood why he was so dear to her and so many others. She thought his story was over. But now, after taking another drink of hot cocoa, Tom was ready to finish the story.

"I wish I could say everything went well after that, but God had to test my newfound faith. It seems I am tested daily, but not like what I had to endure there in Vietnam.

During the rest of our leave, Chi and I busied ourselves by building a playground for the children right near the edge of the village. We fortified six telephone poles with ropes to create tire swings and a mess net to be used for climbing and playing. A couple of huge brightly colored trash buckets were obtained. We cut the bottoms out and made some tunnels with them. The children loved the play areas as did their parents. On the north side of the village perimeter we also created a more permanent baseball field.

With each visit and just before leaving, I would collect the baseball caps to take them back to the post with me. But, one time we were running a little late leaving, and I accidentally went and left the stack of caps in the guest room. Kim and the other kids never did really understand why I was taking them back. When Kim found them, she assumed that I changed my mind and wanted them to keep the caps after all.

Two weeks later was the start of the renowned 'Tet Advancement'. The Viet Cong moved rapidly, invading deep into South Vietnamese territories. Villages across the land were ransacked, and there was so much bloodshed of not only GIs and South Vietnamese militia, but civilians as well. Maimed and dead children were painful to see. The hardest thing though, was not knowing about Chi's village. Were they safe? Did they escape or go unnoticed by the enemy?

Chi had been sent on an assignment up north near his village. As soon as I could get time off, I would be on my way there as well. Then I heard some other officers talk about the activity around the outpost that Chi was assigned to. Fighting was so intense in that area that it seemed imminent that the communication outpost would soon be overtaken by the Viet Cong. Our troops there needed ammunition and supplies badly. I wasted no time. I was naive and stupid. I thought with my new faith that I was indestructible. I pictured myself like David facing lions and bears and like Gideon, facing immeasurable odds with absolute confidence. Surely God would enable me to prevail. My electronic supply truck was loaded with an arsenal of weapons, and all I needed was the signature from my C.O.

He was somber as I approached his desk. He spoke very low, 'I was expecting you. I heard you volunteered to take the needed ammunition to our northern outpost. This is crazy, you know. It will be a miracle if you make it through alive. With the monsoon so heavy in that area, air support cannot supply our compound there with the needed ammo, so I have been directed by the higher-ups to let you go. This is totally against my better judgment for your own safety, but you know that area better than anyone else we have, and if anyone can get through to help our guys there, you're the man. Once you pass the last checkpoint, you will need to take back roads from there to the communication site. These heavy rains have also caused us to lose communication with them, so we don't know their status. We can only pray.'

He had tears in his eyes as he walked around his desk. My stature eased from the rigid attention stance as he approached. He knew this may very well be the last time he would see me alive. His arm gripped my shoulder tightly as he bowed his head to pray for my safety. His praise to God and a plea for a host of angels to guide and protect my mission moved me deeply. That ever so familiar lump in my throat swelled as

I struggled to swallow. I could not speak and he struggled to leave me with these last few words of assurance from Psalm 91 as he spoke:

'He will cover you with his feathers, and under his wings you will find refuge; his faithfulness will be your shield and rampart.

You will not fear the terror of night, nor the arrow that flies by day, nor the pestilence that stalks in the darkness, nor the plague that destroys at midday.

A thousand may fall at your side, ten thousand at your right hand, but it will not come near you.

You will only observe with your eyes and see the punishment of the wicked.

Just remember that God's hand will be upon you just as this Psalm promises.'

From his desk, the Major picked up my orders which would enable me to pass through our checkpoints. I smiled as I thanked him for everything, especially his friendship. We then hugged one another as friends, brothers in Christ."

CHAPTER 11

TOM'S VIETNAM HISTORY
Part 4

"The normal eight hour drive took a little longer. All of the traffic, though, was moving in the opposite direction as many of the tank and armored forces retreated from the offensive to take a strong position further from the front lines. The last few miles were the most frightening. I had to pull off the main highway to take some back roads that Chi pointed out to me on some of our trips. The soldiers at the last checkpoint suggested I not go further. I talked to a tank commander there who told me that his squad was escorting troops from many of the small outposts in the region but had not yet been ordered to help the Signal Corps compound that was near Chi's village. Like the needs of many of the other fortresses in the area, he was certain that the supplies in my possession would be vital for our Signal Corps compound to hold out until the tank squad could arrive.

I could hear the sounds of war all around as I neared the last mile of the trip. My first inclination was to get to the village to see how the children fared, but my orders were clear. I had to ensure these supplies reached the communication compound with haste. Dusk had come all too soon, but not much light was needed to verify the complete destruction of everything there. I was a half mile from the site and from my point of view it looked so desolate. If any of the troops had escaped capture or death, they would be somewhere in the jungle just beyond the perimeter of the compound.

It was a good thing that it was so late in the day, because being on that hill, even with the heavy fall of rain that surrounded me, I would have been a sure target for mortar and sniper fire. I searched the area with my binoculars for signs of life between the flattened comm site and jungle. Nothing! From that position, the tracer bullets and many flashes of light from the rifles of the enemy were all too clear. The risk was too great for me to continue beyond that ridge. Perhaps Chi was able to lead some of the men to his village. Maybe though, he would just go in the opposite direction to protect his family from the Viet Cong that would surely follow. In either case, I had to get to the village. I had to know if they were OK. I prayed without ceasing, 'Please Lord, help Kim escape the terror of the Cong. Help Chi and Chem and the people of the village. Do what you will with me, but please, God, protect them.'

It was dark as I neared the village entrance. There, a few hundred feet from the gate behind heavy brush, I stopped as I noticed four armored transporters forming a square and connected by canvas. This was obviously a command site for the Viet Cong. My worst nightmare came to life in my mind as I thought of the harm done to the villagers. But there was more than fear and sorrow, there was anger. Anger like I had never known before. Hatred like I had never felt. I suddenly had no care for my own life, only thirst for revenge for what I imagined they had done to my friends. I was about to go running up to the camp with my M16 blazing when I came up with a better plan.

The truck was loaded with explosives. There were cases of grenades and high powered shells. I opened one of the cases of hand grenades and carried several to the front seat of the truck. I stared at the group of men huddled around a campfire who were apparently on guard. I tried to remember the amount of time I had once the pins were pulled. I knew I did not have enough time to pull all of the pins and still get away. I grabbed some string from behind the seat, and cut it in two foot lengths. From each of the grenades, I carefully pulled the pin and, holding the lever in place, wrapped the string around the lever and body. I placed them in a stack with the string of each exposed. Just at the right time, I would use my knife and cut the strings, almost simultaneously. The levers of all would be expelled leaving me a few moments to escape from the cab of the truck. If I could time it just right, my truck could destroy all of the enemy in that command site and put a halt to whatever strategy they were planning. I felt too angry to pray, but I found myself praying anyway. Even in this sorrow and pain and anger, I could not completely turn away from my God. Not after all he had done for me. Besides, there was still hope. Not much, but still hope.

I was stupid though. I was no fighting soldier. My skill was with a slide rule and pencil and paper, not these weapons. Still, I thought it could work. Other trucks were driving along the ridge. They were Viet Cong trucks taking part in the offensive. The sound of my truck would not be noticed. The one thing they feared was the possibility of our bombers discovering their command sites. This one lone truck would be a real surprise for them. I grabbed a bamboo stick from the field and jumped into the truck and drove as fast as I could toward the village gate. The men had left the campfire and went inside one of the tents. At a safe distance from the place of impact, I wedged the bamboo stick between the seat and accelerator to insure the truck would continue moving without my foot there. I then took my belt off and tied the steering wheel in place. Then, with a quick turn at the waist, I pulled my knife from its sheath and cut the string of the explosives. The levers sprang from the grenades as I turned to jump.

Something was wrong, something was holding me back. I struggled and fought to free myself. Who could it be? What could it be?! It was a few moments before I realized it was a coil from the seat of that old truck, snagged onto my trousers. In my mind, time was ticking. I had to get out of there. My mouth became dry and fear nearly caused me to panic. Instantly I tore open the front of my pants and jumped from the cab. In my struggle, the belt was snapped from the steering wheel. The truck swerved and hit a stump nearly sixty feet from me. I positioned myself as a fetus, and anticipated the onslaught of shrapnel from the explosion. The ground shook as the truck disintegrated before my sight. I buried my head and waited. I waited for the shrapnel to penetrate my body, and if I lived through that, then the attack from the Viet Cong which would surely follow.

At first I thought I was unharmed. It was just an illusion though. At the instant the metal shrapnel entered the flesh of my thigh, it became numb. My only warning of the injury was from the flow of warm blood onto my other leg. I was fortunate though. Just as the Lord watched over Jonah and caused a vine to grow over and shade him from the sun so had He caused there to be vines under me. I struggled to wrap some of the vines around my leg to attempt to stop the bleeding. Some of the vines broke, and they seemed useless. But as I felt around in the darkness, I found other thicker vines that held as I wrapped my upper leg with them. I pulled gently at first, then harder to slow the river of blood. I was afraid if I pulled any harder they would break. The rain caused a puddle to form around me. I dug for mud and caked the clay-like mud over my leg. The bleeding stopped and I waited for enemy troops to surround me. I could

hear them yelling and rustling in the distance. I was weakening. Fatigue
overcame me. I fought to retain my consciousness, but to no avail. I
realized I had been acting out of revenge and was now this sorry sight
before God. 'Vengeance is mine'; says the Lord. I should have tried to
sneak around and see if the villagers were being held as prisoners, despite
how slim the chances were of that being true. I was so stupid and then I
thought I must pay for this stupidity. Still, God loved me; I knew that. So I
was not afraid. I felt certain I would die that night but I was at peace. There
was no fear. I thanked my Lord for eternal life. I asked for forgiveness and
He forgave me. He always does. He loves me, in spite of who I am and
what I do. I wanted to sing praises, but I was too weak. A smile was on my
face as I hummed a few bars. I felt the warm gentle hand of Jesus on my
face, and I thought of First Corinthians 15:55:

   Where, O death, is your victory? Where, O death, is your sting?

Later I was told that during the time just prior to the explosion, the
Viet Cong had gathered all of the people from the village to the riverbank.
Chi had disposed of his uniform and was there with his people. He had
been beaten and his wife and the elderly were attending him. There were
several boats on the river, one with a large machine gun mounted on a
tripod pointing at those on the riverbank. The soldiers were just waiting
for the final order to execute the villagers. They had cameras set for the
filming of the slaughter to be used for propaganda to blame Americans
for the onslaught. Some of the Cong were dressed in American uniforms
and wore camouflage paint on their faces. Now that the scene was set, they
awaited the call from the command site. The villagers on the shore had a
peace about them. Yes, there were traces of fear, but their faith at whatever
God should decide kept them confident. Suddenly all were startled from
the sight and sounds of the mighty explosion of my truck which the
Viet Cong thought was from a highly explosive bomb dropped from an
aircraft. The darkness lit up like a firebomb. Panic was in the voice of the
commander as he ordered the boats to leave as fast as they could. In their
minds, their position had been revealed. The communication operator
asked about firing upon the villagers, but there was no response. The
command site had already been quickly disassembled. The gunmen did
not know what to do. There were no orders. The villagers on the riverbank
huddled together, praying. There was fear in the eyes of the soldiers as
they kept looking up, anticipating an array of bombs and gunfire at any
moment. The soldiers on shore ran to the boats as they prepared to leave.
They were given one order and one only, 'leave as fast as they could.'

This they did, and the villagers praised God.

Just before I awoke, I felt so warm. The puddle around me had drained away and the sun was shining so brightly. I shadowed my eyes with my hands as I looked about. I couldn't believe it. They were gone! Or were they ever here? Did I just imagine or dream it all? It was all quite real though. As I moved, the pain in my leg was real. I could see the small pile of debris that was once my truck. The trail from the tracked vehicles of the enemy leading away from the village was real. Why did they leave? I would later learn that the explosion caused them to think that it was fire-power from the air. They thought their position had been discovered, so they immediately left. I prayed, thanking the Lord for my life. I tore my shirt to make a wrapping for my wound. I then used some bamboo sticks to keep my leg straight and used some of the vines to hold the sticks in place. I removed the shoestrings from my boots and used them to reinforce the vines to hold the make-due splint. Now I was ready to crawl. Everything was so quiet, it frightened me. Where were Kim and Chi and the rest of the villagers?

I felt a little weak from the loss of blood, yet I managed to crawl to the gate of the village. As I peered toward the village I saw, in the distance, what looked like a group of children beneath the playground poles at the edge of the village? Six poles; six children. It looked like they were sleeping there, each child leaning against a pole. Had they not seen the brightness of the sun or felt its warmth? Why were they sleeping there rather than in their huts? Or were they sleeping? Please God, I pleaded, let them be sleeping!

I was then somehow on my feet running and hopping toward the playground. I kept telling myself they were OK, yet inside I knew. No! No! Surely God would not allow......

I stopped ten feet from the poles. I could not believe my eyes. On each pole was a rustic blade through a baseball cap covered with blood. A single sign was posted, 'GI Go Home'.

I cried out, 'Oh my Lord! No! Not Kim! Father, did I not plead for Kim. Why?'

I looked at the unrecognizable pile of human flesh beneath the poles. Only the long hair of the first pole signified to me that this was Kim. The others were surely Sal and the other boys. I sobbed as guilt and shame and sorrow filled my heart as I knelt before that little child and cuddled her in my arms. Over and over again I said to her, 'I'm sorry, Kim! I'm so, so very sorry!'

I stroked her hair like I would have done that one night had I been her dad. I then sang those Christian songs that she so loved to hear. Those songs that comforted her from the fear of the explosions and machine gun blasts. I whispered to her, 'It's OK now Kim. It's over. It's all over. Now you are where you've always wanted to be. But, Dimples, if I could just see your smile once more. Just once ...... once more!'"

Suddenly Tom was pale and staring at the wall as though he could still see it all. Tears welled in the corners of his eyes until the little pockets there could hold no longer. Now Kelly too was crying. She thought, "How could Grandaddy ever have endured such hurt and sorrow? Indeed, how could anyone?" She was on her knees now, before this man that she adored so and gently took his hand in hers.

After a short time of silence he was ready to bring this story to its conclusion. "I buried the children, the best I could. The villagers were reluctant to return to the village. They did not know why the boats left so quickly. They did not know what the explosion was that brightened the night sky. Chi did not regain consciousness until late that afternoon. By then I was gone. I did not want to live. My leg was hurting, but not nearly so much as my heart. I felt like I did not deserve to live. I did not deserve God's love. And at that time, I didn't even want it. I was weak and exhausted and hungry and angry. There was food in the village, but I did not eat. I believed I did not deserve food or water. I had asked ... begged God to spare Kim. If only he could have let her live, I could have accepted it all. The shame, the guilt. But my last hope had been crushed, along with my spirit and will to live. I stumbled off to find a place to die. It would not be a clean or pretty spot. I did not deserve that. I ran and crawled down a hill as far as I could. I just kept going and going. After maybe a mile, maybe two, I fell and rolled into a murky swamp surrounded by tall weeds and bamboo. Yes, this was the perfect spot for one as wretched as myself. The perfect place for me to die. I banged my throbbing leg to cause it to bleed and waited for the leeches to do their part. If I did not die of infection or loss of blood, lack of food and water would eventually cause my death. I did not pray or even think. My mind was blank as I waited for the end.

In the meantime, our troops had overcome the offensive for that area and re-established control. Chi received word from the C.O. that I had volunteered to resupply them with ammunition and was somewhere in the area. Chi found my cross necklace (the one the children made for me), covered in blood near the playground surrounded by GI boot prints. He saw that the children were buried. He found what was left of the supply truck and pretty much pieced the whole story together. The only missing puzzle was me. Chi knew me well, though. He knew I would be in despair with guilt over what had happened to the children and went out to look for me. The village children arranged a search party of their own among themselves and combed the area to find me.

Chi had sent word to our command site reporting my being MIA. I was given full credit for initiating the drive that pushed the Viet Cong in that portion of Vietnam back across the border. I was also credited with saving fellow soldiers and the entire village from certain death. I was a hero in everyone's eyes but my own.

For two days I was in the murky smelly waters of the swamp. I should have died. I faintly heard voices calling for me but I did not want to be found. Only a few children continued the search for me.

I fell asleep and when I awoke I started to think more about that day I accepted Christ as my Savior. Again Jonah came to my mind. At least he had the wisdom to pray to the Lord for help while in the belly of that fish. But then, I thought, 'Jonah had not seen someone he cared for, even prayed for, murdered, killed mercilessly.' Then within, I heard a voice say,

'Have you considered my servant Job?'

Then I thought, 'Yes Job, indeed.' Even after his own children whom he loved and regularly prayed for were killed, he was able to say with confidence, 'Though he slay me, yet will I hope in him.'

It suddenly came to me, 'Christ is real! God's love is real!' Though it was too difficult to even speak, I prayed. Praising God for his righteousness and asking for the gentle hand of Christ to again touch me and give me strength.

Amazingly, there were no leeches about. I had sunk to my chest in soft mud which kept me upright and prevented my falling beneath the water and drowning during my long periods of unconsciousness. I started hallucinating seeing deer and lions and other animals that really were not there. Then I heard what couldn't be. It was Kim's voice calling me. I knew it could not be her but I found myself calling back to her. Then she was there.

The dimpled face with both smile and tears was unmistakable. She was nearly hysterical with joy. She came plunging through the swampy waters saying, 'Mr. Tum! Mr. Tum! I knew God would protect you under his wing. I prayed for you constantly and Jesus heard and answered. Everyone had given up hope of seeing you again but I kept searching. I knew you were somewhere near and needed help.'

Though my mouth was so dry that my tongue kept sticking against my palate, I managed to sound out Kim's name and reached to touch her with the little strength I had. I wanted to touch her. I had to be sure I wasn't hallucinating again. How was it possible? Surely I buried her! Yet here she was. All of my prayers during the offensive did not go unanswered! The Lord did hear and somehow protected her! I was coming back to life. God had not forsaken me! He loved me enough to do the impossible. Yes! Chi was right! With man it is impossible, but with God, all things are possible! She was dead, but now she lives. I was truly a dead man, but now God had revealed his love for me, and, indeed, I too am alive. We were both flowing in tears of joy as I kept saying over and over, 'We're alive! Praise Jesus my Lord and God! We're alive!'

Kim refused to leave me to get help. She quickly tied bamboo together with vines to create a make-do stretcher for me. We pulled and strained to free my legs from the grasp of the soft wet mud. Then it gave way and we were on the grassy embankment surrounded by weeds and bamboo. As my heart started to beat with strength it had not known for days, my color started to return. It was hard to see the condition of my leg because it was black with mud. I was surprised to see that there was no swelling though.

Once I was on the stretcher, with the help of my one good leg pushing along the ground, Kim hurriedly pulled me up the hill. As we entered the village, we were immediately surrounded first by children and then a host of men and women. It was like a parade. They were singing songs of praise to God for my safe return when Chi came running.

Kim was exhausted and stopped a moment as she saw her father approach. She yelled out, 'Father, it's Mr. Tum!'

Chi was soon at my side. He grasped my hand with both of his and prayed right then and there. He thanked the Lord for this wonderful blessing and asked for a speedy recovery for me. As he prayed, others were praying simultaneously, thanking God.

He and another man carried me on the stretcher into his home. Once I was settled inside, Chi ran to one of the jeeps that was part of the stream of vehicles parked outside his house. He cranked on the military telephone to reach the communication compound nearby. He gave the doctor there the little information he had about my condition and asked if it would be safe for me to be moved to the compound. The doctor concurred that I should be moved to be checked and possibly be transported by helicopter to a hospital.

I was still weak and in much pain. Then I faded into a deep sleep. I tried to fight it though. I wanted to know about Kim. I wondered who it was that I buried in her place and how it all happened. The fact still remained, though, that I was responsible for the life of Sal and the lives of the rest of those lovely children. As horrible as it was, I knew it was something I would have to live with.

Chi, knowing me well, tried to console me as he saw me fading into unconsciousness, 'Tom! You did not harm the children. It was the Viet Cong, not you. You are not responsible for their lives, just the saving of our lives!'

Kim then added, 'You are the bravest man I ever knew. You are my hero, Mr. Tum!'

The last thing I remember thinking was, 'What are they talking about? Me, a hero?'

The next thing I knew, I was in a military hospital in Saigon and Chi and Kim were there when I awoke. It was a difficult story to tell, but Kim told me how her life was spared.

Kim was shaking a little as she started, 'We all decided to play a game of baseball as we waited for daddy to return for a visit. I had just hit the ball and ran toward first base. As I slid into first base, my cap fell off and Chim ran over and she grabbed it. At first I thought she was going to return it to me, but instead, she ran off with it. Just then I saw the soldiers make their way across our field toward the village. Two of them ran after Chim. The rest of us scattered across the field for our hiding places, but the Viet Cong soldiers made sure they had captured all of those wearing the caps. I stayed in my hiding place and waited.

It was almost dark when I heard the screams of Sal and the others. I thought about Chim and how I was the one they should have grabbed and tortured instead of her. I prayed and asked God to relieve them of their pain. No sooner had I spoken these words and the screams stopped. I knew they were then with Jesus. I felt sad because I knew I would not see them for a long, long time. A shimmering circular cloud hovered over the village and then faded. I believe it was angels coming for my friend's souls. I waved and thanked God. I remember feeling a little disappointed that I was not going with them.

I thought that my mom and dad may possibly be dead as well and that frightened me so much. The thought of being alone. All alone. Then, later, I heard that powerful explosion that shook the ground beneath me. You know how explosives always frightened me. I covered my ears and leaned against a tree, pretending the tree to be Daddy. In the breeze the branches brushed against my hair and I pretended it to be Daddy, brushing my hair with his hand. The wind through the trees made a soothing sound, and I pretended it to be Daddy, singing those wonderful songs to me. As I sang along, I fell asleep. When morning came I was afraid to go into the village. Afraid of what I would see. Then after many hours, I saw Daddy coming out of the village looking for me. I was so glad to see him. When he told me you had been there to save us all but were now missing and believed to be hurt, I knew I had to find you. I asked the Lord to please help and keep you safe. I kept looking and calling. I had to. When I found you, it almost made up for:....'

Kim paused for a moment and looked to the ground: 'for losing my friends.'

There was a period of silence that followed and during that time I remember those feelings of guilt starting to swell in my throat again. Chi, though, was quick to remind me of my innocence regarding the lives of his nephew and the other five. No one blamed me, only me myself. I knew it was something I would have to live with, but knowing that those sweet kids were in the presence of the Lord made it a little easier. I believed the Scriptures and I knew that in spite of everything it was true, as Paul states in Romans about everything working for good for those who trust in Christ. Chi then told some of his story of how the Viet Cong took possession of the Signal Compound and then the village. He mentioned that as the soldiers positioned themselves to shoot into the crowd of villagers, the commander offered to spare their lives if they would only denounce Christ and promise their loyalty to the North Vietnamese government.

Chi's last comment was, 'We could not turn from our Lord Jesus Christ. We could not denounce Him even in the face of death, for we know as did the Apostle Paul...

to live is Christ, and to die is gain.'

Though the shrapnel had done damage to my leg, I was finally able to leave the hospital in Saigon.

A few weeks later, General Tailor, who was commander over the US Army Signal Corps, presented me with the Congressional Medal of Honor. In my heart I could not accept it although I humbly pretended to go through the motions. After the ceremony was over, when I was alone, I found a quiet little place and gave it a mighty toss into a nearby pond. Now I kind of wish I had kept it, not as a reminder of my courage, for I had never felt less courageous, but as a reminder of the courage of Kim, Chi, and all those of that village who were willing to die for the truth of Christ. Chi or Kim should have been awarded with honor, not me.

Now you know Kelly-Joy, because of what I had done to Kim, what I had done to cause the death of those 6 children, I can honestly and accurately say that I was the chief of sinners."

Kelly was speechless. She was now sitting on the floor near the chair where her grandfather was sitting. He was staring out the window, looking far into the past. Then, with a quick turn of his head, his eyes focused deeply into Kelly's eyes. Kelly often thought of her grandfather as a man of compassion, and greatness, and tenderness, and courage, but never so much so as now.

CHAPTER 12

KELLY'S SALVATION

An hour had passed, but it only seemed like a few minutes. Kelly was so involved with her grandfather's story that until now she had forgotten about her own secret which her heart was calling for her to tell. She silently thought she could dismiss the idea of telling her grandfather by noting the time. Although it was already too late to go to the early church service, they still had more than an hour before the second service started.

Her grandfather had told her the darkest shadows of his past. He opened himself up before her and knew very well she may reject him and be appalled at what he had done. He trusted her with truth, the greatest gift to share. Could she now trust him any less? But how?! How could she tell her story? Where would she begin? She knew she would, though. Now she knew he would understand her shame and guilt!

Kelly hugged her grandfather and then returned to sit on the floor next to her bed. She leaned against the mattress and stared into the flames of the fire. For a few minutes they delightfully entertained her by dancing from one log to the next. She sighed and turned to again face the gentle man as he patiently waited for her confession.

Tom expected the worst but hoped for the best. His thoughts raced through the possibilities: drugs, alcohol, sexual promiscuity, thievery or perhaps some combination of these. He took advantage of the silence to pray to his God. Again and again he prayed.

"Lord! Whatever this child has done to move her away from you, please help her to repent and give her guidance and direction to know what to do to restore her relationship with you!"

Suddenly Kelly felt a new strength. She leaned forward and wrapped her arms around her knees. She spoke slowly but to the point.

"Grandaddy, I am not the sweet, innocent, little girl you think I am. I have sinned so greatly against God. I don't know how to tell you or where to begin."

Tom moved his chair closer to her and took her hand in his. He leaned close to her and said, "Kelly-Joy, just talk about when it all started. Last year, last month, last week. There is always a beginning."

This wise man was right, and Kelly knew it. The beginning. She wasn't sure what she would say, but as she opened her mouth to speak, a flood of words formed and flowed from her. As they did, a huge weight was removed from her shoulders. It felt so good to release that secret. Not to have to be cautious of every word which might cause a hint of suspicion.

"Grandaddy, do you remember last year when I was here and received that phone call from Daddy?"

Tom answered, "Yes. You were overjoyed that your dad had found a solid mission in prison ministry, completely giving up the idea of ever becoming a church pastor again. He felt it was God's calling for him to continue to preach the Gospel in prisons and get back with your mother, which he was certain would eventually happen. The burdens of a congregation would no longer keep him from his duties as a father and husband, and the prison ministry would help him keep a manageable schedule."

Kelly nodded her head. "I was so happy! Daddy gave me such hope that we would all be a family again. I missed him so much. I was anxious to tell Mom the news and see some glimpse of hope from her reaction. Before I even had a chance to tell her, all of my dreams were crushed by her news. She took me aside shortly after I arrived back home. It was hard for her, and she knew it would be. As carefully and tenderly as she could, she told me that the divorce had been finalized. I nearly fainted. Anger and disappointment just overcame me. I said horrible things to her that I know I shouldn't have. I wanted to hurt her. I blamed her for the separation. Daddy tried to explain to me that he had done Mother a terrible wrong by demanding so much from her and giving so little, but I could not believe it. I suddenly hated my mother. I know it sounds horrible Grandaddy, but at that moment and in the weeks that followed, I really hated her."

Kelly continued, "You know, Grandaddy, the separation had been a year, and Mother had been true to Daddy that whole time. During that whole year, she had not shown any hint of interest to be with any other man. And Daddy has been so devoted to her. He loves her as much as you love Grandma."

Tom squeezed Kelly's hand, "Yes, I know Sweetie!"

Trembling a little, Kelly squeezed the large gentle hands in return. "She was successful at her new job though, which did not go unnoticed by the men there. She is a very lovely lady and men seem to have an instinct about timing. Being in a new location, far from her old friends, she became lonely I guess. My attitude all along, I'm sure, made her feel even more isolated. Several of the men from her work asked her out, regularly, but she continued to decline. But a couple of weeks later, she had car trouble and allowed one of the men, named Bill Purgoe, to drive her home. Then a few days later, they went out to dinner. I was furious.

I was determined to break up this relationship, no matter what the cost. I was on a crusade that would end in destruction. In my own mind though, it was an unselfish and honorable crusade which was intended to bring my mother and father back together as one."

Kelly's throat was getting dry, so she got up and went to the breakfast tray and poured a cup of chocolate from the thermos. After a few swallows she was ready to go on,

"I started forcing myself to be nice to my mother to regain her trust. After she and Bill had a few dates, I encouraged Mom to bring the gentleman home for dinner. I wanted to size him up to determine the best way to break up that friendship. I found out that Bill had been divorced twice before, so I started researching his background. I dropped in a few times at my mother's office and made conversation with some of the people there about Bill, to try to gain as much information as I could. I memorized names that were casually mentioned and carefully asked questions about him. I started talking to some of the kids at school to get ideas on tactics and strategies. I got lots of ideas and many of them I tried. A boy I confided in gave me some very nasty pornographic magazines, and I made mailing labels with Bill's name and address on them. Then when Bill came over to pick up mother, as they were inside, I placed some of the magazines partially hidden between the seat and backrest. I knew this would bug my mother, and at some point she would pull them out and then have different thoughts about this man. I got a newspaper route in Bill's neighborhood, and as I delivered his newspapers, I added porno magazines with labels of his address to his mail. I thought mother might sometime see them too and she did on a couple occasions; usually in his trash cans. I did a lot of other things to discredit him, and Mother finally did believe him to be a pervert and stopped seeing him. But that's not the worst part, Grandaddy!"

Kelly looked carefully at her grandfather to assess if condemnation had yet crossed his mind. She only saw gentleness and understanding in his expression, so she continued:

"I was still angry at Mother though. I thought that it probably wouldn't be long before she would be dating again. I talked more to some of the kids at school who were troublemakers. Boy did they have a lot of ideas. Especially the boy who gave me the magazines. He went by Tab, but his real name was Robert. He said he knew of a sure fire way of preventing my mother from seeing other men. He sounded very confident. He talked like he was very concerned about me and my situation. I was very lonely and starved for someone to talk to. I had stopped talking to Mother. It was horrible. And here was this boy who treated me special. He made me feel like somebody. He came to my house after school, before Mother got home. I knew I shouldn't let him in, but I did. We just talked awhile. We didn't even go in my bedroom, but I did show him where it was because I had to get information about a homework assignment from my backpack that he said he needed. Then he left. I waited for him to call on the telephone, but he didn't. At three in the morning, I heard a tapping on my window. It was Tab. He said he was having problems with his parents and just needed someone to talk to. At the time it seemed very romantic to me. We just stood there and talked through the open window. He was a real sweet talker and I was very vulnerable. Before daybreak, he left.

I wanted to talk with him more. We seemed to have so much in common. After a few days, I wanted to see him again. He finally called me and told me that if I trusted him, I should meet him at his house at 2AM. He said that his parents would not be home at all that night. I know I should not have gone, but I did. It seemed to be so much fun, sneaking out of the house, like on some special secret assignment. You know the imagination I have, Grandaddy.

Anyway, I walked the few blocks to his house. It was not so bad. There were lots of street lights, and I kept my fear down by humming. I stopped in front of his house and waited awhile. I almost turned back, but I thought that since I had come this far, I might as well complete what I set out to do. To the side of his house was a set of sliding glass doors that was an entry into his bedroom. They were open. His lights were on. I cautiously walked to the entryway and there he was with a sweet smile on his face. He had a small table set up in his room with two chairs and a small urn of hot chocolate. It was chilly outside and the steam from the urn tantalized my nostrils. And in the center of the table was a dish of fresh cookies. I couldn't believe that he baked them himself for me.

Well, we sat and ate and just talked for a few hours. Then, near daybreak, he walked me home. I really enjoyed myself. He didn't seem like such a troublemaker. He seemed like a good friend. A good listener. He had a good sense of humor and a cute way about him. I found myself liking him and wanting to see him more. So I did. Once a week for the next two weeks. Mother never suspected a thing. I went to bed very early and made the trip to his house each time. Although his parents were home, their bedroom was up on the third floor on the other side of the huge house. He was always there to greet me, and we would talk. Then one time we did more than talk. We did what I promised my dad I would never do until marriage, what I promised God I would never do until…….."

Kelly broke off in sobs as she fell into her grandfather's arms.

She pulled back a second to finish her story.

"That wasn't the end though. I kept going to his house, and instead of hot chocolate he would have vodka and other drinks for us. And I drank, and we did it again and again. I would drink just until I was slightly drunk and then near daybreak make my way home. On occasions I would tell my mother I was sick and she would let me stay home, not having an inkling of what I was doing. I was wrong. I felt so evil and unworthy of God's love, of anyone's love. Sneaking out of the house, doing what I told myself and promised all who cared about me that I would never do. Betraying my mother, betraying my father, betraying you! Oh Grandaddy, I am so sorry. What do I do? What do I do? Please tell me what to do!"

At this she broke down into long deep sobs. Tom immediately went to her and held her long and hard. She quickly broke away and stepped back.

"How can you hold me like this? Grandaddy, don't you know what I'm saying?"

As she looked at him though, there was no expression of shock or anger, just love. She then remembered his story and the shame he expressed. The remorse and pain and sorrow. Yes he knew exactly what she was confessing, yet he loved her regardless and now she knew that. Realizing this, she stepped back into his arms and continued to sob and weep.

Tom said nothing. There was nothing to say. The damage was done. Now, with God's mercy, there could only be healing. There would surely also be consequences, but truth and honesty and a clear conscience are worth it all. Yes, this was indeed a horrible truth, but it was also a great victory for Kelly because she can learn from this. No longer would the stress and turmoil of trying to keep this secret be a wall between her and God and her mother and her father and everyone. Tom prayed as he held that child. He silently thanked God for Kelly and her courage.

Tom knew there would be many more steps she would have to take in dealing with this problem, but this was a first and mighty step indeed. Now she needed to confess it to God, repent, and work on restoring her relationship with God and with her mother. This was something she alone had to do. Tom was concerned that if he were to even suggest she do these things, it might be out of obedience to him, rather than through sincerity. This beckoning must come from the Holy Spirit. Only then could her efforts be real and her repentance be authentic.

Although Tom's heart ached within him with sorrow, he also felt relief. But at this moment, Kelly's words did not yet have their full impact on him. His heart was too full of compassion to even consider being angry at her or God. Throughout her life, he, Doug and Janet had labored rigorously to encourage Kelly-Joy to be honest, pure and kind hearted in preparing her for the straight and narrow walk with God. Mary, too, although not so emphatically, encouraged her daughter to live a Christian life. Prayers were continually lifted for guidance and support in this effort. Tom would soon be bewildered and wonder how this could have happened. But not now. God had blessed him with an understanding for the hurt she was feeling and the hurt that drove her to such rebellion.

Finally, Kelly's tears subsided. She was glad this ordeal was over but she also knew she had a greater ordeal ahead of her. She knew that she was now going to have to tell her father. How would she? How could she? He had already been hurt and humiliated so badly with the divorce. How could she possibly cause him sorrow upon sorrow now? It did feel good though, to reveal this horrible secret that had been crushing her.

It had been half an hour since she started her confession. Although they still had time to arrive at church for the second service, her enthusiasm was more than diminished. But Tom encouraged her and told her that she would probably even enjoy the service more. Indeed, she would. Indeed, they both would.

Woodridge Falls Community Church was just a few blocks away, so they both had plenty of time to clean their tear stained faces and freshen up. At first Tom felt exhilarated from revealing his secret to Kelly and her confiding in him with her heartbreaking situation. But after climbing the stairs, as soon as he entered his bedroom and closed the door, he fell to his knees.

Hurt and pain overcame him now that he was alone and out of Kelly's sight. How could she have done this and how could God have allowed it to happen? He felt like knives had been thrust into his heart. He suddenly felt betrayed and confused. He thought about his son and knew the pain that this would cause Doug as well.

Could anything have caused him greater pain and anger and bewilderment? Had he failed her? Had Doug failed her? Had they not prayed exhaustively for Kelly? Tom remembered that it was last year when Doug took Kelly out on a father/daughter date. After she promised him and God that she would not have any sexual relationships until after marriage, they both sincerely prayed. Then Doug presented her with a "Promise Ring" that she could always wear to remind her of this commitment. Doug was so excited when he told Tom of the event. Tom remembered how it gave him confidence that Kelly would follow through with that commitment. Was that not real? How could she have ignored it all?

Tom had personally counseled Kelly during the separation of her parents and was certain that, although her disappointment could not be denied, her love for God was steadfast. During one of their sessions in one of the workbooks, they read a story about a girl who had so much defiance that she would sneak out from her bedroom window at night and meet a boy to spend most of the night with. He remembered Kelly saying, "Grandaddy, I would never, never do that. It would hurt too many people I love. No way!"

Was she sincere in that statement or just fooling me? Again feelings of betrayal crept into his heart.

He was suddenly convicted by that word 'betrayal'. Had Kelly's act of betrayal been any greater than that which he had indeed committed against Kim, against Chi? No, indeed far less. Yet, they forgave him. Would he dare do any less for Kelly? He must forgive her once and for all!

As he was thinking about the importance of his forgiving Kelly, he remembered that prior to asking for Kim's forgiveness he had already asked God for His forgiveness and repented before His presence.

Would she really ask God for forgiveness and repent, or go on with this misguided behavior? Although she started this affair out of loneliness, does she now think she is in love with this boy? He hadn't quizzed her with that question, so for the moment it tormented Tom. She mentioned yesterday that she felt strong here on the mountain, but weak away from it. He struggled to remember her words,

"I feel so strong and confident up on this mountain. I feel as though I could tackle anything up here. The wind, the storm, lightning, thunder… anything. But when I leave, I feel so small and helpless, unable to face anyone or anything."

But now she will be facing many difficult situations, and it will be away from these mountains. Would she really be strong enough to face her feelings and this dilemma? The so-called '*magic*' here that she talked about yesterday is the same that exists everywhere, '*God's Love*'. But to use it, she must accept it.

Ever since she was a little girl, praying was as natural for her as singing or walking. Although the past few years have shown her to be less apt to initiate prayer, she still seemed delighted to join in when prayer was spoken. With her relationship with God severed, prayer will continue to be difficult for her. Will she be able to overcome this obstacle and humble herself before God, before our Lord Jesus Christ?

At this, Tom melted on the floor with his face pressed into the carpet and his arms outstretched to both sides. Pain swelled within him from his lower torso up through the rest of his abdomen until it all seemed to settle at the base of his throat, causing him to gasp for air. After waiting a few moments to compose himself, with a soft spoken voice he humbled himself before his God in prayer,

"Lord, please help Kelly-Joy. I believe, but Father help my sudden fear and confusion and unbelief. Help me to know that this will indeed be used for Your Glory, somehow! So often in the past I have truly felt your strength …. but now I am limp. I feel helpless. I can do nothing to help this child without your blessing. Please! Today, give me some sign of reassurance that will enable me to regain my hope. I love you, my Lord Jesus!"

The intensity of his conversation with his God left him oblivious to what was happening around him, but now he could hear Kelly's voice quietly calling him from the other room and the faint knock on his bedroom door.

"Grandaddy! Grandaddy! Are you in there?"

Tom quickly got up to open the door. In doing so, he glanced over at Janet and was relieved to see that she was still deep in sleep. Kelly had a bright smile on her face as she said, "We better hurry to even have a chance at getting to church on time. If we're late, the only seats that will be open will be those right in the front row, causing our tardiness to be revealed to all. And I know how that embarrasses you, Grandaddy."

Kelly was right and Tom knew it. He laughed a little at her knowing him so well, "I'm sorry kiddo. I just need a second in the bathroom to wash my face and then we can leave."

The church was packed, yet there were conveniently two seats vacant in the second row, near the aisle. They were just on time and Pastor Bob Milhorn was making his way to the platform. Tom and Kelly were greeted by several friends and acquaintances around them as they arrived at their destination and sat down for the opening prayer.

At first the service seemed quite ordinary. The announcements of upcoming events and new births and such were discussed, and a visiting missionary from Europe was introduced. Yes, all very much typical for Woodridge Falls Community Church.

While this was going on, Tom was intermittently reading some of the flyers in the church program. Kelly had her Bible opened from the time she sat down. One of her friends who had just greeted her had mentioned that the high school class was studying chapter 4 of I Thessalonians so Kelly wanted to look it over to be ready for the class, which began after the worship service. Verse three immediately caught her attention. She felt very strange as she read these verses. Her father always told her that God speaks through His Word. Was He indeed speaking to her now? Surely He knows the sorrow of her heart and her inner struggle. She knew these words from God were indeed for her and at this moment in time for her alone:

It is God's will that you should be sanctified: that you should avoid sexual immorality; that each of you should learn to control his own body in a way that is holy and honorable, not in passionate lust like the heathen, who do not know God; and that in this matter no one should wrong his brother or take advantage of him. The Lord will punish men for all such sins, as we have already told you and warned you. For God did not call us to be impure, but to live a holy life. Therefore, he who rejects this instruction does not reject man but God, who gives you his Holy Spirit.

She had been acting like she truly had not known God. By initiating and participating in that whole sexual escapade, had she deliberately been rejecting God, not man? Rejecting God, not just her mother? She searched her memory for an instant in time when she had accepted Christ as her Savior, but could find none. She remembered her grandfather's words from his story:

Oh, I thought I was a Christian. I suppose most Americans do. But after being around Major Canter and hearing about Mr. Greg and seeing the faith of those people, especially the children, I knew my faith wasn't real.

Could it be true? Could it be that her faith, too, was not real? Had she fallen into that dilemma of believing herself to be a Christian simply because her parents were Christians? Because she went to church nearly every week? Because she was an American?

Her grandfather had told her of his conversion and it was real. He had asked Christ into his heart and asked for forgiveness for his sins. Had she? No! Not ever! In his story, her grandfather was reborn just as Jesus said in John 3:

I tell you the truth, no one can see the kingdom of God unless he is born again.

She thought, "But how could I be reborn? What could I do right now for God to forgive and accept me the way He did Grandaddy?"

As her mind was pondering over all these things, the church worship team had been playing and singing their series of songs along with the congregation. A new song began though, which immediately captivated her attention. A beautiful melody she had never heard before was beginning. This song was new to Kelly and to the congregation, but it was not new to Tom who was staring at the large wooden cross behind the altar.

Previously Tom had been singing with joy and jubilance at the top of his lungs, but now this song had brought him to his knees in thanksgiving and wonder. He was suddenly quiet and overwhelmed with emotion.

This was Tom's conversion song. He had not heard it since that time and now the message spoke again to him like soft gentle words from an old friend, indeed an old loving friend. Tears trickled down the side of his face as the truth that assured him of God's forgiveness became real once again.

Of course, Kelly had no way of knowing that this was the song her grandfather had just been telling her about an hour or so ago. For herself, though, the message was overpowering! It seemed the sounds were coming from Heaven itself and settled gently within her being. Though the church was full, she suddenly felt all alone right there before God. The words of that song went straight to her heart as deep sobs of thankfulness exploded from the very center of her soul. She had been waiting and fearing God's condemnation. Until now, she was sure she was destined for His rejection as a result of her rebellion and poor judgment. But this message revealed a side of God she had not known or understood. Upon hearing it, she wasn't sure she could ever understand it. "With man it is impossible, but with God, all things are possible."

Tearfully she thought, "Miracle upon miracles, this is proof that with God, indeed, all things are possible. Forgiveness! Reconciliation! Hope! A clean conscience! Regained Trust! And yes, even Rebirth!"

At that moment Kelly asked Jesus to be her Savior. She had confessed her sins to her grandfather, now she was confessing them to God. And now she was ready to do just that. In her confession she stated as King David had done in his confession: *I have sinned against you Lord, and you alone!*

She asked for forgiveness and was ready to repent and take whatever consequences were necessary. She felt God's peace and God's love. She was a new creation bound for heaven to be with Jesus, forever!

The worship team had completed all the verses. Since it was a new song they were now restarting the song from the beginning. Kelly now joined the singing, between sobs of joy, with her beautiful soprano voice! She sang every adjective and verb as she deeply expressed herself before Jesus!

> *Kneeling there, at the cross, with tears abound,*
> *Expecting nothing but some angry words,*
> *My sin so cruel, I'm such a fool,*
> *Such shame I felt,*
> *Then your arms were around me,*
>
> *The Word says, it's your kindness,*
> *Your kindness alone,*
> *That leads us to repentance, Oh Lord.*
> *You love me, and trust me, though my sin was great,*
> *I see now, forgiveness is your trait.*

What can I say, what can I do, where can I go?
You see me now, in the darkest of my ways.
It's Jesus Christ, that paid the price,
And now I'm clean, forgiveness like I've never seen.

The Word says, it's your kindness,
Your kindness alone,
That leads us to repentance, Oh Lord
You love me, and trust me, though my sin was great,
I see now, forgiveness is your trait.

The joy I feel, now that I'm healed,
My soul declares,
I'll live my life with no more strife or shame.
I have this hope, now I can cope,
Whatever comes my way.
For I know that your Spirit's here to stay.

The Word says, it's your kindness,
Your kindness alone,
That leads us to repentance, Oh Lord
You love me, and trust me, though my sin was great,
Forever, forgiveness is your trait.

During the last verse of the chorus, Kelly had stood and walked slowly to the front of the congregation. She had no idea why she was doing this. There had been no altar call, no request from the pastor or worship team for those seeking Christ to step forward, yet here she was. After noticing that Kelly was no longer sitting at his side, Tom made his way down the aisle to stand next to his granddaughter.

The end of this song was to initiate the beginning of a well-prepared sermon. Pastor Bob had done his homework and was ready with a very inspiring message. As he stood there on the platform, though, looking straight into Kelly's eyes, he knew God had a far better message planned for his congregation. She was glowing, and he had witnessed an expression of such peace only one other time. This was special. Pastor Bob held out his hand for Kelly to join him in front of the microphone. Tom followed and flanked her left side as Bob addressed the congregation:

"Good morning friends and welcome! Most of you know Tom Wisp. This is his granddaughter Kelly, and I believe she has something for us. But first, let's thank the Lord for what Kelly is about to share and for God's wonderful forgiveness."

Bob spoke beautifully, giving glory to God, and praising Him with several quotes from the New Testament which spoke of the Lord's promises. Bob had a deep resonant voice that would reach the four corners of the large sanctuary, even without a microphone. There was no roughness in his entire oration; it was smooth and perfectly spoken. Bob had once been a disc jockey with a bright future in radio. But when God called him, he realized it was for an even brighter future throughout eternity. At first, when Bob revealed his desire to leave the radio station and preach God's word, people shook their heads in disbelief, even his own parents. He had walked away from the most popular radio rock station in the Los Angeles area for a small corner church covered with graffiti. But to him, that first little stucco building was like a mansion, and the people there, poor as they were, were like a beautiful field of golden wheat, ready for the harvest. Just prior to his conversion, he had lost everything. That everything was the materialistic everything. But his joy came from what he gained, which was a better everything: eternity, peace, love, a tenderhearted spirit and best of all, a closeness with Jesus. This was real! Eternal! That which he gave up was future dust. Paul expressed in chapter two of Philippians very well what Bob had felt:

But whatever was to my profit I now consider loss for the sake of Christ. What is more, I consider everything a loss compared to the surpassing greatness of knowing Christ Jesus my Lord, for whose sake I have lost all things. I consider them rubbish, that I may gain Christ and be found in him, not having a righteousness of my own that comes from the law, but that which is through faith in Christ--the righteousness that comes from God and is by faith.

With the completion of the prayer, Bob stepped down from the platform and sat in the front row. He had no resentment that his well-planned sermon would now be set aside for another day. The Holy Spirit was about to provide an even better sermon. He could feel it. He could see it in Kelly's and Tom's faces.

Kelly was not at all nervous, although she had no idea what she was about to say. But she spoke with the power of the Holy Spirit. Her voice was soft and in no way earth-shattering, but the words were powerful.

As she confessed to the congregation of all that she had done, her speech was interrupted several times with sobs, and then tears of joy.

After the confession she explained to everyone there that she, at last had given her heart to Christ. She told them that all her life she thought she was a Christian, but in reality was just playing a game with God, just trying to offset the bad in her life with the good, that by doing so she hoped to win God's approval. Before ....she didn't think it was important to actually ask Jesus to be her Savior. Just now though, she remembered how time after time, Jesus stood there at her heart knocking. During the storms he was there, knocking. During the blazing heat he was there, knocking. Calling to her! But she was too proud to answer. Through the shame of her sin, together with the power of the Holy Spirit, she was able to overcome her pride. Now that she had answered and welcomed Jesus into her life, she stood before them as clean, as pure, and as white as freshly fallen snow. As she finished she humbled herself before them and God and melted in her grandfather's arms. The congregation was deeply touched by her courage and the sincerity of her conversion. Tears from both men and women graced the faces of the rows of people there.

Just then a man who had been standing in a shadow near the rear doors started to walk to the front. As he passed each row, heads turned and followed him as he made his way to the couple at the microphone. Kelly looked up as did Tom. Their eyes were focused on this man, and his on them. After a brief moment, they embraced, one with another, and all three as one. God had arranged for Doug to hear his daughter's confession first hand.

It was a touching scene to all who witnessed it. Some of those saw for the first time the goodness of confession. It was overwhelming! It was inviting! It was absolutely awesome!

Sunday was usually a very busy day for Doug who led the worship at several of the prisons, so he was not expected to be there in Woodridge Falls until Monday. But, unexpectedly and miraculously, God had arranged for a very popular college singing group to be available, and had placed in their hearts a desire to entertain prisoners that very Sunday. They even had a speaker who was an ex-convict and anxious to give his testimony to fellow inmates. This made it possible for Doug to be there in Woodridge Falls. He had no idea just how important it was for him to be there. He was so relieved to see Kelly stepping out in faith to fully commit herself to Christ. Sure, her sin was bewildering to him, but her confession was heartfelt, and her salvation a real gift from God. He had witnessed real conversions before in his ministry, and knew Kelly was now a true child of God. In light of this wonder, how could he feel anything but joy? Yes, there would be times ahead when he would blame himself for her misdeeds. After all, her motivation in the whole ordeal was this feeble attempt to help restore his marriage, the marriage that Doug knew he himself was mostly responsible for disrupting and causing to end in divorce. But this was a time for rejoicing and an open opportunity for the entire congregation.

The trio made their way from the platform to their seats. Pastor Bob hesitated in returning to the microphones just long enough for a line to form along the steps to the platform. He had never witnessed anything like this before. Men, women, and other teenagers were coming to the microphone for confession and repentance. For some...salvation, for others re-commitment and rededication. Entire families came to confess their sin, one to another. The sin, shame and pain of even some of the church's elders who came forward to confess, left Bob motionless but not speechless. He was praising God. Shackles were being broken and cast under foot that morning. One could almost hear the chains falling and feel the relief of those partaking in this revival, a revival stirred by the courage and confession of one young girl. Bob knew, though, he would have his work cut out for him. Many would seek his counsel. There was much restoration to be done. Some would need to restore relationships with distant family members. Some would even need to turn themselves over to law enforcement agencies. But the greatest step had been taken. That step of confession and acknowledgment of fault and responsibility. In the past Bob's most difficult work involved counseling those who would continue to deny any great fault, blaming anyone and everyone but themselves. In comparison, this work ahead would be refreshing and a real blessing.

For what was happening here, Bob knew God alone was to receive the glory, and glorify God he did, as did the entire congregation. They had all stayed an hour past the normal ending time of the service. No one looked at watches. Cell phones and pagers long before had been turned off. Even the children were exceptionally silent. The eyes of the people there were fixed on the platform as Bob gave the final benediction of the service. It had been such a meaningful time with God. Blessings abounded as the flock left the small church with a new hope and renewed love for Christ.

CHAPTER 13

A GRANDMOTHER'S LOVE

On the way home from church, Kelly had a long talk with her father and asked for his forgiveness. How could he refuse? The remorse was sincere, and the new confidence she exhibited was something that could not be denied. Even Tom now felt relief and confident that Kelly would be able to face whatever consequences with strength and stamina. He saw in her what Paul expressed in Philippians 4:13:

I can do everything through Him who gives me strength.

Kelly seemed almost ready to tell her mother. Her newfound faith overshadowed her shame. Even though the confession would be painful, the opportunity to share the truth of Christ with her mother was overwhelmingly exciting. Mary did love the Lord the whole time Kelly was growing up, yet lately she seemed to be back-sliding. The concern Kelly had was—would this feeling of strength in telling her about the miracle of God's forgiveness really continue, or would it be dashed beneath her with the passing of a few hours?

Oh yes, she knew, in all probability, her mother would just pass it off as a temporary emotional high. Even so, time would disprove that concept. And the possibility of her mother recommitting herself to Christ after these past couple years of suppressing the Holy Spirit and lacking any faith in God, would uplift Kelly's hopes. Her father had agreed to go with her to face Mary. The immediate confrontation, though, was that of facing her grandmother. Janet had such high hopes for Kelly-Joy and had prayed and hoped the best for her. Kelly knew that in explaining what she had done, describing her role in those sinful and immoral acts, would hurt that lady deeply. But she also knew that God would somehow help her through this as well. Her confidence was at its peak.

Janet was at the door as they all arrived. She was especially excited to see Doug. Doug lifted his mother completely off the ground as he hugged her so dearly. Kelly knew this was not the time to talk to her grandmother, but perhaps after a cup of hot chocolate. She didn't want to wait too long, or she just might lose her courage and confidence. Brunch was on the table, and although Kelly was not very hungry, the aroma of freshly cooked bacon and eggs seemed very tantalizing. They all sat down to pray, and when it was Kelly's turn, she completely overwhelmed her grandmother with praises to God which puzzled her as well. The last thing Kelly requested of the Lord was for her mother and grandmother to be understanding, forgiving and accepting. Janet hated being kept in suspense. She realized she must have missed something by not going to church. She wanted to just blurt out to Kelly, "Just what is this all about, child?" But she knew, as she had learned from Tom, patience is bliss and a very virtuous attribute, especially in dealing with adversities. She suddenly remembered Tom's concern the night before and his assurance that something was very wrong in Kelly's life. Her mind raced through all of the possibilities. It was dreadful and frightening as well, but she realized this sudden change in Kelly's attitude about the Lord gave her a sensation of peace about the whole thing. Janet just sat there, pretending to be preoccupied with her meal and waiting as patiently as she could for Kelly to begin her explanation.

With grace being completed, Kelly glanced first at her father, then her grandfather. She knew, as they did, spoil the brunch or not, she had to confess the whole mess to her grandmother and be done with it. After all, it should not be that hard.

Of all the forgiving people she knew, her grandmother outshined every one of them. The hardest part of the confession was knowing how much it would hurt her. So often she and her grandmother would go on long walks along the forest trails and around the lake, talking, confiding, and sharing. It would hurt that sweet lady to know that she had kept this from her for so long; that she had not called her for counsel or advice. With one phone call, it all could have been prevented. Her grandmother would have made it clear to her how devastating that escapade would be to her young life and the lives of those she loved. Hindsight! As one looks back on mistakes, they always seem so clearly foolish and preventable. But Kelly knew that she must not look back, but rather ahead. Ahead to a life dedicated to Christ. Paul stated it so eloquently in Philippians 4:20:

Forgetting what is behind and straining toward what is ahead, I press on toward the goal to win the prize for which God has called me heavenward in Christ Jesus.

A life full of change and repentance. It would not be easy though. She would surely lose the few friends she had at school. But perhaps there would be other girls she could befriend who would encourage her walk with Christ. She would need to forget about Tab and not let the stories that might be told about her cause her to lose her newfound joy.

Feeling the tension around her, Janet stopped eating and looked directly at Kelly. Kelly's eyes were already speaking to her. Now they were welling up with tears. Kelly wondered if her tear ducts would ever empty. For over a year she had held back those tears of disappointment, pain and sorrow, and here within one day it seemed buckets had flowed. A year's worth of tears pouring out in one single day. Tears of sorrow, heavy and dark, as well as tears of joy, light and shimmering, intermingling with each other as they flowed down her cheeks. Janet said nothing. She carefully wiped her mouth with the napkin from her lap and stood and then walked over to Kelly. Now Kelly was standing as they held each other long and hard. Without knowing the sin, Janet said over and over, "It's OK Sweetie! It's OK!"

After Kelly composed herself, they walked to the bedroom arm in arm. It would be better for Kelly to talk to her grandmother alone. The men knew this, as they slowly returned their attention to the meal before them.

Tom was the first to speak, "I know you must be blaming yourself for this. I can't tell you to stop that kind of thinking, because I too feel as though I share in the blame. Oh, my mind knows that these young people have a mind and attitude of their own that often seems impossible to penetrate. In my mind I also know that I am not responsible for the sin chosen by others. But with my heart I ask, have I not been counseling her? As her mentor, was it not my responsibility to keep her accountable? I was so sure she was handling the many changes in her life so well. She seemed so stable and positive in her outlook on things. Inside she must have been so confused and insecure. For years I have been counseling young people at the church, but she had me completely fooled. I am so sorry, Doug. I know you won't believe this right now, but you have been a great father to her and a great son to your mother and me."

Doug was speechless. He dared not speak, for so much emotion overcame him, emotion over Kelly, over his failed marriage, over his own mistakes, over the love his father had just expressed to him!

Tom continued, "We have seen a miracle today! We have a lot to be thankful for. Kelly is confident in putting the past behind her. We must do the same, you and I. Your intentions have always been good, Doug, and

I believe Mary will come to realize that and have a change of heart but even if she doesn't … even if she does continue to be apart from you … even if the mourning doves never again make their way to Woodridge Falls, we can praise God for what has happened in Kelly-Joy's heart. Yes, even with Christ there in her heart, she will still make mistakes. She may even still be easily swayed by her peers in making wrong decisions. She will need us even more now in her walk with Christ, but the miles separate us. There is only so much we can do, and then the rest we must pray for and trust in God."

Doug had suddenly stopped eating and made direct eye contact with his father. "I know you're right, Dad! I just love both Kelly and Mary so much, yet I feel I must have somehow failed them both so greatly. A father is supposed to be a knight, ready to defend and protect the purity of his daughter even to his death. I had treasured the thought of walking down that aisle with my daughter one day, arm in arm, proudly showing off my little Beauty, in her lovely white wedding dress. Showing the world that I had not only done my part in protecting her purity, but also in instilling within her the wisdom of choosing abstinence until marriage. Since her infancy I have prayed for her purity. Since my own wedding day, I have prayed consistently for my marriage and Mary's happiness. I trusted God with both of those prayers as I have labored in doing what I thought was the best I could do to help these two things happen. I wanted to show my Lord that I was willing to do my part and trust in Him to do His part. You and Mary have both helped me see my wrongdoing in regards to my marriage. But I still have difficulty in understanding where I failed Kelly. Could any father have loved a daughter more? Throughout her childhood I devoted myself to building her self-esteem. I taught her the Scriptures well. I encouraged her with each step of every edifying venture she undertook. Yes, I was pouring too much of myself into my work and neglected to fulfill many of the needs of my wife, but I truly believe I have not neglected my daughter in that way. God Himself can testify on my behalf concerning this."

"So often I hear my colleagues, as well as many Christian psychologists, profess that a teenage girl will seek sexual affection from a boy or man because she had not received proper affection from her father. They seem to blame every improper sexual attitude and choice a young girl makes on her father as a result of either his neglect or sexual misconduct with her. It's a lie! Dad, it's a lie! I have taken special care to love Kelly in a godly way, in a proper way."

Doug looked down at his empty plate and whispered, "What could she have been thinking? How could she have been so stupid?"

These last questions echoed over and over in his mind. He suddenly felt ashamed of himself because he still obviously had not really forgiven her and had put more concern over what people would think and say about him rather than the difficulty and hurt she was undergoing. Oh, he said he forgave her on the way home from church, but now his injured pride had changed his attitude towards Kelly. Had she not asked for forgiveness? Did she not take a great step of courage in telling the entire congregation of her misconduct? Did God not show His blessing on her decision to confess by encouraging many of those in the congregation who also had hidden sins, to openly confess and repent as well? What she did with that boy was wrong and it was stupid, but it is done. He must not let his damaged ego and disappointment in Kelly cause bitterness in his heart.

Of course, the boy was not just an innocent bystander and what must be done with him would soon need to be determined. But for now, Doug's greatest concern was Kelly. His father was right! He must trust God. He knew what he had to do, at this very instant. He looked up and said to Tom as he often did when he was a child, "Dad, would you pray with me? Right now!"

Tom scooted his chair next to his son and approvingly placed his arm around him as they both bowed to pray. Each prayed sincerely and openly to their Lord. First, praise was given for the goodness of God and many of the good things that had occurred that morning. Then with much emotion, requests were asked of the Father. Each of the men referenced Scripture with their prayers. Tom concluded with the following:

"Lord! Lord! We seek and expect your promise of hope and guidance. For as it is written in Philippians 4:6:

Do not be anxious about anything, but in everything, by prayer and petition, with thanksgiving, present your requests to God. And the Peace of God, which transcends all understanding, will guard your hearts and your minds in Christ Jesus.

After a few moments of silence, they heard laughter from the hall. It was a welcoming sound. A welcoming sound, indeed, that made its way into the dining room and felt as refreshing as a cool, spring breeze full of the aroma of fresh and blossoming wildflowers. The men now had smiles on their faces as the ladies entered the room.

Janet was always the optimistic one and had a hat full of delightfully funny short stories to lighten the mood at the end of even the most serious of conversations. Kelly adored this about her grandmother. If only the rest of society had her optimism and calmness, life would be ever so much less stressful.

During their time together in the bedroom, Kelly had once again described the series of events that led to her hideous misbehavior. Her grandmother listened with an understanding heart. Although Janet was an optimist, she was also not afraid to face the consequences of any decision. She had then asked Kelly a question that the young girl had not really thought much about, mainly because it would be too difficult to face: "What if a child should come of this?" Indeed. What would she do? They discussed the possibilities. Adoption, relatives caring for the child for a period of time, Kelly and her mother raising the child….

One option was not even considered, for it was one that neither one believed in any way to be an option, that of ABORTION. It was a foul and ugly word. To even regard it would be like cursing God.

They both knew the topic of what to do about pregnancy may need to be discussed in greater depth, but it could wait until tests were done and results received. Kelly also knew she needed to face whatever would come of this. Yet it encouraged her to know she had the full support of her grandparents and father. The one question remained: What about her mother? How would she take the news? Mary had already been through much emotional duress with the divorce and the additional responsibilities of a new job and the relocation. This would certainly be a real shock to her, sorrow upon sorrow. Kelly was determined, though, to do the right thing from now on, and perhaps things would still work out OK.

That night, as Kelly laid in bed, her mind raced through several scenarios in telling her mother what she had done. With each, she tried to imagine her mother's reaction. It seemed hopeless. Of course, she would have to tell the truth, but no matter how she set the scene or arranged the words, the reaction she imagined was the same: anger, hysteria and pain, followed by a series of ugly words. She had already said her prayers to her Lord and Father, but just now she was compelled to pray again. This prayer would not just be words, but an expression of her feelings to the One who knows her better than she knows herself. She slipped from under the covers and knelt beside her bed. Her voice was tender and laced with the humility of a small child:

"Lord, I'm so sorry! I have caused pain to so many, but mostly to you, my Father. I know it was because of this sin, that Jesus died, for the wages of sin is death. To others I tried to justify my actions.

I was this lonely, helpless victim. But the truth is, I wanted to hurt my mother. I blamed her for all that had happened, and I wanted her to feel pain, like the pain I felt. I knew this would hurt her, but I didn't think about the hurt it would cause others and myself. I do not know what will happen now. I do not know what my mother will do. I know I don't deserve any special favors, but would you … could you … somehow work it out for Mom to love Dad again and for us to be a family again? I know my mother said: 'The skies of Woodridge Falls would have to be filled with mourning doves before I have any love for that man!' I keep waiting and looking for those doves. I know it's silly. Just an expression. But you know what I mean when I say, 'They are truly your doves, Lord. Please bring them back!'"

With this Kelly knelt there silently, whispering that last phrase over and over: "Please bring them back! Please bring them back!" Soon she was asleep, her knees on the floor and her shoulders and head draped across the side of her bed.

Suddenly a set of strong arms lifted her and gently laid her on the bed. As he carefully covered her in the comforter and placed a pillow under her head, Doug, in a broken speech of hope, reiterated his daughter's request, "Yes L … Lord, please bring them……. please bring them back!"

CHAPTER 14

A PLEASANT DAY *at* FERNVIEW COTTAGE

Monday came at last. It had been a difficult weekend for the Wisps. Tom had been up for hours praying to his Father on Kelly's behalf, for his other grandchildren and many other individuals for whom he felt a burden. He especially had a burden for the many babies who may be in danger of possibly being considered for abortion that day, and the great guilt the mothers would undergo as a consequence if they followed through on that decision. By now he was weak and drained from the emotion of it all. His prayers were sincere, and his praise of God's wonder and goodness was absolute.

He suddenly realized that he hadn't even looked at his planner yesterday, and now wondered what he may have forgotten regarding this day's activities. There were no court hearings to attend this week, but there was a rescue planned at an abortion clinic tomorrow morning. Although Tom participated in some of the pickets at the homes of abortionists and never missed a Walk for Life or Life Chain event, it had been a long time since he played an active role in an Operation Rescue event at an abortion clinic. He had reservations about being involved in such recent activities. He understood that some of the graphic pictures of aborted babies were necessary to convict the hearts of certain people and to stress the horror of it all, but that was actually not his approach. During marches and previous Operation Rescue events, Tom carried a beautifully hand-drawn sketch of a sweet, adorable baby who had an expression of hope as a single tear streamed down his tender cheek. The words above the baby read, "Take my hand, not my life!"

He had drawn the sketch from a picture of his own Dougie. Tom went to the closet and dusted the old picket sign. He had used it for years, yet it still looked newly drawn, fresh and preserved. Often as he carried that sign for a Walk for Life event, reporters would approach him with questions regarding what a lot of people would consider difficult circumstances, in hopes of catching him off-guard. Questions like, "What is a young girl to do in the event of a pregnancy as a result of a rape or incest?" He would answer simply and to the point: "Two wrongs don't make a right! It never has. It never will!" They never liked this response because it would actually catch them off-guard and leave them speechless. A good reporter never likes to be speechless.

Janet would not be with him for these events. He was concerned for her safety. He also knew he could not trust himself to control his temper should she actually be mishandled by the riot patrol. They were trained to treat all civil disobedience the same, as a dangerous disturbance to be quickly dispersed with whatever force necessary. All those participating in a "rescue" were made very much aware of the risk and possible consequences. He knew, though, that the saving of even one child was worth the risk.

Tom was usually cheerful and optimistic, but the weekend's awareness of Kelly's circumstances left him feeling a bit down and sad. He tried to shake it, but just couldn't. He thought, "Where is my faith and trust in my Lord? Why can't I just do what I can do and hand the rest of it all over to Him? Hasn't He proven himself time and again? If only there were some good news. Something to regain my hope. Good News. Yes, the Good News!"

He immediately thought of the Bible and how he had not yet started his morning study. As Tom turned to the marker in his Bible, he read from Romans 12 verses 11-15:

Never be lacking in zeal, but keep your spiritual fervor, serving the Lord. Be joyful in hope, patient in affliction, and faithful in prayer. Share with God's people who are in need. Practice hospitality. Bless those who persecute you; bless and do not curse. Rejoice with those who rejoice; mourn with those who mourn.

By now it was 8AM. He was pondering over these words. The message was clear. In spite of Kelly's situation and in spite of what may happen tomorrow at the clinic, he must maintain his zeal in serving the Lord. Yes, tomorrow he may be afflicted with brutality, but he must not curse those who persecute, but rather bless them. There may indeed be mourning over those infants who are aborted, and he is to mourn as well.

There may indeed be rejoicing over those infants who are spared, and he too will rejoice. This message was encouraging, but he still felt a little depressed. Suddenly the telephone rang.

Tom answered the phone, "Good morning and bless you my friend!"

"Hello and good morning to you, Mr. Wisp!"

The response was from a child full of excitement. "Mr. Wisp! Mr. Wisp! I have my own motorcar! Thank you! Thank you so much! You're the best!"

Tom was quick to answer, "Reggie, is that you? Wait a minute. What are you talking about?"

Reggie was too excited to say any more. Betty accepted the receiver from the boy and happily greeted her friend, "Good morning Mr. Wisp. As you heard, Reggie is really excited about the gift. Mrs. Parks came by this morning and personally escorted the delivery of the motorized wheelchair to our doorstep."

Betty paused as she wiped the tears of happiness from her own face. "She told us that you suggested that this would be a big help for Reggie and me in transporting him about. Boy! Is it ever! Mrs. Parks apologized for being misinformed of our situation as well as her negative attitude towards me and her actions in tricking me into signing the release forms. We talked about my reading classes, and I impressed her with my progress. She was like a different person. It's a miracle, I tell you. A real miracle! And this wheelchair. Wow! Again I am lost in finding words adequate to thank you."

Tom was speechless. What could he say? His thoughts went back to that verse from Romans that he had just read:

Rejoice with those who rejoice!

Yes indeed! Rejoice! Tom was laughing and crying at the same time. His tears were mainly in thanksgiving to God and his laughter completely chased away the blues. Again God proved himself. In his moment of despair, his Savior was there. Everything was like a puzzle being carefully placed together before his very eyes, revealing God's faithfulness. Tom was himself again, solid in his trust in his Lord.

"Betty, I am so happy for you and Reggie, but please, don't give me the credit. This is all a miracle all right, but nothing of my doing."

Betty answered, "Yes, Mr. Wisp, praise God! But I still want to thank you for allowing God to use you in this way. You are a blessing to all!"

Betty was suddenly distracted by her son's plan to exit the front door on his own, "Reggie! Reggie! Wait for mommy before you go outside. I'm sorry, Mr. Wisp, but I need to catch that boy before he hot rods all over town. Goodbye and thanks again."

Tom hung up the phone and ran downstairs to the kitchen to give the good news to his darling wife.

Janet welcomed the news. She, too, was feeling a little depressed over all that Kelly had been involved in. She had not even met Reggie, but felt she knew him anyway from the many conversations with Tom about him. Tom and Janet embraced each other and lingered in each others' arms for several minutes. Both of them needed that firm but gentle hug of affection. It was a reminder to them both that, in spite of surrounding trouble, they still had each other. Together, hand in hand, with one another and their Lord, they could face anything.

Suddenly Janet burst into a series of sobs. Last night she could laugh with Kelly and tell some funny stories, but now she just needed to cry. Tom remembered a quote from a speaker he had once heard, "Sometimes it seems like there is nothing else to do but cry." This was one of those times. But after the tears come acceptance and healing, and then once again, contentment. No, not that oblivious "Happiness", but that refreshing and mature feeling, 'Contentment'. Paul said it quite well in Philippians 4:11:

I am not saying this because I am in need, for I have learned to be content whatever the circumstances.

Janet stopped just as suddenly as she had started. As their embrace became relaxed, she remained silent, but looked deeply into Tom's eyes. They mirrored the tenderness and strength that was such a part of this man. As her stare caught Tom's attention, he quickly reassured her, "Everything will be fine in God's time. Just wait, you'll see."

She smiled and gave him a quick kiss. "Enough of this, my knight in shining armor. Doug and Kelly will be getting up soon. I must be getting breakfast started. And you, my darling, have some catching up to do with Doug. I see you have the equipment for making fishing flies all set up. This will be a good opportunity for the two of you to talk. Oh and remember, tomorrow you have some dragons to slay and some babies to rescue from certain death. Please be careful, my love, and remember the Apostle Paul's wise advice of Philippians 3:2:

Watch out for those dogs, those men who do evil, those mutilators of the flesh.

Tom thought, yes indeed. Though this was a good description of those abortionists, they too still have the hope of salvation. He at once thought of Bob Logan. If that man could just get a grasp of the message of Christ. Tom knew he must try to do what he could and leave the rest to God.

Suddenly he had an idea. "It is still quite early. How about I help you with breakfast. We could throw the lot into the oven to keep warm and then take a nice stroll around the lake. The air is a little brisk, but that bright sun will soon put a stop to that. Those little ducklings will be right there ready for your gentle touch. We can stop at Turner's Cove, sit on the bench swing and watch some of those Canadian geese gracefully skim across the surface of the water as they lift off to make their homeward journey north."

It all sounded lovely to Janet. They worked marvelously as a team, and soon the kitchen had a delightful odor of bacon, French toast and coffee. With great haste, Janet raced to the living room closet for her shawl and handed Tom his denim jacket. All along the path towards Turner's Cove, patches of irises and dark green fern flanked each side of the trail. The fingers of Tom's large hand folded gently around and over the soft warm hand of his spouse. Tom slightly quivered as her fingers stroked and followed the lines within his palm. This was just one of her ways of displaying affection for him.

As Tom had predicted, the air was brisk, but little rays of sunlight streaked across the sky as the sun was just beginning to peek over Arrow Ridge, giving an encouraging sign of a warm day ahead. Before they even reached the bend, they could hear the flock of geese, honking orders to one another, which echoed throughout the cove.

When they reached their destination, they took their place on the bench and awaited the beginning of the maneuvers. As the first flock proceeded past them, Tom squinted at the lead goose and then turned to Janet and winked, "Well lookie there! If it isn't Major Black himself taking Point."

For five years now, the same bird led the initial liftoff. His distinguishing markings were matchless. The tops of the feathers that lined the upper portion of his wings and group of tail feathers were black as coal, while the layers beneath shimmered streaks of white and gray. His voice was exceptionally deep with periodic bursts that echoed across the lake. All the geese flew in unison across the top of the water, allowing their webbed feet to skim the lake's surface. Not one of them in the ranks would dare liftoff before the lead goose. The flight into the air was as graceful as any Tom and Janet had ever witnessed. Just as they became airborne, their landing gear was quickly tucked beneath the down feathers that covered their lower extremities. With their necks stretched as straight as an arrow, they moved as one, masters of flight.

After a few moments, the 'V-shaped' flock of geese were soaring through the sky. The couple watched carefully as the spectacle faded in the distance. This moment filled their inner beings with peace. A moment remembered and shared by both husband and wife. There were many others, of course, but this one had its own uniqueness that was worth remembering. Tom squeezed Janet's hand gently three times, and she expectedly responded by squeezing his with a familiar four. The code was clear, "I ... Love ... You!", "I... Love ... You ... Too!"

They gazed into each other's eyes a few moments with as much awe as they had for the vision of flight that they had both just witnessed. Their love for each other was deep and strong and healthy. This love continually boosted their confidence in themselves and in each other over whatever they would do. Then they hugged tightly, and each quivered a little at the joy it all brought. They, too, were now as one. Could any two people ever be as close?

All too quickly, they reached the front door of Fernview Cottage. As they entered they could hear the faint sound of the hair dryer from the downstairs bathroom. Janet rushed to the kitchen to complete the preparation of breakfast.

Tom went over to poke at the fire a little and add a few logs as Kelly was just exiting the bathroom. She was wearing a light blue tee shirt and blue jeans shorts. She chirped a cute, "Good morning, Grandaddy!" as she passed her grandfather to help in the kitchen with the drinks.

Tom smiled as he twisted about to return the greeting. From looking at her, he could tell the night's sleep had done her well.

Just before entering the kitchen, a thought came to Kelly, and she reacted instantly. She made a quick turn for the family room, and there in the corner, was a special little crate box where wild animal food was kept. She carefully lifted the lid and reached for the bag of peanuts. With a handful cupped in her grasp, she headed for the front window. It was already slightly open, so she opened it a little more and nudged the window screen, which flew open on its hinges. She then tossed the nuts, and patiently waited there at the window with her elbows on the window sill and her chin resting in the palm of her hands. A gleaming smile of excitement quickly came to her face as she saw a little squirrel make his way from cedar to cedar and then to Fernview Cottage. He ran right past the scattered pile of peanuts and right below the window. Looking up he made chirp-like sounds, bidding Kelly a "Good Morning," and then turned sharply to chase away the Stellar Jay birds that had spotted the food supply there on the ground. This was Dusty. His right ear had a distinguishable little split at the top and his tail was very bushy. Kelly knew Munchi would soon be there as well. Munchi was small and very shy. But at Dusty's calling, she came rushing to the scene. She stood up a moment on her two hind feet and balanced herself with her stubby little tail as she twitched her nose towards Kelly. Although Munchi was indeed usually shy, she had no fear of Kelly and waited for the young lady to hand-feed her. Kelly giggled as she taunted the little squirrel with a large peanut. Kelly reached out further and further, but then was momentarily startled as Munchi jumped right on her forearm. Munchi then laid her front torso across Kelly's hand, grasping the nut tightly with her front paws. The bushy fur tickled Kelly's wrist and arm as the squirrel twitched her whole body in excitement at both being there with Kelly and having the tasty snack. Carefully and gently the sensitive girl petted the animal with her other hand.

Kelly enjoyed that moment. As she hummed a little tune, two pretty goldfinches landed right there on the window sill and bounced across the frame. Kelly reached down for some seed and placed a little on the window base. The little birds waited a moment, as though saying a little prayer, and then hopped over and pecked their beaks on the window sill, to pick up as many seeds as they could.

Janet started to call Kelly to get her to help with the drinks, but once she noticed that Kelly was with her friends, she went back to the kitchen to finish the work herself. She felt Kelly needed that time with her wildlife friends. It didn't matter to them what Kelly had done. They had no pity, or worry, or strife with her, just love for her. Their love for her was like the affection of Christ Jesus. They did not come for the food, although that did get their initial attention. They came to be with the girl. Laugh with the girl. Cry with the girl. They did not worry what others would think of them by what she had done. The squirrels and birds only wanted the joy of her company and the tenderness of her touch. At that moment, she needed that, and they were glad to give it. "If only my family could be as loving and forgiving," Kelly thought. Oh, she knew her father, grandfather, and grandmother were trying, but their disappointment was still quite obvious.

Tom had a karaoke tape player near the entertainment center. He slipped into the family room and placed one of Kelly's childhood favorite tapes into the player and turned it on. As she heard the music she slowly turned her head with a smile. She looked up to God with all sincerity as she sang. Her voice sounded like an angel in heaven and Tom imagined birds lingering in the trees nearby, accompanying her in this delightful praise to the Lord. The song she sang, 'As a Deer Panteth for the Water,' was a warm welcome to all who heard. It had been many years since Doug had heard his little girl sing that song. Just now as he entered the room, he marveled at the beauty of her singing and the strength of her voice. Could anyone have sung it better or with more feeling? Then he thought, "She surely has her mother's gift for singing."

Doug remembered his first pastoral assignment in Golden, Colorado and the many solos Mary performed in her desire to use her gift to praise God. This was long before he took advantage of her good nature and desire to give. Those were the fun days. The happy days. They both longed to make each other happy. He remembered the little things he would do for her. Often on his way home to dinner, he would stop and buy her some cashews or peanut brittle (her favorite). A couple of times a week he would rub her feet as she read a book. She would sigh with thankfulness as he gently engulfed a tender foot in his hands and moved his finger firmly but carefully over each muscle, pressing and then stroking with care. Back then he regularly sent postcards, thanking members of the church for various things. With that stack of cards he would have a letter enclosed with a special poem addressed to Mary. He learned this from his father. But he would go a step further and make the hour round trip drive to Loveland, Colorado just to get Mary's card stamped with that special Love stamp that Loveland is noted for. Some evenings after arriving home from a Bible Study or social event, he would pick her right up off her feet at the front door and carry her inside over the threshold, like he did on their honeymoon. They would laugh, and she would say, "Let me down, you silly romantic!" But in her heart he knew she was saying, "Don't stop and the honeymoon will never be over." Why did he stop? This suddenly occurred to him. Why?

With the song completed, Kelly turned from the window and was happy to see her father right there next to her. She hugged him and whispered in his ear, "Daddy, I love you!"

This moment was interrupted by the sound of a little dinner bell. Tom was doing the honors, and Kelly laughed seeing her grandfather hold up that little metal triangle and carefully striking the inner bar with the miniature hammer. "Come on you late risers, let's sit down here for a tasty treat."

Tom sat at the head of the table. As they sat he winked at Doug. Doug knew this meant his father would want him to do the honors of saying grace.

They all held hands and Doug started the prayer. It was well thought out and the words flowed like sweet butter from his lips. Doug included a request that Mary be understanding and forgiving with Kelly. Kelly silently added a similar request in her own words. When the eating started, Tom talked about the morning at the lake. Kelly and Janet giggled as Tom went on about Major Black. He humorously imitated his honk, and to each he added an interpretation as he would imagine it: a series of preparatory commands followed by commands of execution, as any well trained officer could expound.

The meal went rather quickly and soon the women were busy clearing the table and cleaning the kitchen. Tom and Doug took this opportunity to spend some time together. They both went into the basement where Tom had the fly-tying rigs all set up for the two of them in anticipation of this moment. Doug sat and studied the variety of flies attached to felt material on the wall next to him.

Doug started the conversation, "Dad, why don't you participate in the fishing contest this year? I know you have your license. Did you see the grand prize? Wow! The lift kit on that pickup is something else!"

Tom responded, "Yeah. Couldn't you just see me climbing into that tree-house on wheels? I'd need a ladder to make it to the driver's seat."

They both laughed a bit and then Tom continued, "I may just enter that contest, if your brother could bring Ronny and Joshua by for a few days. Those boys always bring me good luck!"

Doug responded, "I expect to see Don tomorrow. I'll pass on the word. I'm sure he would make a point to bring them up, and he might even try a little casting himself."

With concern for Don, Tom spoke, "It's been a long while since Don fished here at Woodridge Falls, but if you take a picture of the grand prize to him, that certainly might get his attention. It would be good for him to come up for a little relaxation. He works so hard. Too hard!"

"And you didn't, Dad? Come on! I can remember several times when you were at work overnight, doing integration thirty-six hours straight." Doug had a tinge of pride in that statement about his dad. Tom had worked hard, but not at any expense to his family. He made sure he had plenty of time set aside for Don, Gretchen, and Doug. There were times when he stretched himself, but he always took equivalent time off to be with his family.

"Well, Son," Tom went on, "I had to do something. I was not as smart as the rest of the guys, so I just worked a little harder."

Doug grinned as he looked at his father. He loved that very humble man. He knew his dad was not just saying that, but really believed he was not as smart as the others on his team. Just then Doug remembered a company deep sea fishing trip he and his dad went on. He remembered how proud he was to be with his dad, and especially as he overheard some of his father's co-workers talk about his dad. He could sense the respect and admiration they had for him. He remembered his father's manager coming up to him and quickly ruffling his hair as he spoke, "Young man, that father of yours is the best man I've got, so you keep a close eye on him and make sure he doesn't fall overboard."

The other men laughed because they all knew how excited Tom would get over the team accomplishing goals and the way he would laugh in the lab and slap his knee in jubilation at the success of completing some software functionality that was weeks in the making. They just imagined Tom with a large tuna on his line and getting so excited that he would fall over the helm of the small ship and into the water. They could also picture him in the water still struggling to pull in that tuna, having the time of his life, oblivious to the danger of the sea and the possibility of being left behind or drowning. They chuckled as this picture faded from their thoughts, and then went about preparing for the day's catch. Just then the memory faded for Doug as reality recaptured his attention.

Now Doug's thoughts moved to a more pressing matter as he spoke, "Dad, do you think I should be with Kelly as she confesses everything to Mary?"

Tom had no intention of advising Doug as to what he should do, unless being asked. Now that he was asked, he was confidently prepared to respond, "Yes, I do. Considering your position as father and the embarrassment this places on you as a pastor, your attitude of forgiveness and confidence in Kelly to do the right thing might encourage Mary to be more understanding. Mary may try to downplay Kelly's confession in church, but you were there and can testify to Kelly's sincerity. Doug, regardless of what Mary thinks of you as a husband, she very much respects your integrity and honesty."

Doug did not respond right away, but let those words sink in. He thought, "Could it be true? Does she respect that about me? If she really does, is that not possibly a starting place for growth into something more? After all, Jesus never commanded a wife to love her husband, just respect him. However, He does command man to love his wife as Christ so loved the church. I do love Mary!"

Just then he silently spoke to God, "Lord, You know I do love her. Search my heart, Father, and tell me if this isn't true. You know all things, Lord. Look into my heart and help me see all that is not glorifying to you, that I might pluck it out. My Friend, it would not be so painful to do this. Nothing could be more painful than this rejection I feel from Mary. Neither physical ailment, nor financial ruin, nor the rejection of anyone else who knows me could weigh heavier on my shoulders, my heart, indeed, my very soul."

Doug finally spoke, "OK dad, but if I have the handles of a rolling pin sticking out of each ear the next time you see me, don't even ask what happened."

They both chuckled as a picture of that came to mind in the form of a cartoon. Yes, these men did think a lot alike.

For the next hour they talked as they went about creating several superb fishing flies. Then they exchanged their products with each other. Studying the detail and artwork that went into each fly while making gestures, they rambled on with interest and admiration.

By now it was late afternoon, and the girls were just placing the dessert on the table as the men reached the top of the stairs. A wide grin came across the faces of those guys simultaneously as they peered across the top of the table. Tom was the first to speak, "Yahoo! Ice cream and pudding. What a combo!"

Doug echoed the compliment, "Treatment like this can make a man stay, even just at the point of leaving."

Janet replied, "Well, you boys were working so hard down there, grunting and struggling in toil, I just took pity on you."

Kelly laughed as she added, "Sure, Grandma, just like you struggle and moan so much over playing the piano."

Kelly knew her grandmother loved playing the piano as much as her grandfather loved making flies. She then continued, "Come to think of it, I haven't heard you play a tune all weekend. Please Grandma, play something for us."

Janet needed no other coaxing. She immediately rushed to the ivory keys and tickled the ears of everyone there. Momentarily, Kelly imagined colorful smiling notes emanating from the soundboard of the piano, like bubbles from a bath. The music thrilled her so, that she sighed to take it all in. Janet smiled as she looked at Kelly. It pleased her so to bring a little joy to that child. She knew Kelly would not have an easy time telling her mother all that had happened. But as she played, she silently prayed for God to show mercy on her granddaughter.

The men were just finishing their dessert as Janet slowly ended the tune which genuinely glorified God. For a few moments it was silent, for they all knew that the time had come for parting. No one wanted to hurry or even suggest it, but the "tick tock" of the hall clock spoke ever so clearly.

Finally, Doug walked to the piano to give his mother a hug and tender kiss goodbye. "Thank you so much, Mom!" Doug, gazing at his mother, pointed to Tom and said, "I hope this old fisherman here realizes what a catch he has!"

Tom quickly responded, "A real keeper, she is!"

Doug turned to hug his dad. For just a moment he felt like a little boy again, hugging his dad before leaving for camp. The two of them had a real bond. Just before parting, Tom placed his large hands on Doug's shoulders, as so often in the past, and gave them a slight shake. "You take care of yourself, now. God be with you!"

Doug responded in his usual fashion, "And also with you, Dad."

Now it was Kelly's turn to bid her farewells. Yes, there were tears, as they all knew there would be. It was hard for her to leave the safety and peace and love ever so prevalent there at Fernview Cottage. She thought, "If only I could feel elsewhere as I do here." In her mind, she quickly responded, "But then, perhaps, I would take it all for granted and not really appreciate it as I do. It is so good to have a place like this, with people like these, that makes 'Hellos' such a joy and 'Goodbyes' such a sorrow."

It was easier leaving, knowing how joyful she would feel with her next visit.

As she entered her father's car, she said a quick little prayer, "Please, dear Lord, let the return be soon!"

CHAPTER 15

The UNGAME

Again Tom and Janet were alone. Janet made some tea for both of them, and they went outside on the patio for a cool evening chat. Tom was the first to start the conversation. "I wonder if I should have asked Kelly if she would want me to talk to her mother first. You know, to sort of, prepare Mary for what Kelly would have to tell her?"

Tom was just thinking out loud and Janet quickly responded. "No, Tom. Even if you had asked, I don't think Kelly would have wanted you to do that. She knows that this is something she must do, and your trying to make it easier for her would just make things worse. Oh, Honey, I don't mean to say that you aren't capable of helping Mary understand how repentant Kelly is and how much she has changed. But, Mary would probably think that Kelly put you up to it to save her own skin, and that would put Mary right off in a disrespectful attitude toward Kelly. Don't you see, Dear?"

Tom pondered on this a moment. He realized how wise his sweet wife was and he felt so grateful for her. Janet was careful in choosing her words so as to prevent Tom from feeling foolish. She knew him well. His intentions were always so good. Good intentions, though, are not good enough. Even the best of good intentions must have a little help to guide its actions, and Tom knew this. He took her counsel very seriously, the same as she took his.

Tom winked at Janet and got up to get a board game. He was not able to get his fill of games with Kelly, so now Janet was to humor him. She was glad, though, because she felt very much like playing a board game with Tom. It was one they had not played in a while, the Ungame.

Luck had it that Janet was to go first, so after the roll of the dice, she took her card. The question on the card took her back many years. "Tell about an adventure you had on a bicycle." She thought to herself, "My shiny red Schwinn!"

She smiled as she looked at Tom and showed him her card. He laughed and said, "You aren't going to remind me about that nature trail bike trip we took just outside of Vail, are you? That sure was something else. Remember, we stopped for a rest under a tree, and when we awoke, we were completely surrounded by huge porcupines. I mean huge! Well, what was I to do, I mean their quills were like daggers and ……"

Janet cut him off short, "Hey mister, this is my card, remember! What are you doing talking out of turn? The rules are very clear, 'A player is only permitted to speak during his or her own turn!' This is my turn. I'll admit that was a very funny adventure, but I have one to top it."

Tom raised his eyebrows and shifted his eyes from one direction to the other. "Are you talking to me? Am I to understand that you have a story that can put the porcupine adventure to shame? Hmm, I've got to hear this! I'm all ears, Duckie."

Tom slightly stood and turned his chair completely around from under him so he could fold his elbows across the top of the chair's backrest and lay his head on his arms. To Janet, his expression reminded her of an old hound dog resting his head on his front paws in front of a warm fireplace, while gazing into the fire.

She started her story by telling Tom about how she would ride her bike to school. "I lived a few miles from school and there were no buses, so I either walked or rode my bike. I was ten years old when Dad bought me the bicycle to help me get to school quicker. It had long plastic fringes hanging from the hand grips, a nice wide seat and a cute little basket. I also had a beautiful golden retriever, named Angel. On Saturdays, Angel would go with me as I rode my bike. She would always run right alongside me. On weekdays, though, she knew I was going to school and that meant she had to stay behind. I loved Angel so much. I was sad to leave her while I went to school.

My teacher, Mrs. Cross, was very upset when students arrived late, and I never wanted her anger directed at me, so I was very careful not to be late for school. Well, as you might suppose, my friends and I were about to be late for school one day. I had one chance to make it on time, but it would mean passing through El Morte's court. El Morte was a huge black Brahma bull. In the cold air his breath looked like smoke from his nostrils, and I could almost imagine fire trailing behind him. His eyes were black as coal. That day I happened to be wearing a bright red dress,

I kid you not, Tom. I didn't plan on it. I never expected a choice like this: Mrs. Cross's ruler or El Morte's sharp long horns. I knew I would be caught by Mrs. Cross, but with El Morte at least there was a chance of making it. Cutting across that pasture would save me a good five minutes, if I didn't stop right in the middle of the field, stiff from fright. Sometimes for the fun of it some boys would dare others to carry their bikes over the fence and try to ride to the other side. The response was always the same. 'No way! I'm not committing suicide!'

I had to move quickly, because I knew if I waited another moment, I would lose my courage. I said a short prayer to the Lord for help. Soon I was pedaling across the pasture, trying to avoid lumps of El Morte's droppings. Even before I saw him, I felt the ground move and shake from under me. It may have been my imagination, but I'm sure I felt it. Then the sound of a short repetitive cycle of a heavy burst of breath and dead silence. The cycle of breathing was shorter and shorter as he moved closer, sounding like an enormous locomotive engine. As I peered his way, he looked much the same. The wind was blowing the ruffles of my dress, which, I'm sure, taunted the bull like a silk red flag, daring his approach. At first I could hear all of my friends shouting at me, encouraging me, and even pleading with me to peddle faster. Before I closed my eyes, I looked at them and many of my girlfriends had their hands over their eyes, anticipating the bloody clash about to take place.

I'm not sure what happened, but I do know God had his hand in it all. When I closed my eyes, I suddenly didn't feel the wind in my face, or hear the shouts from my friends, or even feel the pedals beneath my feet. I felt the warmth of the huge arms of God around me. It was the sound of Angel barking that quickly caught my attention. How did she know I was in danger? How did she get there so quickly? She was no match for El Morte but that didn't stop her. She leaped right at the face of that ugly beast and clamped her canines deeply into the flesh of the bull's lower face. El Morte stopped just a few yards short of me, and shook his head violently, trying to free himself from Angel's tightly clenched teeth. The bull shook Angel like an old piece of carpet and ran back towards the barn with Angel still hanging from his face. I dropped my bike and started running after the bull. On the way I picked up an old piece of fence post. Tears were running down my face as I feared for Angel's life.

I stopped suddenly and looked in horror, as Angel fell from that beast and all four hooves appeared to trample the dog asunder. El Morte turned around and started to head back for another go at the dog. But seeing the dog was still and lifeless, he just trotted off towards the barn. I ran as fast as I could to Angel, if only to get there in time to thank her and give her a last kiss goodbye. But I stopped a few feet from her and walked slowly towards the carcass of fur mixed with blood on the ground. She was breathing heavily, and right when I was about to lay down next to her, she leaped right on me, knocking me backwards. As I lay there, she was licking my face. The blood on her fur belonged to the bull. She was apparently as glad to see me as I was to see her. She wasn't even hurt. She must have somehow eluded those huge hooves and was just pretending to be dead, when the bull came back for a second stomping.

By now all the children were there, laughing and looking at me and Angel in amazement. The best part was that I didn't even get into trouble with Mrs. Cross, since so many of us were all late for school. For the next week though, my dad gave me additional Bible lessons which took most of my free time to do. The lessons all had a message of being cautious, only willing to risk death on the most important of issues, and being late for school wasn't one of them. I remember one of the lessons was about Shadrach, Meshach and Abednego from Daniel 3:16 where they were to be put to death for not bowing down to an idol. Their response was clear:

O Nebuchadnezzar, we do not need to defend ourselves before you in this matter. If we are thrown into the blazing furnace, the God we serve is able to save us from it, and he will rescue us from your hand, O king. But even if he does not, we want you to know, O King, that we will not serve your gods or worship the image of gold you have set up.

See, I still remember those verses. And I remember Angel and how she was willing to risk her life for something that she felt was very important. Me!"

Tom had listened very attentively and was much entertained by the remarkable story. At its completion, he quietly clapped his hands in expression of his delight and remarked, "Well, you sure showed me. That adventure had me on the edge of my seat. Why is it you never told me about Angel before?"

"I don't know, Dear. I guess the subject just never came up. Isn't it nice though that, after all of these years, we don't yet know everything about each other. You see, this gives us years and years to learn so much more about each other. And the more I learn about you, the more and more I love you."

"Yes." Tom remarked, "And so much more that I love you, Duckie! Now tell me more about your youth."

"I'll save that for my next turn. It's your turn now to roll the dice and let me learn a little more about you."

The evening went by quickly, and soon the two were by the bedside praying. Praying for their Kelly-Joy, praying for Doug and Mary and Gretchen and Don and on and on. Wherever two or more are gathered in Christ's name, Christ is there, and so there was He. They cast their cares before His feet and went to sleep, rest assured all was well.

CHAPTER 16

The CONFESSION *to* MARY

As Doug drove down the hill, he and Kelly were very quiet. Too quiet. Suddenly Doug had an idea to break the silence. "Hey, what am I doing driving, when I could be sitting back enjoying the scenery!"

He then pulled the car to stop at the side of the road. Before getting out, he sat there a few minutes, looking at Kelly. A large welcoming grin came over her face.

She was laughing and shaking her head at the same time, "No siree, Mr. Preacher Man! I'm not driving all the way down this snake of a road. The turns are so sharp! No way! No No No No No!"

She was saying no, but in her mind, she was thinking, "YES!"

It was an older Chevy Caprice, but in very good shape. Kelly was a little hesitant driving her mother's car because the city where they lived was so busy with people always in a hurry. Her mother did let her drive fairly regularly, although she always felt nervous behind the wheel. But here in the foothills, she felt very confident driving her dad's jalopy. The Caprice handled like a dream, and she grinned as her father set the seat back to its full extent and pretended to be ready for a nap. He even took off his shoes and wiggled his toes as he crossed his legs.

Kelly slightly held her nose and started to giggle, "Whew, really Dad!"

"Very funny!" he responded. "Now I'm going to be watching you from the corner of my eyes, so don't get wild on me."

Doug had his old fishing hat partially over his eyes and peeked out to wink at Kelly, just as she looked his way. She remembered the long rides they took years ago and spontaneously spoke, "Dad, why don't you tell me one of your stories. It will make the trip go faster. C'mon! It'll be fun."

"I've got a better idea." Doug was now sitting up with his elbow on his knee and his right hand stroking his cheek as though a beard was there. "You're the driver. You tell a story. C'mon! It'll be fun. Right?"

Kelly squinted her eyes as she thought. Then she said, "Ok. I can do this. It won't be easy, but I can do it."

"Sure you can!" said Doug. "I've never seen you at a loss for words."

She started her story and it was as exciting as any her father had ever composed. She had captured the art from her dad, mixing hilarious parts with the very sad. It was a story about Ireland and two families caught up in the war-torn street battles. One Protestant and one Catholic. The oldest son of the Protestant family fell in love with the lovely and spirited daughter from the Catholic family. It was like a modern day Romeo and Juliet. Except, instead of dying at the end, they were joined in marriage, and the two of them led the entire town to stop fighting and unite as one for Christ.

They were near Kelly's home as the story ended, and Doug was moved to tears from the message of the tale. "United as one for Christ," he thought. "What a lovely message. After all, the love for Christ is supposed to bring Christians together, not separate them in war."

Then he thought of his own family. Once united in Christ and now separated as though in war. It made him feel sad and sorry for his part in it all. Could there really be a happy ending for his story as well? Only God knew. At any rate, he knew the Lord was good and only had good things in store for him and his family. He just needed to trust and have faith in the Almighty. He suddenly remembered Psalm 118:29:

Oh give thanks to the Lord for He is good.

His thoughts were interrupted by something Kelly had said. "Dad, are you alright?"

Doug quickly sat up and wiped the tears from his eyes with his shirt sleeve. "Wow! That was a beautiful story. You should really think about going into writing. You are so articulate. I never realized that about you before. Thank you."

Kelly did not know her dad was comparing the story to his life. She just thought the tears were from the joyful ending of her story. She knew him to be very sensitive and that he was often touched by romance, especially if it blended with a relationship with the Lord.

Then she questioned, "You're not just patronizing me, are you dad?"

"Of course not, Sweetie. I meant every word. You are gifted, and please think about using that gift."

As they entered the driveway, Kelly stopped the car and sat there a while without moving. She stared at the steering wheel, as though wishing she could stay there. That the next few minutes would not have to happen. But she knew the inevitable awaited them. She turned to look at her father, who now was looking upon her with concern and interest.

"Kelly, don't be afraid. If you like, I could initially explain your situation and let you complete the story."

"No, Dad!" Kelly insisted, "I'm the one that got myself into this, and I must be the one to drop the bombshell and face the consequences."

Although he didn't show it, Doug himself was a little apprehensive about being there. He wondered, "Would she blame me for all of this or perhaps just go into hysterics with disgust at Kelly's behavior."

At any rate, he was glad he could be there for Kelly's sake. He kept thinking about what his dad had said before they left Fernview Cottage: *"Considering your position as the father and the embarrassment this places on you as a pastor, your attitude of forgiveness and confidence in Kelly to do the right thing might encourage Mary to be more understanding. Mary may try to downplay Kelly's confession in church, but you were there and can testify to Kelly's sincerity. Doug, regardless of what Mary thinks of you as a husband, she very much respects your integrity and honesty."*

"Before we go in," replied Doug, "I think we better ask for the Lord's help in explaining this to your mother."

They both bowed their heads and spoke quietly and hopefully to their Lord, first Doug, then Kelly.

Mary had a big smile for Kelly as she opened the door for them. Kelly just had her hand bag, and she threw her arms around her mother. Mary enjoyed the hug, but as she pressed her lips against Kelly's cheek, she felt the taste of wet salty tears.

"What's this?" Mary questioned, "Did you miss me so much even with all of the attention I'm certain you got at Fernview Cottage?"

She pulled Kelly slightly back to look at her and instantly saw it was something else. It was a face of humility and sorrow, not one of joy at being home. Then she quickly glanced at Doug as if to say, "What is going on here?"

Kelly didn't look at her father or burst into sobs or even run upstairs to her room crying hysterically. Instead, she looked straight at her mother, which caught Mary off guard, and said, "Mother, I have done some horrible things, and I must confess these to you and be fully prepared to take my punishment as you see fit."

Mary instantly imagined many awful scenarios that she might possibly be about to hear, but nothing that raced through her mind was nearly as terrible as what Kelly was about to tell her.

The three of them sat in the living room as Kelly began her tale. Kelly said all that she had done and miraculously told the story just as she had told it to her grandparents. Strangely enough, Mary did not interrupt her. It was partially due to shock over hearing of the awful events and partially due to her surprise at the change in Kelly's attitude. From her behavior over the past several months, she would have expected Kelly to put the blame fully on Tab or her or Doug, or the move. But to accept the full responsibility of her actions was unlike the Kelly she knew.

She was also surprised at her own attitude. Why wasn't she raging mad over this? How could she herself just sit there and listen, as though it was some made up story about someone else? This is Kelly, her only daughter, whom she loved and cherished. Why wasn't she interrupting, and shouting, and hysterical as she surely should be?

And Doug, for goodness' sake. How could he accept this from her, of all people? How could he look so peaceful about the whole thing while she was being wrenched inside? OK, he apparently knew the whole story and had time to simmer down. But hearing it again should surely have grieved him. What's happening here? She suddenly decided to stop thinking so much so she could listen more clearly. Although she did not want to hear any of it, she knew she must!

At points in the story, Kelly would suddenly stop to think of the next series of happenings or just pause to clear the lump in her throat. Mary would ponder the thought, "And what should I do about all of this? How should I punish her? What should I do with that boy, Tab, this low-life of a boy who has ruined my daughter?"

She had already discovered that Tab was not anyone she would have wanted Kelly to associate with. She glanced at Doug, who was just sitting silently, waiting for Kelly to continue with each pause. Somehow this gave her the patience to sit and wait as well. She was glad she did, though, because she knew she would need this information in order to even have an inkling at knowing what to do and where to go for advice.

Then she thought, "Is Kelly really so sorry, or is this all just an act?"

Kelly couldn't believe her mother was actually letting her complete the story. This wasn't like the mother she knew. In the past, any disagreement they would ever have, she was hardly able to get a word in. Her mother always seemed to have a pre-assembled lecture and disciplinary plan for each misbehavior. Yet there she sat, trembling a little, yet silent. It gave Kelly the courage to continue and finish with an attempt at explaining her experience at the church. The forgiveness from the Lord that she felt upon her confession. The sorrow she felt that any of it happened. The assurance that this would never ever happen again. That she would be faithful to God, and adorn herself with celibacy until marriage. Kelly finally finished and now all eyes were on Mary.

Mary didn't know where to begin her outburst. She had so much to say, yet wanted to say it all at once. Where would she start? Did Kelly really just expect her to say "it's OK"? It's not OK! Mary wanted to scream and cry and yell and point her finger at the child. Kelly's humility was very convincing, but it was not enough. She must pay for this and so must Tab. It would take forever for Kelly to re-earn her trust. That girl will surely be grounded for years to come.

She wanted to express all of this and MORE. Yet Kelly's words of sorrow really touched Mary's heart and threw her mind into a state of confusion. She surprised herself by suddenly looking at Doug and saying, "What do you think of all of this?"

Doug was astonished at the question. He had to ask himself, "Was she really so interested in his opinion and feelings and concerns?"

It wasn't even said sarcastically! It was just a question that pleaded for an answer. He was not at all prepared, yet he was a pastor. As a pastor, he knew how to console, counsel, listen and express himself when asked. And now, to his surprise, he was being asked.

His response was quick and gentle.

"I understand neither the mind nor the heart that would even contrive such a plan of disgraceful activity. It is unthinkable and unbelievable that Kelly would do all of these awful things. If only she could go back in time and undo what was done. But she can't. Mary, let me tell you about my first reaction to this. I wasn't planning to be at Fernview Cottage until this morning to bring Kelly here. However, a miraculous series of events occurred to free my entire day Sunday, so I left early to get to Woodridge Falls in time for church. I was running a little late, so I went straight to the church. Even then I was late for the beginning of the worship service, but just in time to hear Kelly's confession to the entire congregation.

It took courage and a great deal of humility to do what she did and say what she said. All I could do was walk up and hug her. I felt the Holy Spirit there. He was in the air and all around. The reaction of the congregation was remarkable … Entire families coming forward and asking for God's forgiveness and each other's forgiveness for deeply hidden secrets of sin and misbehavior. You could almost feel the burdens being lifted from shoulders and floating up and out like balloons. As horrible as Kelly's story had been, God used it because truth had been put in its proper place—out in the open. God loves truth, as awful as it may be, and He is glorified when it is revealed in the proper way, when sin is confessed in sorrow and with a penitent heart. I believe Kelly does have a penitent heart. Don't you?"

Mary answered honestly, "I don't know, Doug. I really don't know! Is she acting? Is she being completely honest with us? Is she really sorry and if so, how long will that sorrow last? Is she sorry she did it at all, or just sorry that it was revealed? Confessing is one thing, but now she has to be able to pick up all the pieces and try to resolve all the trouble she has caused. What will people think and say? About her? About us? Is she really penitent? Will this happen again? How can we be sure it won't?"

Kelly thought, "These questions should be poised to me, not Dad! They should be '*Are you being completely honest? Are you really sorry?*' It is as though I'm not even here."

Mary looked deep into Kelly's eyes, trying to see the little girl she longed to see. Although Kelly would have liked to turn her head away because of the shame she felt, she knew her mother would have misunderstood, so she maintained eye contact. The young girl knew, by the yearning in her mother's eyes and her mother's expression, that she was being asked for a better explanation for what she did. Although she had no idea what to say or how to respond, the Holy Spirit guided her tongue for more truth. Maybe it wasn't what her mother wanted to hear, but it was what she needed to hear.

"Mother, I hate all that I did. I knew it had to be told, but I didn't know how to tell it. If anyone could get me to confess, it would be Grandaddy. Don't you realize that? Don't you remember how determined I was to visit Fernview Cottage? He would notice my sorrow and shame. He would probe and gently touch my heart until I would have no recourse but surrender to the truth. Although I wanted to tell him, still I was determined not to. He was so high on that pedestal of righteousness and goodness, 'How would he ever understand?' I never thought it possible for him to ever have done anything that would even come close to the evil I had done and hidden. It was only until he confessed his past to me that I realized the real truth that Paul stated in Romans 3:10:

There is no one righteous, not even one.

I was not alone in my shame or hurt. Grandaddy hurt so much and also had many regrets of his own. Pain he had caused others because of his weakness. Pain that hurt him so. It was only after learning about the hurt he inflicted on others so long ago that I understood the need for confession… the truth he had to confess to them, even at the risk of losing his life. His confession encouraged me to make my confession to him and to God. Who would have guessed that the same song of God's forgiveness brought to me in my greatest need was the same song that brought Grandaddy to his knees decades ago. The freedom of releasing the burden of my sins to Jesus far exceeded the humility I felt. Mother, it wasn't an act, it was an action and one in response to God's message of forgiveness!

It was Grandaddy's story of his salvation that shed light to me on what being a Christian really meant! Not just dos and don'ts (as I used to think), but commitment, and faith, and trust and the pure joy of giving and forgiving. Giving to others and forgiving others. Giving, as Grandaddy has been doing all his life, with no expectation of getting anything in return, in fact, hoping not to. Not getting anything in return would not take away from the joy of giving, but in actuality increase that joy. I remember when he would give a gift anonymously to one thing or another, and I would tell others what he did. I didn't know that I was taking something away from him. I just assumed he would want me to tell others, because that is what I would have wanted someone to do if I had given something to someone secretly. *After all,* I used to think, *what good is it to give something, if no one knows about it.* But God knows. He always does. That is the important thing, because that makes the gift something given to Him. What greater thing can there be than that.

"I'm glad you know what I have done, because now you will see the difference in me. The difference only Christ can make in a person's life. Kim, in Grandaddy's story of himself, had wished by some other means her 'Mr Tum' would have been saved. Still she was glad to be used by God to bring Grandaddy to his salvation. In this same way, I wish that by some other means I could have been saved, like perhaps the way you were, Dad, at five in Grandaddy's lap with tears of repentance running down your face. But for me, it took this horrible act of deception, defiance and rebellion. But the wonder of it all is that the result is the same. Eternal life! I actually have eternal life with God! I know that He loves me! Nothing, absolutely nothing that happens now can take that away! Not one iota of what Jesus did for me can be taken away! I'll hang onto it and cherish it forever as Grandaddy cherishes his salvation and as both of you cherish yours! I put my trust in what God's word says. What Paul stated in Romans 8:

Who shall separate us from the love of Christ? As it is written: For your sake we face death all day long; we are considered as sheep to be slaughtered. No! In all these things we are more than conquerors through Him who loved us. For I am convinced that neither death nor life, neither the present nor the future, nor any powers, neither height nor depth, nor anything else in all creation, will be able to separate us from the love of God that is in Christ Jesus or Lord.

I love you Mom!"

Mary couldn't believe that all she heard was coming from her little Kelly-Joy. Her little girl sounded more like a crusading evangelist. Those last words really struck Mary's heart. The anger was gone. She was no longer tense about this situation. Amazing! It seemed so amazing!

Mary still had doubts though. There was a definite change in Kelly, but was it real or just an act to throw her into confusion, which is definitely the state she was in? Mary was confused about what to do and how to react. Was Kelly just moving the focus from her sexual misconduct to her more pleasant experience with God to get out of punishment or at least reduce the trouble she was in? She just wasn't sure. She did know one thing though. If it was just an act, Kelly would be true to her old self in a few days. In the meantime, other issues had to be resolved. Like, 'what to do with Tab?', and 'would this result in a pregnancy or some form of VD?' She also knew that she would need to apologize to Bill for some of the things she had said to him the last time they were together. So much embarrassment and so many questions. So many decisions. Mary suddenly felt very tired. She felt it would be better to get a good night's rest, if that were possible, and start with first things first in the morning. The very first thing would be to have Kelly tested physically.

What about tonight though? Kelly seemed to be asking what I was about to do, regarding discipline. Again she decided to ask Doug, since he was here, and had such a wealth of training in psychology. "Doug, what's your suggestion in regard to disciplinary actions I should take?"

Again surprised, Doug crossed his arms, leaned forward a little and motioned with his eyes towards Kelly, "Maybe we should hear what Kelly thinks ought to be done for us to regain her trust and provide sufficient punishment for what she did?"

After a few moments of silence, it was apparent that this was a cue for Kelly to respond. During that period of silence, Kelly thought about what she should say, but again drew only a blank. Still though, when she did speak, an amazing burst of wisdom proceeded from her lips.

Kelly tucked her bottom lip under her front teeth for just a moment, then responded, "Well, for one, being grounded is definitely in order. Perhaps even leaving the length of time open for evaluation week-to-week. Once a week I think we should have a talk, Mom. You could get me put on the accountability program at school, where I have to have teachers verify each class attendance on a daily report to you. Until you get home from work, I should prepare meals, do all of our laundry and clean the house. I must keep my room spotless, which I know I don't now, but I will. This ought to occupy my afternoons until you get home from work."

She took a hard gulp before the next suggestion, because she loved talking on the telephone, "My cell phone should be taken away as well as telephone privileges, except for talking to family members. My computer modem should be confiscated so that I will no longer participate in the 'Chat Rooms' and ensure I have no access to pornography on the Internet. All of my rock CDs should be taken from me. I should only be permitted to listen to Christian music—which is all I really care to hear now anyway. Whenever I have extra-curricular activities at school or wherever, I should report to you by phone upon arriving and before leaving. My allowance should be cut to just handle bare essentials and, of course, I must give up my paper route. Jimmy Talbert has been filling in for me from time to time, so I'm sure he would do well to take it over. No more driving the car. I should not be permitted to visit my friends nor should they be permitted to visit me until you feel I've earned your trust. Again, we should talk about this and evaluate it weekly. You may want to nail my windows shut. Not that I will ever sneak out again or even be tempted to do so, but it may ease your thoughts as I am in the process of regaining your trust. I really need to confess all of my misdeeds that I have done against Mr. Purgoe to his face and apologize to him. I can't think of anything else right now."

She lowered her head at the last words, almost disappointed that there were no further suggestions.

Doug added another suggestion, "It might also be good to get you a pager, so that we have direct contact with you at any time. And to be sure others aren't using it to contact you, we can have the paging service report to us on every call to you."

"That sounds reasonable." Kelly said seriously.

Again, Mary was more than surprised at Kelly's suggestions. Do the laundry? Clean the house? By herself? She would do some of that work regularly before, but only with Mary there helping her. Even then she would complain. She has never kept her room clean. So many changes. Could she really do all of this and handle the restrictions without complaining or begging for a compromise? It will be easier to justify holding her to the arrangements, since they were her ideas. Would it really work? Mary also wondered why most of her own anger was gone. Shouldn't she still be cross with Kelly, to place an emphasis on the firmness the child needed? Kelly had definitely made her punishment challenging for herself, but was it really enough? She still wondered if a beating would be better for her. Something at least to help the girl understand how much pain she has caused. None of what was suggested had anything to do with pain, just work and restrictions. Was it enough? Really! Was it enough?

Doug seemed to sense some of the turmoil Mary was going through. "None of this can eliminate what has happened, Mary. Nothing can. The pain, the problems, the consequences are all still there. We can't change what Kelly has done. We can only deal with them now as maturely and wisely as we can and take whatever steps are necessary to ensure they don't happen again.

Mary, I don't think they will happen again. Kelly is a different person. She has accepted Jesus Christ as her Savior. Don't you remember when you accepted Christ and the difference it made in your life? You yourself have shared that story with so many people in so many Bible studies. You were no longer angry when you had to clean up your father's messes when he would get drunk. Through the change he saw in you, your father was converted to follow Jesus.

Of course, you have major custody of Kelly so I can only offer my advice as her father and as someone who has counseled others with such problems. What Kelly has suggested is a just and good form of discipline. I think it would be good to get it all in writing and have her sign it as a binding agreement."

Mary reluctantly agreed. Doug took advantage of this moment to openly pray for Kelly. The three of them held hands as he spoke and praised God and lifted Kelly's concerns up before their Lord. The evening had finally come to a close and Kelly was blessed with such peace. For the first time since this discussion started, Mary smiled at Kelly. It was plain to her that Kelly was exhausted.

The teenager then gave her father a warm hug and kiss on the cheek and turned to her mother and did the same. She was relieved that the evening had not been wasted in arguing and screaming. Her mother had been more understanding than she ever expected. She thought, *Prayers really do work!* Her father's prayers, her grandaddy's and grandma's prayers, and yes, her very own. God had performed a miracle that evening and she knew it. Now, she thought, *if only the Lord would get her mother and father back together.*

She pondered about how well they both acted to one another during the difficult discussion and heavy subject matter. Maybe this was the start of something very wonderful. As awful as it had been and all that she had done, maybe God will use this to help their love for each other to return. Kelly remembered the look her mother had as she listened to her father. So intense. So respectful. It had been a long time since she saw that in their relationship. *Maybe!* She thought, *It could happen!*

With those lovely thoughts, she scurried up to bed. Doug talked with Mary awhile, and then left for his long trip home. They planned to make arrangements to see this Tab fellow and his parents together.

As he pulled from the driveway his mind raced, replaying all the events of the weekend. The wonder of Kelly's return to the Lord and the tragedy of what brought her to the feet of Jesus. He knew he had to have a talk with the Lord. He knew he had to ask his Father, who withheld nothing from him, to help him deal with some of the things he was feeling. Doug understood that Kelly provoked the misconduct of this boy, but he couldn't help feeling some animosity toward this guy. Indeed, maybe almost hatred. He never envisioned himself hating anyone until now. As he dwelled on it all, he surrendered to his Lord,

"Father, as I contemplate the whole matter, I must take part of the blame myself. If I could have been more of what you wanted me to be in my relationship with Mary, all of this never would have happened. The divorce, the breakup of our family, Kelly's feelings of insecurity, it's MY FAULT. MY FAULT AND MINE ALONE. You know my heart, Lord! You know I was just trying to be a good pastor to my congregation. Although from her attitude, it occurred to me that Mary was feeling a little like being taken for granted, but I didn't realize she resented being the church's organist, your organist. I just assumed she enjoyed serving you in that way as much as I did as a pastor."

Now Doug pulled to the side of the road. His feelings were such that he could no longer drive. He had to devote his whole self to this discussion with his Father. As the car came to a stop, he folded his arms over the steering wheel, and rested his head upon them as he continued.

"Dear God, I tried too hard. I allowed the congregation to depend on me too much. I sinned against you and you alone. Please forgive me. Please help Mary to forgive me. Look at this sorry sight before you. I am crushed and in deep sorrow. Those who know me could not believe Mary was divorcing me. How often I was complimented by others for my dedication to Mary and my support of her. They thought, as I did, that we were the most likely to succeed as a long term married couple. During counseling sessions, I was told that I needed to say NO to her more. Say NO to paying for her education. How could I do this? I applauded her for her intentions of becoming a school teacher. Oh Lord, whatever happens, whatever becomes of me, I will continue to praise You and seek Your will for my life. Thank You for Your love and the hope You have given me. You are my joy and my strength."

After a few minutes, Doug was ready to proceed to drive home.

CHAPTER 17

The BUS TRIP *to* SCHOOL

Kelly awoke to the sounds of a woodpecker in the tree just outside her window. She grinned as she watched the bird awhile. Then she wondered why the woodpecker was adorned beautifully with such brilliant colors all about his head, shoulders and breast, while the sparrows, crows and so many other birds comparatively looked so commonplace. She sat at her desk with her elbows on the table and her hands cupped under her chin and around her cheeks, supporting her head. She smiled and then thought, "Surely the Lord honored that woodpecker because of his hard labor. I wonder if that bird ever has a headache after a long day of hammering the hard tree trunks."

Then her eyes turned to the painting her grandaddy had given her. Her heart longed to be back there at Fernview Cottage. It was good to have the painting, though, for it so expressed the beauty of that wonderland. And the love that was put into that work of art seemed to just flow out from it, engulfing her with a mighty hug. She definitely needed that. She thought of Grandaddy and how he always prayed as soon as he awakened from his sleep. It encouraged her to do the same just then.

Actually she had so much to be thankful for. After all that she had done, she knew she deserved to be put away somewhere. And she knew very well her mother could have been angry enough to do just that. But miracle upon miracle had followed her the whole weekend. And here she was, at peace with her mother, father and grandparents. "How could it be?" she asked herself and then the Lord. "How did it all happen? When did it start? Was it Grandaddy's willingness to share his shame that caused everything to turn out so? Was it her own confession?" As she thought about this, she concluded, "No, it is all due to God's grace, that Amazing Grace!"

Whatever and whenever and however, she knew one thing and one thing only. God loved her. And she was determined to try to remember that, whatever circumstances may arise. Her prayer was simple, but sincere. After praying she went over to the wooden cross that hung on her wall above her bed and kissed it ever so softly and said, "Thank you Jesus. You are my hero and my Savior. Now and forever!"

With that done, she busied herself cleaning her room. At first she thought, "Oh my, where do I start?" But once started, she was surprised how little time it took to have it looking almost perfect. She was glad that the woodpecker got her up early so she could get it all done. She knew her mother would not be so impressed until she had done this week after week. But that is exactly what she knew she would do. She had already surrendered her cell phone and telephone the night before as well as all her non-Christian CDs, and asked her mother to scrape them up and throw them in the trash. She felt a good sense of accomplishment as she rushed downstairs to greet her mother.

Mary was in the kitchen. Kelly's breakfast was set there on the table. A bowl of her favorite cereal, juice, toast and hot chocolate. Mary was still contemplating whether or not she made the right decision the night before by allowing Kelly to choose her own punishment. She wondered if Kelly's behavior was just an act. "Was the child really sincere?" she thought.

"Is she really remorseful? Has she really changed with the conversion? Was the conversion itself real?"

So many questions cluttered her mind. She felt so unsure of it all.

Then she felt two loving arms wrap around her. She turned within the circle of limbs that encompassed her to see a smiling face looking at her. She wanted to smile back, but felt that she must show the girl that she did not intend to be a pushover.

"Kelly, I have all the things we discussed last night, about your discipline, written down in a contract form that I want you to sign."

Kelly felt a bit of rejection from her mother's tone, but knew her well enough to know that she was just trying to prove that she meant business. Kelly could almost feel her trying to be so tough, yet wanting to be so loving. She never thought of this before, but suddenly realized how hard it must be to be a parent. Then a bit of fear crossed her mind to think that she, herself, may be pregnant. She may very well be a soon-to-be parent.

"No!" she thought. "Surely God would not strap her with such a difficult ordeal. Not after all of the sorrow she had already been through. Not after she had really and truly, with all of her heart, accepted Jesus and had been saved once and for all. No! It can't be. I'm just worrying about nothing."

With that she regained her smile and replied, "Sure Mom! I'll do it right now."

Kelly took the pen and started to sign the single page, formal-looking document.

Her mother quickly turned and sternly replied, "I want you to read it first. Completely!"

Then she smiled and added, "Don't forget the fine print stating that you are to be handcuffed to your bed each night."

Kelly was relieved to see that her mother's smile and sense of humor was returning. She played along...

"Yea! And bars on my windows! A dead-bolt lock on my door! And a sign reading, 'UNCLEAN,' which is to be announced verbally wherever I go! You really outdid yourself, Mom!"

"Very cute, Kelly-Joy." Mary chuckled.

Then she added as she walked over to Kelly and stooped to meet the girl eye to eye, as Kelly sat there at the kitchen table, "I really do love you! I just want you to know the seriousness of all that you have done."

She gently brushed the hair from the girl's lovely face with her fingers and continued very softly,

"We will need to have you tested to see if you are pregnant or have VD. We will need to confront this boy and talk to his parents. There are a lot of issues we will have to face. This is very complicated. It will be a long time before I feel I can really trust you. I will be questioning your every excuse or statement regarding where you have been and what you have been doing. You will feel your privacy invaded and I'm certain this will cause many arguments between us. Even more than there were before. You will plead with me for exceptions to this agreement, but you need to know right now, I will not budge. Not an inch. For your own good, not an inch! I don't want our relationship to worsen. I want to trust you and have your help in this situation with the divorce. I know you love your father and want us to be a family again, but you must face the facts and understand that this will not happen. I respect your dad and we are friends, but that's all! We both love you and we will help you because we want you to succeed in life. You have a very bright future, in spite of all of this. You are very intelligent and pretty, and are a very sweet young lady when you want to be. Those so-called friends at school that you talked about are not good for you. You must stay away from them! "

Mary stopped there and waited a second for Kelly's reaction, which really surprised her.

"No problem, Mom. I have already decided not to hang around them anymore. I will speak to them only to tell them that I have accepted Jesus and how He's changed my life. I will explain to them that I will not be permitted to spend time with them anymore. There are other kids that have gotten into trouble partially because of them and have had to avoid any contact with them, so I'm sure they will understand. They may not like it and think it's unfair, but that's the way it is, and they will just have to accept it."

After signing the contract, Kelly then quickly finished breakfast, kissed her mother goodbye, and left to catch her bus.

The bus stop was the worst place for school kids to congregate. There was absolutely no adult supervision there. The bullies would get there early to make the best of their domain. For them it was like a delicatessen. So many vulnerable kids to choose from. The freshmen were their favorites, though.

Kelly approached the same bus stop she had known from her elementary school days with caution, yet confidence. She was a sophomore. It didn't completely protect her from those who would try to intimidate her, but she had also been a good friend of Tab's. Tab was one that none of the bully jerks wanted to deal with. He had a look of vengeance about him that frightened them.

Butch Atkins watched Kelly and another girl intently as they approached with a slight smirk on his face. He was a jock as well as a jerk. He placed the cigarette that was in his hand to his lips and inhaled with great intensity. The combination of the colorful gel over the unnatural bright red streaks in his hair with the bright morning sun rays made those streaks appear to blaze like the end of his cigarette. The girl behind Kelly was Jennifer Wilson. She was a freshman and a little overweight. Kelly walked by Butch to stand near the tennis court of the small park. Jennifer followed and just as she neared Butch, he formed a perfect circle with his mouth and blew out smoke in a series of O's that drifted between the girls. Jenny fanned her hand in front of her to clear the smoke from her path.

Butch stepped in front of her to block her path and stood there as she apprehensively looked about for another route to her destination.

With a wide grin, Butch said, "C'mon now, Jen! Don't tell me you've never lit up. Not just once? I think you should live a little. Here, take a drag."

Butch's real name was Richard but everyone called him Butch. As Jenny thought of a response that would not bring more trouble upon herself, Kelly noticed Butch's skateboard was half on the grass that surrounded the telephone pole and half on the sloping parking lot. Butch had his full attention on his victim. As Jenny stuttered a few words, Kelly slowly bumped the edge of the skateboard with her umbrella.

Then she quickly stepped forward near Butch and gently said, "Why Richard! Isn't that your skateboard rolling down the hill?"

Butch quickly turned and without a moment to spare ran down the street after his treasured skateboard, dodging in and out of traffic. Several of the kids burst into laughter. Kelly had mixed feelings about herself. She was glad she could help the young girl, but she also felt a little sorry that she pulled such a dirty trick. What if Butch should get hit by a car or something? She hoped he would be safe, but she also just couldn't help but chuckle a little. He looked so amusing and the thought that he was getting perhaps his just consequence for harassing young girls made her feel a little justified. Still, she silently asked the Lord to forgive her, should it offend Him.

The bus came and all were loading aboard, except Butch, who was retrieving his skateboard from a dirty drain ditch. After the last student had taken his seat, the driver prepared to drive off.

But Kelly shouted, "Please Mr. Walker! Please wait just a moment for Butch Atkins."

Mr. Walker, for an instant, thought of just pretending he did not hear the young lady. Leaving Butch behind would sure make his job easier. It was hard enough to concentrate on driving with a load of noisy kids without having a troublemaker like him to boot. Kelly was sitting right behind the driver.

She asked again, since Mr. Walker was still preparing to take off, "Please, Mr. Walker."

Butch had now made his way to the bus.

As he climbed the stairs to enter, Mr. Walker said, "Hurry along there! You've held me up long enough. Lucky for you, Miss Wisp here asked me to wait. Although the way you treat other people I'm surprised anyone would be looking out for you."

Butch stared at Kelly and took the vacant seat next to her. He was speechless for a long while.

He looked a little bewildered and then spoke softly, "A…Um. Thanks for speaking up for me. No one has ever done that for me before. I thought you were angry at me for the trick I played on you last week."

Kelly grinned a little and replied, "Oh, I'm not angry at anyone Butch. Well, it looks like you got your skateboard. I'm sorry you had so much trouble."

Butch looked her straight in the eye and said, "I don't get it! Last week you were yelling at me for using your hat like a Frisbee, and today, when you could have gotten even by letting the driver go off without me, you didn't. Why did you help me? What do you want from me?"

Kelly had been looking down at her lap, but now was looking directly at Butch, " I want your forgiveness."

Now Butch looked confused, "Forgiveness! Forgiveness for what?"

"Six years ago, one icy morning you came to school with your hair messy and your hands dirty. You were late and didn't even stop at the restroom to clean up. Mrs. Lee scolded you right in front of the class for coming to school dirty. I laughed at you. I had no right to do that. I'm sorry. Really!"

Butch remembered it. He remembered it all too well. He hated that teacher for humiliating him. And he hated the kids, all of them. His home was old and broken down. It had an outhouse in the back and an old pump in front of the house for water. That morning the pump froze, and he couldn't prime it to get water for the family to clean themselves and drink. They all had to go to school dirty and messy. The teacher didn't ask if anything was wrong at home. She didn't even ask! If only his father didn't leave them, he would have known what to do. He would have known how to make that old pump cough up water. But he did leave just the day before. He left Butch, his other sons and his daughters, his wife, everyone. And Butch hadn't seen him since.

Kelly's words were gentle and Butch felt his hardened heart soften a little. He didn't want that. Hatred made him strong. Sure a bully, but strong and fearful.

With a bit of bitterness in his voice from remembering all of it, he said to Kelly, "Why shouldn't you have laughed. The whole class laughed. They thought it was funny. You thought it was funny. So why should you be sorry!"

Kelly had tears in her eyes now, "Because I knew your family was hurting and your father had left you. Because I saw you, so frustrated, trying to get the pump to prime that morning on my way to school. But I didn't say anything. I just let them laugh. And what's worse, I laughed too. I have regretted that ever since! Please forgive me, Butch."

The kids sitting near them were silent at this point and their eyes were fixed on the front seat. Some of them remembered that day. They were expecting the worst. Surely now, with Butch knowing Kelly could have prevented that humiliation so many years ago, would that not cause him to explode into one of his wild tantrums? Butch and Kelly did not even notice the attention they were getting. They were both wrapped in emotion. Then Butch noticed the stares of those behind and around them.

He shouted, "Mind your own business or you will surely regret it!"

Immediately the group looked away and stopped their focus on the two in the front seat.

Butch saw the tears of remorse in Kelly's eyes and quietly pulled a clean white handkerchief from his rear pocket and handed it to Kelly, saying, "Yes, I forgive you. I've done a lot of stupid things too. But why did you wait until now to tell me that you understood how I felt and how wrong Mrs. Lee was."

She continued, "Because yesterday I accepted Jesus Christ as my Savior. He changed my life, Butch. And he can change yours too!"

Butch retorted, "No one can change mine. I am bad to the bone. At least I know it and admit it. I'm no hypocrite. People fear me and I like it."

"No, I don't believe you do like it." said Kelly quietly. "It doesn't have to be that way. You could be a friend and have friends. Jesus could help you like he did me. Honestly!"

With this said, the bus came to a stop in front of the high school. Butch was silent as he pondered all that Kelly had told him. She was right. He didn't like people fearing him and being afraid to get close to him. He wanted friends. He just didn't think it was possible. Then he thought, "Or is it? Is it really possible? Kelly really is different. Something happened to her. Maybe there is hope for me!"

Butch decided right then to have another talk with Kelly sometime. Sometime soon.

CHAPTER 18

THE PROTEST *at the* ABORTION CLINIC

Mary was just about to leave for work when she received a telephone call from Doug. After greeting one another, Doug quizzed Mary about the morning, "So how was Kelly this morning? Did she seem depressed at all?"

Mary responded, "No, she wasn't depressed, that I could tell. In fact we had a nice adult conversation and she had no problem with signing the contract. After she left for school, I made an appointment to have her tested. I will be taking her to Dr. Flemming right after school tomorrow."

Doug was relieved that Mary decided to have their old family doctor examine Kelly. He was a good Christian and friend of the family.

After a period of silence Doug spoke quietly, "I have the phone number of the boy, Tab. I also have his father's telephone number from work. His name is Tony West. I will call him this afternoon and try to make arrangements to see him and his wife. I think you and Kelly should go with me. Should this boy try to deny any of it, I will need Kelly there to verify her story."

Mary reluctantly agreed, and after completing their conversation, each slowly placed the receiver in its place. Doug wished that he could have added some humor or something to lighten the conversation, but there was nothing to be humorous about. The situation was downright grim. He wished he could have thought of something very wise and encouraging to say to Mary, but no such thing came to mind. He felt so ill-equipped to handle this situation. Well, he had his task at hand to perform. It would be a difficult evening, but he knew his Lord was standing by to guide him, strengthen him and help him. He took a moment just then to pray and set about his task of scheduling the next day's visitation to two of the correctional facilities in the area.

It was a beautiful morning at Fernview Cottage. Tom and Janet were scurrying about. They usually had devotions together before breakfast, but this morning they decided to read and discuss the topic of the day during breakfast. Before eating, they prayed. The prayers were much longer than the grace that was normally spoken. It was very special. The subject of the devotion dealt with combating anger, God's patience with us and the need for us to be patient with others.

Each of them could share so much regarding examples of poor and good dealings with anger, from others and attitudes they themselves had had. Tom was the first to begin. He tried to remember a time when he was very angry. He recalled a skiing trip that they had all gone on.

"Duckie, do you remember the time at Snowflake Valley when I got separated from Don and Gretchen?"

"Tom!" Janet replied, "That was so long ago! Doug was only in the fourth grade and Gretchen in first. They looked so cute in their ski outfits. Didn't the chair lift break down or something and you couldn't get to them?"

"No my Dear, it was that chair lift attendant! Those two little ski munchkins of ours went on ahead as I was helping Donny get his skis back on after a little spill. By the time we were on our feet again, they were on their way back up the hill before I could signal to them that the lift was about to close. I remember yelling to them as they were riding up the chair lift, that I would be at the top as soon as I could and for them to wait for me. They heard me alright, laughing and waving to me.

Well, by the time I got to the chair lift, the attendant was just tagging the seats with red flags, indicating to the top the OK to shut her down. I told him very nicely that I had to get up that hill because my kids were too little to take those slopes alone, especially since the easy runs already had their lights off.

He just shrugged his shoulders and said, 'It's time for me to go home, I'm cold!'

I could have strangled him. Too cold indeed! I nearly cursed the man, and if Donny hadn't been there, I probably would have. I should have made him restart that chair lift. But I hoped for the best. I started to climb up the hill sideways on my skis, but then I was worried about leaving Donny alone, and I knew it would take too long anyway!

I didn't know what to do! What a dilemma! I just stood there waiting and looking. I told the kids I would be there, but I couldn't.

As the last group of skiers made their way past me, I shouted, 'Have you seen two little kids up there, a girl with a lavender parka and a boy in navy blue?'

They just shook their heads as they passed. It seemed like an eternity before I saw the silhouette of Doug and Gretchen at the top of the ridge. I was so glad to see that they were smart enough to not try and ski it, but walk all of the way to the ridge instead. I told Donny not to leave that spot, and I ran up after them.

Wow, I can't tell you how relieved I was to be there with them and how angry I still was at the attendant. On the way back, I reported him to the office. Boy, did I give them a piece of my mind! You remember that, don't you Duckie?"

"Well Tom," Janet replied with a bit of a pout on her face, "I was in the lodge, nursing a swollen ankle. Don't you remember that? My first run of the day, and there I was, incapacitated. I was so jealous of everyone else on the slopes. And lonely!"

"Duckie!" Tom remarked with his eyebrows raised in surprise, "Why then did you tell us to go on. You said you had some reading to catch up on anyway, as I recall!"

"Yea, I did say that," Janet responded, "because I didn't want the rest of you to miss out on the fun on account of me. And we had paid so much money for those lift tickets. I sure missed being with you all during that time. But, tell me more about what you told the office personnel. You didn't feel much like talking about it when you got to the café."

"I really don't think you want to hear all that I told them. But I made it quite clear that if anything had happened to my children because of that lazy attendant, heads would have gone rolling!" Tom spoke with his eyebrows lifted to their max, his arms folded over his chest, and his head slightly tilted.

"Wow! Look at the time. I need to get down the hill and make my way to the abortion clinic in Tustin Heights. The sit-in begins at ten."

Janet had a deep look of concern on her face. She was so worried about what might happen there today. The city police departments were cracking down very hard on the abortion protests. She feared for Tom. How could she stop him? Or should she even try? No, she knew being a Christian meant taking risks and standing up for what is right no matter what the consequences. She would be there herself, but she knew Tom would not hear of it. Besides, she was not sure she could keep her composure as Tom surely would. In the midst of those abortionists and knowing the horror of what was happening behind those doors, she may very well break inside and ruin the whole protest. But Tom would be calm but firm. Just then she brightened her face with a slight smile and leaned across the table to give her wonderful man a light kiss.

As they parted from each other, Tom gave her a little wink and said, "Duckie, you bring me such joy! Maybe tomorrow we can go for a delightful walk around the lake. What will you be doing while I'm gone today?"

She thought for a moment and then responded, "I'll be at the school all morning. It is my turn to help in the office and library."

Janet then looked a little melancholy and said, "Tom, I really think we should pray just now."

Tom grinned and gently took her hand, as he prayed for her day and his. He also prayed for all who would be participating in the demonstration. He even prayed for the police and the opposition. There would be many hecklers and troublemakers from the opposite point of view and he knew he would need much help from the Lord to be pleasant to them, in spite of their unruliness. Tom softly squeezed her hand as he finished. Janet felt so much more relieved, knowing the Lord had heard those prayers and would keep Tom safe and secure in His tender care.

As Janet stood on her tippy-toes to hug Tom, he quietly chuckled with joy. He was glad she was so short and had to stretch on the tips of those lovely feet. She suddenly looked like a little ballerina, even from that angle. They said their goodbyes, and off he went.

As Tom arrived at the clinic, a crowd of protesters was gathering for prayer. Tom jumped in and joined the circle of hands held together in outstretched arms. There were many different churches represented there for the same purpose: saving babies. As they finished their prayer, the clinic door opened and a doctor rushed out to warn the intruders, "You people have no business here! I have already called the police, so you had better go home now! I mean right now!"

He knew there were no worries about trouble from the crowd except the hindrance they made. Keeping his patients away infuriated the doctor. Being too impatient to await the police, he immediately turned on a water hose and sprayed the group with water. Being wet was the least of their concerns. As the wet spray covered them with water, they laughed and sang an appropriate hymn, "Showers of Blessings."

This just made the doctor even angrier, and in frustration he returned the hose to its place and went back into the clinic to prepare for the day's work. But he knew that business would be nil until these pests were dispersed.

He smiled as the riot squad pulled up, all dressed in the most current anti-riot attire, complete with shields, helmets and bullet-proof jackets. They carried stun guns and belly clubs. There was no need for any of these and Captain John Lewis knew it. He pulled up in his Ford right between the squad and the protesters.

He yelled at the squad to "Take-5" as he approached the protesters.

He walked to Pastor Bob Milhorn and shook his hand, "Pastor, you know I agree with what you are trying to do, but this method is just not the right way. There is nothing I would like better than to see these butcher-houses eliminated, but my job right now is to protect them. There are some laws in the state committee even now that hopefully will someday snuff these places out. Until then I must ask you to leave. I don't want to see anyone get hurt here. If I had my way, I would give you a few hours and let the day end as a success for your cause. However, the Chief has been pressured to take a hard stand on this. The publicity of the recent bombings of abortion clinics has really stirred the beehive. The press is on its way right now to slant your protest to the most negative way it can. And you know they have ways of doing just that. Why don't you all go home and return in a few weeks when all of this blows over. I might even be able to get a restraining order against those pro-abortion hecklers that have been pestering you."

The pastor responded with a huge smile, "I appreciate your concern and your motivation to help Captain. I really do. I know there are bills in committee and the only reason they are there is God's will and His blessing upon our protests which have initiated those bills. But those bills right now will not do any good in helping the babies entering that torture chamber today. If we can spare just one child, it will be worth whatever we have to go through. As profane and despicable as the enemy is, it will not prevail. In the end, right will win, and we will be here time after time applauding it on, praising our Lord."

At this the crowd praised the Lord with the lifting of their arms and shouts of AMENs!

"Nice speech, Pastor." commended the Captain. "Well, I'll do what I can."

As Captain Lewis approached the riot squad, he cautioned them to be easy on the crowd. Many of the protesters were old and many were women. He was in the process of ordering the clubs, stun guns, and shields to be put away when the chief pulled up. By now the press was there and bombarding the chief with questions as he was getting out of his car. The chief was very intimidated. As the camera focused on him, the chief rapidly changed his expression to that of an angry coach whose team had just been given a bad call by the refs.

"Lewis, what in Sam's hill are you doing?" Before Captain Lewis could answer, the chief called Sergeant Hogan to his side.

"Sergeant, get your men in position with full dress. I want these protesters on those paddy wagons in less than an hour! I don't care how it's done, just do it!"

"Yes, Sir!" the sergeant responded and went about ordering the men to form the line.

As the cameras were moved away and the press raced to be in position to get a good shot at the arrests, Captain Lewis confronted the chief, "Nice show, Chief! I just hope your Aunt Milly isn't amongst the crowd!"

In quick response, the Chief glanced over what he could see of the nearly one hundred Christians now sitting and singing on the sidewalk leading to the clinic. Slowly he walked away and softly said, "So do I."

The sitting crowd locked elbows in preparation of making their removal as difficult as possible. Pro-Choice hecklers were now there swearing and spitting at those sitting. One of the Christians stood as though in retaliation. The press hurried to get the confrontation on film. The man just smiled and said, "Jesus sure loves you!" as he wiped the clump of spit from his face. This scene would surely be edited out.

The sergeant announced that a ten minute grace period would be given for the crowd to disperse peacefully and unabated. But after ten minutes, the crowd remained.

The press was anxiously awaiting some reaction or reprisal from the crowd, but it remained peaceful. Even when the police became frustrated at the crowd clinging together with locked elbows and used their clubs to bruise arms and legs in attempts at quickly getting everyone into the police wagons parked along the curb, the protestors remained peaceful. The riot squad was ruthless.

As one of the clubs swung towards the arm of a woman sitting near Tom, he thrust his shoulders in the way to take the brunt of the blow. After four hours all of the protestors were loaded in buses and police trucks. This ordeal did not reduce the enthusiasm of the Christian protestors. As the vehicles drove away, the Christians were singing and rejoicing over the lives that were saved. Tom's great baritone voice was a foundation for the whole group. His shoulder ached a little, but he wouldn't have missed this for the world.

Even though the riot squad had not wasted any time dispersing the protest, the sit-in had been a success. It was now early afternoon and not one child was killed at that abortion clinic. The protestors were finger-printed and booked for a two night stay at the jailhouse. Had the picket been anything other than against abortion or anywhere besides the entrance of an abortion clinic, they would have been left completely alone and not attacked or disturbed in any way. But the laws were clear and strict against would-be abortion protestors. With pressure from pro-choice activist groups, Governor Alan Blantz had signed several laws into effect restricting pickets in front of abortion clinics. Tom and his fellow servants would be arraigned individually. They were neither worried nor disturbed in any way. In fact, bruises and all, they felt joyful and understood the blessing Paul and Silas must have felt after being beaten and jailed for their obedience to God.

Sam Diggs made his way through the crowded hall outside the jail. After a few words with the jailer, he went into a small conference room across the hall from the rows of jail rooms now packed full with protestors. He felt disheartened at the conversation that was about to take place. He pulled a chair from the table and slowly let his weight fall into the solid oak frame. Folding his arms comfortably on the top of his large belly, he thought carefully, trying to recall if there were any subclauses to this most recent enactment that would alleviate the full effect of the consequences. Tom was handcuffed and accompanied by a guard as he entered the room.

With authority and disgruntlement Sam shouted to the guard, "Take those shackles from this man this instant!"

The response came respectfully, yet with just a tint of sarcasm, "I would really like to oblige you, Sir, but I have my orders from the Chief."

"You may leave now!" ordered Sam.

"No problem. I'll be right outside the door when you're ready to go."

As the door closed behind the guard, Sam smiled at Tom who was slowly seating himself at the table across from his friend.

Then Sam spoke quietly, "Just like old times, Tom."

Then his expression turned a bit more serious. "Except these days they do a bit more than slap your hands and tell you not to do it again. Laws have changed a lot in the past few years, but I know you already know this. You did what you knew was right and are now ready to face any consequences that may come of it, but I sure wish those consequences weren't so severe. How many babies do you think were saved?"

Tom's grin was from ear to ear as he reported, "Sources tell me that there were twelve abortions scheduled at that clinic for the morning, two of them partial birth abortions. Those babies are alive and well right now. Praise the Lord! Of course, they most likely will be rescheduled, but perhaps something will happen to change those young girls' minds. We can only pray. We must pray!"

"I'm with you on that!" Sam replied.

With that said both men leaned forward on their chairs to quietly pray to the Lord and praise Him for the success of the protest and for the lives of the unborn that were saved.

CHAPTER 19

MEETING *the* WEST FAMILY

The day at school for Kelly was quite a change for her. She saw Tab before school and told him that she confessed everything to God and to her parents.

He responded, "Confessing to God is cool, but why did you have to tell your parents? That can be a drag. Next they will be wanting to talk to me and get me in trouble. I don't need that!"

"Tab!" Kelly replied, "You're already in trouble and so am I. What we did was wrong and now we must do whatever is necessary to make up for it."

To this Tab said, "It's not so bad. No one got hurt. It's cool! We will just lay low for a few weeks and then after you regain your mom's trust, we can start over – but this time no more squealing!"

Kelly was not surprised at his response. "No Tab! We are not going to start over. It's finished. I made a promise to my Grandaddy, my father and to God that I am going to remain pure until I get married."

"Remain pure? You never were pure, little lady! And a little confession and promise isn't going to change all that's happened. You want me and I want you. That's all that's important." Tab's tone was confident and demanding.

Kelly responded, "No! I don't want you. Not the way you think. Jesus is real to me. I know He's not real to you, but someday He could be and that could make your life so beautiful. There is such joy in knowing Jesus, Tab."

Kelly reached for her little booklet of the Gospel of John. "It says here in John 6……."

Tab pushed her aside and said sarcastically as he was leaving, "Save it for Sunday, preacher girl!"

Suddenly, Kelly had strength she never knew. Before this, if he had talked to her in that way, she would have been crushed. But now, it didn't matter. She didn't feel hurt or rejected. Just sad that he could not understand. She remembered in John 1:4 it said:

In him was Life and that Life was the Light of men. The Light shines in the darkness but the darkness has not understood it.

Then she remembered something else and found the place in the booklet, John 3:19:

This is the verdict: Light has come into the world, but men loved darkness instead of light because their deeds were evil. Everyone who does evil hates the light and will not come into the light for fear that their deeds will be exposed. But whoever lives by the truth comes into the light, so that it may be seen plainly that what he has done has been done through God.

"Yes!" she thought, "And from now on I will live by the Truth and stay in the Light, your Light Lord, so that it will be seen that whatever I do, I do through you, Father!"

During the day, she no longer had groups of friends about her. Tab spread the word fast and most of the day she heard little whispers and saw grins about her. She paid them no mind though. She thought that it was probably a good thing anyway because it will be easy now to stay away from those so-called friends, as she promised her mother she would do. It did hurt a little to see how few, good, real friends she actually did have. Last week she was the chatterbox of the group. Now she was alone and quite quiet. But she kept her head held high and her smile as bright as ever. She looked about and actually noticed those quiet kids that often went unnoticed. Gerry Woods and Linda Colt were two of those students. She walked over to Linda and made light conversation. Linda was overjoyed to have someone to talk to, although at first she was reluctant, fearful of Kelly's motives. But Kelly had such a trusting ease about her that quickly relaxed Linda's anxieties. Linda was very shy and ordinary. Kelly found her very interesting and they soon became friends.

Doug was able to contact Mr. West and arranged a meeting that evening. So there they were, the three of them in Doug's car on the way to the Wests' home. Kelly was the first to speak.

"Dad, I told Tab at school today that I had confessed everything. He didn't take it very well. I tried to tell him about Jesus."

"What was his response?" Doug asked.

Kelly said, "He didn't like much of what I had to say, with the change in me and all."

Then with a little smile Kelly looked at her shoes as she said with a half-giggle, "He called me a preacher girl."

Doug smiled as he said, "Well, I had a few of those responses myself when I was your age. What do you think his reaction will be tonight?"

She looked a little puzzled as she responded, "I really don't know. Typically I would expect that he would think we are making a big deal out of some small thing, as he sees it, but with his parents there, I'm just not sure."

Mary just sat there thinking about the evening. Not saying anything, just thinking.

Mr. and Mrs. West were cordial to the Wisp family as they introduced one another. Tab was a little sulky but polite. Mrs. West asked about drinks. Doug and Mary requested coffee and Kelly just asked for a glass of water.

With the drinks served, Mr. West got right to the point, "Your call, Doug, sounded very serious and urgent. That is why I agreed to meet with you. I can't get much out of Robert, so you will have to clue me in."

Doug looked seriously deep into Tab's eyes and then looked back at Mr. West. Doug was about to start when Kelly spoke up, "Dad, may I explain?"

"Sure, Honey. Maybe that would be best," Doug responded.

Kelly began her story, "Mr. West, last December I met Tab for the first time at school. We talked of some of the problems I was having at home. A month later, January 12th, Tab asked me to meet him at his house the next morning at 2 AM. He told me that his parents wouldn't be home and we could just talk. Well, I did come here and we did talk, until nearly daylight. After that, I came here about once a week until just a few weeks ago. For the first couple of months he had hot chocolate. But then he had vodka here for us to drink. I drank some with him and we had intercourse, many times in recent months."

Mr. West waited, as though there was something more to be said. When Kelly continued to be silent, he glanced disappointedly at Tab and then looked back at Kelly and quietly said, "Are you trying to tell me that you are pregnant with Robert's child?"

Doug quickly responded, "We don't know yet. We are going to take her to see our family doctor tomorrow after school."

Mrs. West looked horrified while Mr. West looked a bit put out. He said, "Why in thunder didn't you wait until tomorrow then to spring all of this on us! We don't know the damage done yet."

Doug said in a stern way, "I had expected that you would like to know as soon as possible about wrong doing in your home! The immediate concern is not if Kelly is pregnant, but the fact that your son has enticed my daughter, a minor, into his room, has given her alcohol to drink, and has had intercourse with her! The damage has already been done. My daughter has been violated and I hold your son at least partially responsible!"

Mr. West glared at Tab, "What is your side of the story, Robert?"

For the first time since initial greetings, Tab spoke up, "Kelly said she had problems and wanted to talk to me about them. I told her she could come to my house so she did and we talked. She did this many times, and then we started kissing. One thing led to another and we started doing it. I didn't force her to drink or to have sex with me. It was her choice. It's no big deal! All the kids these days are doing it. I don't know what everyone is so concerned about. If Kelly is pregnant, she can have an abortion."

It was Kelly who now retorted, "Tab, it is a big deal! You messed up and I messed up. What we did was wrong! You know that if you had not gotten me nearly drunk, I wouldn't have allowed you to do what you did. And I will not have an abortion! That would be murder!"

Kelly then burst into tears. Mary tried to console her and Mrs. West took them both into the kitchen. She was apologizing for Tab's behavior as the kitchen door was closing.

Tab rolled his eyes as Mr. West began to speak, "Why don't we all calm down? Robert! Kelly admitted to making a mistake. Are you man enough to admit you're wrong-doing and take responsibility for your actions?"

"Dad, what does all that mean? What do you want me to do?"

Mr. West spoke firmly, "I want you to admit that what you did was wrong, apologize, and take full responsibility for your actions. You know this is serious, Robert. You are over 18 and can be charged with rape and supplying alcohol to a minor and you yourself are not of drinking age. You know what you did was wrong. You had no right inviting Kelly here in the middle of the night and doing what you did!"

"OK, OK! I was wrong. Alright! Are you happy now! I am sorry. I won't do this again. But I won't take the responsibility for paying for a kid until I'm 92 that can otherwise be taken care of by an abortion!"

With that said Tab stormed downstairs to his room and slammed the door.

Mr. West called out to him, "Come back here, Robert! I'm not through with you yet!"

As Mr. West left to see about talking more to Tab, Doug had a mixed feeling of emotion well up inside of him. He actually wanted to run his fist right through that boy's face. He was also embarrassed for himself, Mary, and Kelly. This was a very awkward position for all of them. He thought for a while and then prayed silently,

"I wanted this to be different, Lord. From Kelly's description of Tab, though, I should have expected as much. Well, at least this is done. Maybe not the way You nor I would have liked it to have gone, Father, but I tried. This is very hard. Hard for Kelly. Hard for me. Hard for everyone."

Doug sank into the living room couch as the ladies were coming from the kitchen.

Mary quietly asked Doug, "What happened?"

Doug responded, "Robert just half-heartedly apologized and left to his room with his father close behind."

It was Mrs. West who now spoke, "That boy! When is he going to grow up! I'm so sorry for all of this. Tony and I are stumped on this one. We had no trouble with April or Jan, but this boy is unbelievable. "

Doug said, "I would like to talk with Robert privately in a few days if that is OK with you and your husband. He doesn't grasp the seriousness of the sin. I don't know if I could help him, but I would like to try."

Mrs. West responded, "I will talk with Tony, but I'm sure that would be fine. As a prison chaplain, I'm sure you've dealt with the worst of young men. Maybe you can help Robert. Are you going to press charges against him?"

"We'll wait on that call. If he's not held accountable, I'd be worried about his next victim. God only intended sexual activity for the marriage bed, but he doesn't see it that way. I think the only thing he is sorry about is getting caught."

The evening was getting late and it was clear to Doug that it was time to leave. Mr. West made his way to the living room, and he and Mrs. West cordially walked the trio to the door. The ride back to Mary's house was very quiet, but all were relieved that at least this part of the ordeal was over. They all wondered what was next. The results of the visit to the doctor's office would determine that. But that was tomorrow's worry. It's ironic but they were all thinking of the same verse, Matthew 6:34:

Therefore do not worry about tomorrow, for tomorrow will worry about itself. Each day has enough trouble of its own.

Kelly was thinking, "It sure does, Lord. But I will trust in you!"

CHAPTER 20

OUT *of* PRISON

The judge set the bail high, but all protestors were able to post bail and be released after two days. While they were in the county jailhouse, they received many visits from family members and friends and members of their various churches. Usually visitation for inmates was very limited, but Captain Lewis pulled a few strings to increase the number and frequency of visits. The children of the protestors were well cared for while they were away. Most of those with children had only one spouse involved in the protest. Each protestor would be arraigned separately. Janet arrived at the county jailhouse early to pick up Tom.

This was not the first time Janet had to make this trip to pick up Tom. Several times in fact she had to wait it out while Tom served time in the state penitentiary for a sentence decreed from his pickets at abortion clinics. During the trials he always served as his own lawyer. This enabled him to personally cross-examine the doctors at whose clinics he conducted peaceful protests.

During each occurrence he would ask the doctors the same question, "Do you enjoy what you are doing?"

After some jargon about service to the public, they would all eventually confess their distaste at what they do for a living. In fact, they all hated it, but there was no other way they could otherwise earn the kind of money they were making. Greed! It all boiled down to greed.

After parking the car, Janet went inside to meet and talk with Sam as Tom was in the process of being released. On seeing her, Sam's eyes brightened with that Irish beam about his face.

With a smile he shouted, "Well, if it isn't the lovely queen of Fernview Cottage. What a joy it is to see you, Darlin'!"

He rushed to her and gave her a slight hug and kiss on the cheek. He chuckled as he jokingly said, "Here to pick up that scalawag of a husband are you?"

Laughing she responded, "Yes, well I thought I'd better come down and take him off your hands. You know what a commotion he can bring about in this whole establishment."

"Oh yes, Lassie! Like the time for entertainment he used a beam of light and shadows from his hands on the wall to create a whole theatrical performance for the entire ward of jail-mates. Everyone was laughing and shouting with delight. Even the guards! The commander of the watch had to make the trip downstairs himself to stop the whole affair and get things back to drab normalcy."

Janet giggled at the recollection of previous tales of this event as well as others that came to mind.

Just as Sam finished his last remarks, Tom walked in and added, "The truth of the matter is, it was not the commander of the watch that made that discovery and put all to rest, but rather the Chief himself. By coincidence he happened to stop by that night to pick up tickets to the opera that he left in his desk and forgot to bring home. Was he ever angry with me! After he ordered me to be brought upstairs he wanted me to show him what I did to cause all of that noise and racket. I tell you he was ready to have me put into confinement. Well, I did so, and in the process he got so involved with the show, he started laughing just as the phone rang. It was his wife, and boy was she mad to hear him up there laughing as she waited in the car with the cell phone for his return. I've never seen a chief act so sheepishly!"

With this tidbit completed, Tom rushed over to Janet and gave her a squeeze and a quick kiss. "Good to see you, Duckie!"

Janet responded, "Are you ready for the long drive back to Fernview Cottage?"

Tom answered, "We will have so much to talk about. Our being apart these past couple of days will make the time just fly by. I can't wait to tell you all about the rally and the blessings from our Lord, even while in prison."

Tom winked at Sam as he reached for a handshake. "Good to see you again, Sam!"

The drive home did not seem long as Tom was making up for lost time with his lovely wife and recounting the time away. Only when they reached the foothills did Tom's stories slow down to allow Janet an opportunity to share. She told Tom about Doug and Mary's meeting with the West family. He suddenly became very silent as though deep in thought. Janet became very curious about what was going through Tom's mind.

CHAPTER 21

A VISIT *to the* DOCTOR

At school the next day Kelly was her cheerful self. It didn't take her long though to find that Tab had started spreading more bad rumors about her. Being new at the school she did not have many friends and now most of the few she had seemed to ignore her. She looked around to see Linda Colt who, she knew, would pay no attention to those rumors. Not finding her, she smiled as she thought to herself, "This is an opportunity to meet new people and make new friends!"

Though many looked sternly at her, she just continued smiling. Before the bell rang, Tab met her in the hall and pulled her aside.

He spoke rudely, "I didn't think you would be in school today. Didn't your mom say she was taking you to see the doctor?"

Kelly replied cordially, "We are going to my family doctor right after school."

"That's good," approved Tab. "The sooner this is over the better! And if you are pregnant, then don't get any grandiose ideas about keeping the brat. I've got plans and they don't include paying for some kid for the next 18 years of my life. You know, last night was no picnic, so tell your dad to forget about any more family gatherings. My mother mentioned that he wanted to counsel me. Tell him to forget that too. I don't need no jail-bird preacher telling me what to do! Got it?"

Kelly answered firmly, "Yea, I got it!"

She knew it wouldn't be any use trying to talk any sense into him with the attitude he had. Butch Atkins was just around the corner and heard all that was said. Kelly stopped quickly as she rounded the bend coming face to face with Butch.

Her face was red as she spoke, "Well, I guess you heard all of that before. I imagine most everyone has."

Butch had not talked with her since that day on the bus and just now felt something he hadn't felt in a long time, concern and sorrow for someone else's hurt.

Butch spoke softly to console her, "No, not everyone. Don't worry, Kelly. I'll see that no one bothers you. If that Tab gives you any more trouble he will have to answer to me!"

She was taken back and a little surprised at his response.

She managed a slight smile and said, "Oh, you know Tab. He is pretty much just all talk. Anyway he has already done his worst, not that I'm innocent in the whole matter."

She started feeling her face flush again.

Butch retorted with an unusual seriousness in his expression, "Look, Kelly, you're not the only one who has made a few mistakes. We all have our short-comings. I sure know that. But I have been thinking about what you told me on the bus about my not liking the person I am and the things I was doing. You're right. I don't like the way I am. I just don't know how to change. I've had this chip on my shoulder so long that it seems like such a part of me."

Kelly really perked up now. "That is where Jesus can help!"

Knowing that Butch might not understand, she said quietly, "At least He sure has helped me. I don't ever want to be the way I have been these past few months, and I know I never will be that way again. It won't be easy to live this down, but I have confidence that Jesus will see me through this. He can help you too."

"I don't know about that," said Butch.

Just then the first bell rang.

"Well, I will see you around Butch."

As they parted, Butch just remarked, "Yeah, see you around."

Kelly was thinking, "It sure is strange. One moment you're ready to cry in despair and the next after talking about Jesus, you feel such a sense of joy and peace. Thank you Lord!"

The day at school went by quickly enough. Doug and Mary arrived an hour before the end of school to take Kelly to the doctor. Doug had called Dr. Flemming earlier in the day to further explain the situation although not in great detail. He wanted to thank Dr. Flemming for making time in his schedule to see Kelly so early. Dr. Flemming was a good Christian man and was a member of the church where Doug was once a pastor. His medical assistant, April, led the family to an examining room when they arrived. Dr. Flemming met them all with his cheerful smile. After words of greetings he asked his assistant to take Kelly in another examining room for prep work prior to his examination. Normally in these cases he would quietly say a short prayer for God's will in the outcome of the tests but with Doug there he asked Doug to lead in prayer. Doug did so and concluded with, "Not our will but let Thy will be done, Oh Lord!"

Mary asked how long the tests would be and how certain the results were.

Dr. Flemming hesitated a moment and casually said, "Well, the pregnancy test will be quick in doing and the accuracy quite certain. The tests for various venereal diseases are a different matter. The blood samples and cultures will need to be sent to the lab for tests which may take several days."

Mary felt a little embarrassed and Dr. Flemming was perceptive and compassionate enough to help try to ease her feelings.

"You know, these days this sort of thing is unfortunately quite common. But I know Kelly. I've seen her grow up. I was with the youth group on one of the mission trips to Mexico and noticed Kelly's maturity and concern for others. She is a delightful young girl. I hope you don't mind my asking, but as I would like to pray for her during my quiet times, how is her spiritual condition?"

Though Doug had been a little gloomy up to this point, he suddenly brightened as he responded, "Well Bill, to tell you the truth, there has been a wonderful blessing from our Lord that came out of this. I am glad to tell you that just last week Kelly accepted Christ as her Savior. She made a public confession in front of the entire Woodridge Falls Community Church, and I am convinced that she has sincerely repented. As strange as it may sound, I can honestly say that I am glad this happened because now all of my doubts about her salvation are gone. She is truly a child of God bound for heaven!"

The doctor smiled and was about to say, "Hallelujah," when Mary suddenly burst out with a stern hard look at Doug.

"Well, I am not glad this happened. Not glad at all. I'm not so sure her choosing Christ is not just an act. I must admit she has been sweeter than ever lately, but I know Kelly too. And I know she can be quite convincing in her performances, believe me! Time will tell and you'll see!"

She suddenly blushed that all this came out with Dr. Flemming right there, but her emotions were so strong she could not hold it back.

This caught Dr. Flemming off guard and he wasn't sure what to say. He just excused himself to go to the next room for the examination. As he was leaving, Mary was facing the window with her back to them.

Dr. Flemming then gently placed his hand on Doug's shoulder as though to say, "I feel for you brother!" He then called out to April and asked if all was ready and requested that she assist him.

Though both Doug and Mary were deep in thought, neither said anything.

CHAPTER 22

KELLY *is* PREGNANT

Tom woke up before the 5:30AM alarm and went right to praying. It had been only a few days since Kelly's confession and so much had happened. He was anxious to hear the results of the doctor's visit, but being aware of his anxiety reminded him of Philippians 4:8:

Do not be anxious about anything but in everything by prayer and petition with thanksgiving present your requests to God. And the peace of God which transcends all understanding will guard your hearts and your minds in Christ Jesus.

After praying Tom felt more relieved and sat down to read a section of the Gospel of John that he was memorizing and then read some of Romans chapter 8. Such a message was just what he needed to hear. Just a little after Tom's reading, Janet was up and exercising in the basement and praying all the while. Tom smiled as he heard the faint sound of her praying. He was so thankful to the Lord for such a wife. Tom then washed up for breakfast and headed to the kitchen to make Janet's favorite morning dish—a western omelet, home fries with onions, toast, fruit, and orange juice. He liked making breakfast.

Although the breakfast was a tasty meal, there was not much rejoicing. Both Janet and Tom were a little solemn.

Then Tom burst out, "Why are we so anxious? We should be glad! Glad that Kelly-Joy has truly accepted Christ! Glad that Doug and Mary are actually talking to one another. We have so much to be thankful to the Lord for!"

Just as a smile came to Janet's face and she was about to say, *Amen to that!* the telephone rang.

Tom answered the phone with his usual, "Wisp residence, Tom speaking. I'm happy you called!"

Doug was on the other end of the line. He spoke with mixed emotions, "Dad, I don't know how to tell you this, but you are going to be a great-grandfather."

It took awhile for that remark to sink in. When it did, he too had mixed emotions. "Do you mean to tell me, Doug, that Kelly, our Kelly-Joy, is pregnant?" The last word trailed off as though it had fallen from his face.

Janet reached over and grabbed the phone. "Doug, what were your words to Kelly on hearing this?"

Doug answered quickly, "Well, Mom, I surprised myself. I just smiled at her and said, 'Well, young lady, we have some decisions to make now that the Lord has made His will known concerning this matter.'"

Then I kissed her on the cheek and gave her a hug. I couldn't bring myself to say *Congratulations*, but I did want her to know that I love her and firmly believe that God has a good plan for all of this."

Then Janet asked, "What was Mary's reaction?"

There was a moment of silence as Doug reflected, reviewing all that had happened the night before. "She wasn't happy about the whole thing, I can tell you that. She sat down and cried. I wanted to take her in my arms and tell her that it was all going to be alright, but I could tell by her expression that she didn't want that. We have been getting along pretty well these past few days, but this brought a cold look to me. I'm sure she wanted me to get angry and give Kelly a scolding. Mom, she seems so different."

Janet responded, "Doug, Honey, you did the right thing! I'm very proud of you. Kelly-Joy will get enough rejection from the rest of the world, she must not get that from us. As for Mary, well, I'm sure she will come around. I know she is disappointed, but I believe her love for Kelly will overcome her bitterness. How did Kelly take the news?"

A smile suddenly came to Doug's face. "She surely surprised me. She immediately, gently placed both hands on her tummy and had a little, dreamy smile on her face. She just said in a very low whisper, 'Oh, I had a feeling someone was there!'"

Then later she said, 'Well, no matter how this turns out, I'm glad for this little baby! Dad, will you pray over this child right now!'

Of course I did, and the words just flowed from me. It seemed to even soothe Mary's distress a little."

Now Janet had placed the phone on speaker as Doug continued. "I'm not sure what to do right now. I've been praying most of the night as to what to do. I'm concerned that Mary's bitterness may grow more as the time for the baby's birth approaches. Do you think I should talk to Mary about having Kelly stay with me, at least for a little while?"

Tom was waiting patiently, but now this question gave him an opportunity to speak. "It may be a good thing to suggest to her, but you must be on your guard. She may take it to mean that you don't think she is competent to handle the situation. Also, she still wants to do what she thinks is best for Kelly. Now I know, Son, a new life being formed, no matter what the circumstances, is something to celebrate, but it may take Mary awhile to see it that way. Mary wasn't there to see God's miracle in moving Kelly to confess to the entire congregation her sin and sorrow. She didn't see how God used that confession or may not yet even believe it to be real. She may be thinking that Kelly is just pretending, living on false pretenses so she can have more freedom and take advantage of another opportunity to do just as she pleases."

Doug replied, "Well, Dad, it is just as you say. She does believe Kelly is just putting on an act! I know this discourages Kelly, but she is more determined than ever to prove to her mother and everyone else that she is sincere in her faith. Some of her new friends at school remarked to me one day how different she is. Her old friends are really out of the picture and she is really glad about that and so am I."

Tom then asked, "Have you discussed with Kelly and Mary about keeping the child or considering adoption?"

From the silence, Tom knew it had not yet even been discussed although it was surely on everyone's mind.

With a sigh Doug replied, "No. I thought it was just too soon. I know that adoption is the first thing on Mary's mind, but the look on Kelly's face when the doctor told us she was expecting told me she was thinking, 'This is a keeper!'".

Tom took Janet's hand and quietly said to Doug, "Son, let me pray for you, Kelly, Mary and our new little one."

By the time the prayer was over they were all in tears but their hearts had a calm peace within. Tom and Janet smiled at each other, and Doug thanked his dad for his faithfulness to God and support to him and his family.

As the conversation ended, Tom parted with, "I love you, Son!" and Janet warmly repeated those same words.

Tom and Janet sat awhile and cuddled. He then let Janet lie on the couch while he massaged her feet. She felt so relaxed with Tom right there beside her.

Then she sighed and said with a grin, "I sure hope they decide to keep that darling child."

Tom looked at her with that twinkle in his eyes, "So do I, Dear!"

CHAPTER 23

A DISCUSSION ABOUT *the* BABY

It was a few weeks before Doug called Mary to set up a meeting to talk with her and Kelly about what the plan was to be for the baby.

Mary was cordial but direct. "Yes, that is a good idea," she said. "The sooner we work this out, the better."

They made arrangements to meet that Saturday. Saturday came all too soon and Doug found himself in Mary's living room with Mary across from him and Kelly who was sitting beside him on the couch. Kelly had a little anxious smile, whereas Mary looked stern. Tom closed his eyes and said a prayer for unity, God's will, and the best decision to be made for all concerned, especially the baby.

It was Mary who started the conversation. "Kelly, I can tell by the look on your face that you would like to keep this baby and raise the child to be your own, but I think your father will agree that this is not best for you or the baby."

Her voice was somewhat gentle. More gentle than Doug expected. Kelly didn't respond right away, so Doug jumped in and carefully said, "Mary, please, don't put words in my mouth. When we talked about this I said it was an option for the baby to be adopted, but we all must be in agreement. Kelly, what do you think?"

Mary wanted to take control of the conversation, but Doug held his hand up and said as he looked at her, "We must hear what Kelly has to say!"

He knew from his years of counseling that in a meeting like this everyone must have their say, especially those affected most by the decision. He said, "This is a decision Kelly will have to live with for the rest of her life so it must be carefully considered, especially by her." There was a long silence.

Kelly knew that what she was about to say would not meet with her mother's approval, but she knew it had to be said.

She loved her mother and father and didn't want to show any disrespect so she spoke softly as she reached out and firmly grabbed her mother's hand, "Mom, I know you think I'm too young to make such an important decision and in reality I probably am. This isn't the way God wants things to happen. I was stupid and irresponsible, but I don't intend to be like that anymore."

She now glanced at her father. "Dad, Mom is right about what I want to do. I want to do the right and responsible thing. I loved this baby even before the doctor announced it because I just felt like I had a little wonder within me. My wanting to keep him has nothing to do with Tab. I want to keep him for the both of you and Grandaddy and Grandma and Uncle Don and Aunt Maggie and Aunt Gretchen and all our relatives. Don't you see! I'm sure he has your wonderful blue eyes, Dad, and your sweet smile, Mom! God is designing him to be a masterpiece. We just can't give him up!"

She had tears in her eyes.

Doug spoke, "Why do you say 'he'? It has only been a few weeks, and you have not yet had an ultrasound to determine if the baby is a boy or a girl."

Kelly smiled as she said, "Oh, I'm very certain I'm carrying a boy. I just feel it. I won't be disappointed if it's a girl, but I really think this little one is a boy."

Kelly's speech was touching, but Mary was ready to say her piece and Doug saw it coming and motioned it on.

"Kelly dear, I know you think keeping this baby is the right thing to do but just think of the baby. Think of that couple out there trying for years to have a child, losing one baby after another from stillbirth. What joy we could bring them with this child. Don't you think that would please God? And the baby will have so much. A loving mother and father and a great future. They can give this child so much. Do you want to deprive your child of what an older, more responsible set of parents can give?"

Then Mary pleaded, "Doug, talk some sense into her!" Now it was Doug's turn.

He spoke softly, "Kelly, all that your mother said is right. You can give this baby so much love, but you can't give him or her a father during these formative years. I can give you statistics of the difficulties children have, especially boys, who grow up without a father." Doug stopped for Kelly's response.

"Well, Dad, I don't have any statistics, but I know several kids at school who were adopted, and every one of them is planning to go out and search for their real mother to ask why she gave them up. They have difficulties too, because they were cast aside by the one who should have loved them the most! They have real nice things and what would seem a good life, but they are hurting inside. I don't want that for my son. We can have all kinds of ideas of what the future could be like for this child, one way or the other, but the truth is we really just don't know. I want to be on the safe side for him. And I want to do what is right. But you are my parents, and I love you both. You have heard from me, but the decision is really yours. I can't have this baby on my own, and I must obey you as God declares. I will do whatever you say. I'm just thankful I have the two of you and not parents like my former friend at school whose mother and father made her get an abortion. I couldn't endure that."

There was a long period of silence. Even Mary had never looked at this situation from that point of view. But Mary was still determined to be done with this child right after the baby was born. She was glad Kelly would accept their decision without rebellion. She was certain Kelly was sincere about that.

Doug surprised her by saying, "Well, we don't have to decide this right now. We will pray about it and your mother and I will have some discussions. We will need to come to a conclusion about this soon."

Kelly was feeling so much better. She knew her mother had her mind made up just by the look on her face, but her dad seemed to be much more sensitive to her feelings.

"Oh well," she thought, "I do want this baby, but I will leave it up to the Lord. I will pray about this as soon as I go to my room."

Doug said a prayer for God's guidance and afterwards Kelly kissed her mother and father good-night and went up to her room.

Mary was a little upset with Doug. After Kelly was gone, Doug was putting on his jacket to leave.

As he turned to say good-bye, Mary said, "I was hoping we could settle this tonight. All we had to do was to say that we believe putting the child up for adoption will be best, and that would have been it. All settled. Why did you prolong this ordeal?"

Doug gently placed a hand on each of Mary's shoulders and replied, "This isn't a decision about whether she should go to summer camp or on a mission trip. I have counseled families with this situation, and the decision was about 50/50. You know Mona Trift at the New Life pregnancy center. She has dealt with this situation on a regular basis. I think we should discuss this with her. She knows Kelly, and she has personally seen results from this decision. She may also have some candidates in mind for parents if we decide to go that route."

Mary was suddenly impressed with Doug's demeanor and how clever he appeared. She thought, "Maybe a talk with Mona would be good. I hope she doesn't try to change my mind. It will be good, though, to get a jump on prospective parents, and she would be the right one to find them."

Mary said to Doug, "OK! I agree that a talk with Mona would be good. But let's not prolong this. The sooner we get Kelly's mind settled on adoption, the easier it will be for her to accept it."

Doug kissed her on the cheek and said, "Please, Mary, pray about this!"

And then he left.

CHAPTER 24

A VISIT *from* GRETCHEN

Three months later Fernview Cottage was bursting with excitement. Tom had just come from the post office after picking up their mail. He was too busy to stop by Saturday so he went by right after church. A letter from Gretchen had arrived telling of her return to the Los Angeles area to give a presentation about her work at the orphanage and Christian school in Brazil, the Brasil Orfanato Cristao Central. Her work had come to the attention of an organization that was interested in providing some funds for the school and orphanage.

"This calls for a celebration!" said Tom with exuberance. He continued, "We should have had a celebration with Kelly's Born Again experience and the revival it caused at Woodridge Falls Community Church, but the way it happened sure put a damper on things. But now with Gretchen coming home we can get the whole family together for a real prayer-fest and singing celebration. This will also give us a chance to break the news about Kelly's pregnancy to Gretchen in person. "

Janet added, "And present the new Christ-centered Kelly-Joy to her. As much as she loved the old Kelly-Joy, she is going to really love the new one. It will be so good for Kelly-Joy to have Gretchen here even if it is for a little while. Gretchen will be such an encouragement to her. Now we only have a few months to get this celebration planned."

Tom eagerly asked, "When did she say she would be arriving?"

Janet answered, "The trip is three months away. She will arrive on a Saturday, at the Ontario Airport at 2PM."

Janet continued. "I need to get a list as to all that needs to be done. You know how she loves to ride her bicycle around the lake, so you will need to get it all checked out. I will also need to plan for her favorite meals. Her old room also needs some preparations. Oh, there is so much to do. My, it will be so grand to have her home again! Do you think we should have told her about Kelly-Joy sooner?"

To this Tom remarked, "No Janet! We talked about this. Gretchen has enough on her plate right now. It will be better to talk about this when she is here."

The months flew by, and then the time arrived, and Tom and Janet were at the Ontario Airport just waiting for the arrival of Gretchen's plane to be shown on the terminal display. As they were sitting there at the very clean and busy airport, Tom was remembering the trip to the train depot several months ago to pick up Kelly-Joy. He remembered the sparkle in Janet's eyes as she spoke and laughed about a previous trip to the train depot when he had danced with her in the rain. Just as he looked into her beautiful face and then glanced at the dull, warm day outside, he thought how lovely it would be if suddenly it would rain. He would then take her in his arms and dance right outside the window for everyone to see how much in love with her he was, creating another wonderful memory. He liked creating memories they could later laugh over and chuckle about.

"Well Duckie, our little chick is on her way home! This reminds me of the trip to pick up Kelly-Joy. My, how I wish it were raining like it was then."

Janet responded, "Why in the world would you wish that on such a lovely day as this?"

Tom spoke in his unique, crafty way, "I would love to dance all the way to the car singing that same song and dancing the same dance we did so long ago on your birthday!"

Janet smiled as she remembered that day again and said, "Oh you Silver-Silly you! I'm sure you would like that, with Gretchen on one side and me on the other. Now that would be some fine homecoming for her! What would she think? You still think of her as a little girl in pigtails, don't you?"

As he lifted his hand and pointed his index finger up in the air, Tom replied, "I'll tell you what she would think! She would love it, and you know it. And you would love it too! We are all hopeless romantics, and I hope we always stay that way. That is how God wants it, and I am so glad He does."

Janet was smiling and spoke sincerely and quietly, "Well yes. You are right. We would love it. But it is not raining, so you can just get that idea out of your head, my sweet Sir Gallahad! You know you really are my hero. I sure love you."

She jokingly elbowed him a little and then snuggled up to him and kissed him on the cheek. She didn't often show such affection in public, but he just touched her heart so.

At that moment Tom was in paradise. He smiled as he squeezed her hand and silently spoke to the Lord, "Thank you Father. You sure know how to brighten a dull, dreary day even in the midst of this busy heartless flow of foot-traffic. I just wonder how many of these poor lost souls hunger for such a relationship with you as Janet and I have. But just what can I do here?"

Then they heard that there was a delay in the flight. For some unknown reason, it was coming in late. As a result, they still had over a half-hour before the plane would arrive. As Tom was digesting that news, he looked across the aisle and noticed a little boy and girl sitting next to their mother looking very bored and fidgety. He thought they were probably waiting for the same late plane. They looked so sad. He then had an idea. Out of his pocket he pulled his harmonica and started to play a lively tune. Janet knew what was coming, so she was not surprised.

The two munchkins across the aisle were looking at him with interest as smiles appeared on their faces. Suddenly Tom jumped to his feet and started dancing to the music. He sure knew how to move those feet so much in step with the sound from the mouthpiece. Janet, not to be outdone, stood along to the side of Tom and did a little tap dance right in step with Tom.

The kids were giggling now as others were taking in the entertainment as well. It wasn't long before the children were dancing right along with Tom and Janet. Of course their movements were not nearly as graceful as the old couple, but to that crowd of tired and bored onlookers, the four-some were a delight and joy to behold. After a few minutes the song ended and so did the dancing for the aching legs of the seniors. But the kids were not so ready to stop.

"Mister, that was great!" said the little boy who Tom later learned was Jimmy.

"Please play another!" pleaded the girl whose name was Anna.

Tom looked over to the mother, whose face was also egging him on. Tom told them his name and asked for a song they might know.

They shouted a few common songs and then went dancing again as Tom played to their wonder and excitement. For nearly the whole half-hour Tom played and they danced. Their mother was glad to see their energy being used in a productive way. When the last piece was played, they finished with a bow as the crowd cheered, and the two munchkins sat down without a fidget in their bones. Their mother looked so relieved, and Tom again thanked the Lord. He then went over to the kids' mother and introduced himself and Janet to the lady. They had a nice short talk, and Tom handed the lady a Christian tract as they were leaving. She smiled and placed it in her purse. Tom was wishfully thinking that she might read it after boarding the plane.

A few minutes later Gretchen was coming down the escalator with a smile on her face. She saw her mom and dad right away and waved both hands wildly and happily.

"She sure is her father's daughter." Janet said under her breath. Tom just chuckled. Soon Gretchen joined the two in a huge group hug. When Gretchen was excited she talked very fast. She was talking faster than ever then, which didn't surprise either of her parents. Her legs were twitching too, another unique sign of her excitement.

Tom let his cane rest on her suitcase as he picked her up and twirled her around like he used to do when she was a little girl. Gretchen was giggling, not at all shy or embarrassed over his actions, but Janet was.

"Now Thomas Wisp, you put her down this very minute. What do you think you're doing! Gretchen is a grown woman not to be thrown about like some rag doll. Look at the disturbance you are making!"

Gretchen was laughing as she whispered, "Oh who cares!" Then she looked about at those staring and waved her hand and said, "Hello, hello! Sorry, no more rides today!"

The people then just grinned and carried about their business.

Gretchen was speaking fast again, "You haven't lost your touch Daddy. As strong and fun as ever."

Just to get her mother going she said, "Maybe we should try that again right over there in front of the fountain!"

Janet put the matter to rest, "Now Gretchen, don't egg him on so. We have already made enough of a spectacle of ourselves today."

Gretchen's eyebrows rose, "Oh, we have, have we? Now what have you two been doing to make such a spectacle of yourselves?"

Janet smiled and said, "We will tell you the whole story on the way home. Let's get you into the car before your father tries some more shenanigans."

As she reached for her purse, Gretchen responded, "I sure can't wait to hear this!"

The ride to Fernview Cottage was a joyful one. As they started to enter the foothills of the San Bernardino Mountains, Gretchen could smell the sulfur from the Hot Springs of the beautiful Campus Crusade for Christ facility. She remembered the many Easters of visiting the Grand Lodge there and the wonderful Easter banquets they had. The speakers were so thrilling to listen to as they shared their experiences on college campuses across America. Then they passed the huge billboard, and Gretchen quickly looked to assure herself that the Bible verse was still on the great billboard.

John 3:16—For God so loved the world that He gave His one and only Son that whoever believes in Him will not perish but have everlasting life.

She sighed as she recited that powerful verse. Looking across the valley as they rode through the foothills of the San Bernardino Mountains reminded Gretchen of the valleys of Brazil. The streams and orchards from a distance were breathtaking. It was strange not to hear Gretchen speaking fast and excitedly during the past few minutes as she was taking in the scenery with the thrill of seeing it all.

Janet broke the silence, "Tell us more now about the … ah, what is the name of the foundation that funded you to come here?"

Gretchen was off and running again, "Oh, Mother, I just can't believe it all. If we get that support, it will mean so much to those children. The organization is the Ellenbelt Foundation. Mr. Grump is the CEO and board Chairman. He sounded so interested and friendly as we talked, and his emails were so encouraging. I sent him loads of pictures and many videos of the orphans and school children. He wanted to know how much land we had and how close we were to surrounding cities. From our communication it sounds like he would like to help us upgrade our facilities and even provide additional buildings. I'm not getting my hopes up too high about this though, and I am not naive either. I've been approached by other organizations that wanted to help but also wanted to remove the whole Christ-centered focus of our work. When they tried to pressure me or bribe me to change, I just brushed them off like an old pair of shoes. And I will do the same if Mr. Grump tries to weasel in any compromise to God's work there."

Tom gave a hearty laugh and said, "That's my girl!"

Janet was impressed at how Gretchen had matured in her business-like conduct. She knew Gretchen was quite the organizer and her charm was unsurpassed. Janet enjoyed just watching her daughter as she turned this way and that to observe every bit of scenery. Her green eyes flashed brilliantly with each sight. She had always been an alert, bright, little child grasping every detail. At times she could also sit very quietly and intently study a painting or ponder over a Bible verse or bit of poetry. A remarkable child, well, woman actually. But to her, Gretchen was still her little girl with all her grace and wonder.

As they turned to enter the gates of Fernview Cottage, they all sang the home's theme song that Tom wrote decades ago, each one taking turns at a line, trying dramatically to outdo the other. What fun they always had with this song!

> *Fernview, Fernview—to see our very home,*
> *Fernview, Fernview—why bother else to roam,*
> *Her beauty captures every heart and causes one to dream,*
> *Her fragrance sends you in a whirl of splendor so supreme,*
> *The mountain air is fresh and clean with raindrops pure as gold,*
> *In this land, though one may age, you never will grow old.*
> *I say, you never, never, never, never will grow old.*

When the car stopped, Gretchen suddenly stopped laughing and tears welled in her eyes.

Then she spoke softly, "That song must be true because you two are so vibrant and so much in love with each other like you are still newlyweds. Though the years pass, that about you never changes."

Janet saw an opportunity and spoke, "Speaking of romance, Dearie, how is Joe these days?"

Gretchen's smile quickly returned, "Now Mom, I like Joe Turner, but he is just a friend. I've been looking but I can't find anyone like Daddy!"

Janet returned, "And you never will, Sweetie, so don't bother trying. God broke the mold when he made that one. He is a joy, but he is also quite the handful you know! But God has just the right man for you all planned out. So don't worry."

Gretchen responded, "Oh, I'm not worried! I trust the Lord, and I have my hands pretty full anyway right now too, with all those kids. But the time will come. I know Kelly-Joy thinks I'm an old maid, but I still have a few good years ahead of me."

She laughed as she thought of Kelly-Joy's idea of her as a hopeless case.

"Speaking of Kelly-Joy, I got the feeling from your last letter that something was troubling you about her. Is she doing OK?"

Tom had finished unloading the car just in time to hear Gretchen's question. "In one way, Praise the Lord, she is better than OK!"

Gretchen asked, "What do you mean by that, Dad?"

"What I mean to say is, our Kelly-Joy has accepted Christ as her Savior and I was right there to witness it at Woodridge Falls Community Church and so did Doug! And the testimony she gave brought the whole church to their knees. I have never seen such a revival! But I guess it would be better to start from the beginning."

Well, Tom did and before long Gretchen was laughing, and then crying, and then uncertain just how to react.

Gretchen responded, "I was worried that the divorce would have a horrid effect on Kelly-Joy, but I never expected this. I mean, I'm really very happy about her conversion, but I thought she accepted Christ a few years ago at the Christian camp at Hume Lake. I'm sure it felt so good to get the truth out, but how is she handling all of this? And what about the baby? What is she going to do?"

Janet responded, "Mary is expecting to have the child adopted by someone, but Kelly-Joy has the strong desire to keep the baby. I really don't know how this is all going to work out but the Lord does. We must trust in Him."

"You're right about that, Mom!" replied Gretchen. "I know we are all hungry, but I really feel we need to take some time right now and pray for Kelly-Joy and this whole situation. Dad, would you start us out?"

And start them out he did. They all held hands and Tom started with Psalms 51, which he had memorized, and then talked to the Lord from the depth of his heart.

"Dear Lord, Creator of all things, Master of the universe, Giver of life. It is with joy that we praise you and thank you. Our lives are in your hands, just as they should be. We praise you and want to live for your Glory. Through Jesus Christ we know we have the promise of eternal life, not by our works which in comparison to your work are like filthy rags. No, we don't boast in our works but only in Christ Jesus. Right now, we lift up our Kelly-Joy and the sweet baby she carries. Thank you for her salvation and the testimony she presented, drawing many closer to you. She is in distress not knowing what will happen to the child within her womb. Whatever is decided, let her be at peace and trust in you, knowing that you are the Lord of her life. Dear Father, be also with Doug and Mary as they pray and discern what is best in your eyes. In the name of Jesus Christ we pray."

Then Janet and afterwards Gretchen expressed the desires of their hearts regarding Kelly-Joy and the baby.

As a final gesture, they hugged and said in unison, "Amen!"

That evening, the rest of the clan started to arrive to see their much missed Gretchen. Tom welcomed them into the castle, "Fernview Cottage."

"Come in, ye lads and ladies. You mustn't keep the princess waiting!"

As Don and Maggie stopped at the door, Tom threw his arms around the two of them and then his grandsons.

Josh was the first to speak, "Ronny said that he was going to try to get you to tell another story about "The Lost Land Within the Center of Mt. Gear." But Grandy, I was hoping for another "Frank and Bill" story!"

Ronny and Joshua had always called Tom by the name of Grandy because it rhymed with Dandy, and that is how they always thought of him, a Dandy Grandfather!

Tom chuckled as he spoke, "Well, I'm sorry to disappoint you boys, but the spotlight is on your Aunt Gretchen tonight. I'm sure you must have a bunch of questions for her about life in Brazil, and she is as fine a story teller as they come."

"That's a good idea!" said Joshua. "For a school assignment I need to write about a missionary in a foreign land. Aunt Gretchen is perfect for my topic."

Then Ronny asked, "Is Brazil a 'for-din' land?"

Joshua smiled as he got Ronny's head in a bear hug and said, "It's foreign land and yes, it is, silly, 'litter' brother!"

At this they all had a little chuckle. The boys rushed through the door, each hoping to be the first to see their aunt. The meal was just being placed on the table when Doug, Mary, and Kelly-Joy arrived. As they entered, they were singing the Fernview Melody which stirred the whole group into singing that song – even Joshua and Ronny tried to have their childish voices be heard among the hefty baritones and delightful sopranos.

They all greeted the new arrivals with hugs and kisses. The boys used their fashionable 'Hi-Fives', of course. The meal was tasty and delightful to them all. It was a memorable evening with lots of conversation, catching Gretchen up on all that had happened in the states, from political changes to various Christian ministries.

Then Kelly-Joy bravely gave an announcement about the baby she was carrying. Of course, she knew they had all already been told, but she thought it right to apologize for the embarrassment her actions brought on the family name. Her expression was sincere, and they all felt it. An ultrasound had recently revealed that the child was a boy, just as she suspected. She smiled as she pushed slightly on the sides of her belly to introduce her son to the family and especially Gretchen, who by her expression, Kelly thought, did not know, but actually Gretchen had no idea how far along the baby was. Then each shared a little spiritual blessing they had received over the past week. As the ice cream was being passed out, each settled down in the family room for a video Gretchen had brought about the work she was doing in Brazil.

Afterwards they broke up in little groups to discuss little and joyful things in their lives. Mary felt a little uncomfortable and made her way to the kitchen to do cleanup and dishes. This caught Maggie's eyes so she followed along behind her. Maggie was a dear, and Mary really loved her. Maggie was glad to have Mary to herself for a little while to discuss the baby, if Mary was willing to talk about the subject. As they were cleaning, Mary started the conversation, asking about the boys and the plans for them during the summer at Hugh's Lake.

"Oh Mary," she exclaimed, "You know all about Hugh's Lake with all of our summers of counseling there when we were in high school."

"Yeah, but I'm sure it has changed a lot in the many years since then!"

Maggie giggled a little, "Well you don't think Don is going to miss out on the action, do you? He has talked the Board of Directors into letting him do a session on GPS and Geocaching. Of course, the boys know all about that, so they are going to be his little helpers. Ronny is really excited about that. He tried to convince them to give him a ranger hat to wear like all of the other leaders, but Don told him that he and his brother would have to settle for a leader's neckerchief to be worn only when they were helping him. Well Ronny thought that was still pretty cool."

Mary's little laugh suddenly stopped, and she became very serious as she spoke, "You have been my best friend nearly all of my life and I love you dearly, but I feel so uncomfortable being here. I should have just dropped Kelly off and let Doug bring her home."

It was Maggie who now had that serious look in her eyes, yet her smile sparkled, "Mary, there is no one judging you here. Not I, nor Don, nor Gretchen. Not even Mom and Dad. You are part of the family and we love you. Didn't you see how Gretchen beamed when you entered the room? There is a lot we don't understand about your situation with Doug, but it doesn't mean we think badly of you. How could I, of all people, do that? Of course, we hoped and prayed that all would work out between the two of you, but that is because we love you both so much."

Mary looked deeper into Maggie's eyes, "You think I'm wrong to insist that Kelly have the child adopted, don't you?"

"Do you know what I think? Well I think you are a wonderful mother who is just trying to do what is best for her daughter. It's not like you're wanting her to abort the child. It is a good thing to give a couple who are starving for a child hope for a little baby all their own. And Kelly won't disobey the decision you make. You know that!"

Maggie's eyebrows lifted as she ended her remark.

"I know," said Mary, "But she may go on living the rest of her life regretting that she obeyed me, and that may cause her to eventually hate me! You know how hard it was for me to get pregnant with Kelly, and I haven't been able to again since. What if she is never able to have another child? What if this is the only child she would ever have? How can I live with that even if Kelly could? I love Kelly and I don't want to bring any more sorrow into her life than that which she is already having to deal with. It must be my fault! All my fault! Everything that has happened! Why did God let it happen so? I've prayed and prayed! It just doesn't seem to do any good! I used to have such faith but now it is fading so fast. So very fast!"

Mary then burst into tears as Maggie put her arms around her and led her to the kitchen table and they both sat down.

"Do you know what your mother told me about you in her hospital bed? It was her last remark to me. She said, 'Maggie, watch over my Mary! She has so much faith, perhaps too much, if that is possible. Satan may wish to sift her of it! But there is one thing I want you to do. I can't tell her now, because she will not understand. Even in my condition, I see how strong her faith is! We talk about heaven and though she is tearful because she will really miss me, she smiles, knowing I will be there with her father and without pain. But someday she may come to you in tears, feeling empty of faith. When that happens, tell her that her mother at that very moment is in heaven praying there before Jesus for her, praying that her faith will be strong and not be overshadowed by the woes of the world she is living in. I will be longing to see her again. Tell her she must remain faithful no matter what, for my sake, if not for her own. As wonderful as I know heaven is, I can't see how I can live there in joy if Mary should lose her faith in Jesus. She may wonder, as I did at the passing of her father, why God would allow awful things to happen. But God is good, and as I prayed, He helped me through that great ordeal. God's promise comes through Paul in Romans 8:38:

For I am convinced that neither death nor life, neither angels nor demons, neither the present nor the future, nor any power, neither height nor depth, nor anything else in all creation, will be able to separate us from the love of God that is in Christ Jesus our Lord.

Tell her, if she remains faithful, God will surely help her through any ordeal. The night is cold and dark, but light, such warm light, comes in the morning. I have felt that warm Light of God and she will too, but she must not lose faith!'"

On hearing that, Mary cried all the harder for a little while. Then she grinned and hugged Maggie and thanked her with tears of joy mingled with those tears of sadness about Kelly and those tears of sorrow over missing her mother.

As they sat there with arms over each other's shoulder, the words of Mary's mother reminded them of their favorite childhood song, and so like years ago they sang:

When the morning breaks through and I'm praying to you,
You are Oh so good.
In the midst of the day and I'm working away,
You are Oh so good.
Lord I know that you care, and I know you hear every prayer,
And the best I can do, is give glory to you
Cause you're good.
But how can this poor girl, reflect your light,
And shine like the stars, in the midst of the night?
How can this poor girl, reach out to the lost,
And carry forth your word, no matter the cost?
When I feel my faith gone, and I'm just carrying on,
You are still so good.
Then you just speak it out, and make joy come about,
You are Oh so good.
I just don't know how to express, as you change me when
    I'm such a mess,
I love you, I do, as you carry me through,
You are good.
But how can this poor girl, reflect your light,
And shine like the stars, in the midst of the night?
How can this poor girl, reach out to the lost,
And carry forth your word, no matter the cost?
I will carry forth your word, no matter the cost!

Maggie and Mary were best friends while growing up and here they were—as best of friends as there ever could be! And best friends they would remain—no matter what!

CHAPTER 25

The ELLENBELT FOUNDATION

Monday morning came so soon to Gretchen, but she was ready and excited to get to meet the board of the Ellenbelt Foundation. She had a detailed powerpoint presentation to submit and felt more passionate than ever about the work of Brasil Orfanato Cristao Central. Janet's car was cleaned and full of gas for Gretchen's trip to Los Angeles. Gretchen had the attire and step of a truly confident business executive. She prayed with her mother and father before heading out the door. Then away she went with a hopeful smile on her face.

Mr. Grump looked over the schedule of the day presented by his secretary. It had only been a few months since he was hired from outside of the organization as CEO of the Ellenbelt Foundation. The foundation itself was not a Christian organization, but most of the board members were Christians, and many of the programs that they solicited funding for were faith based. It was their focus on humanitarian aid to foreign countries that brought in most of the support from the many household name companies. Mr. Grump was aggressive and had a remarkable business record. One of his goals was to increase the medical support to their programs which were mainly based in South America. His recent accomplishments in many of the South American countries were to add abortion to the procedures of the medical facilities they supported. This, however, met with a lot of resistance from some of the board members who tried to keep abortion out of the program. He had a plan to correct this situation by submitting names for additional board members who would support his goals. His first candidate was one Dr. Robert Logan. The board was in the process of reviewing his application. Mr. Grump arranged for Dr. Logan to be a part of the meeting with Miss Wisp. Brazil was the one country that was blatantly against humanitarian aid that included abortion as part of the medical package. If he could get in with an organization that was already established in Brazil, he could promote his agenda without the knowledge of the Brazilian government. Brasil Orfanato Cristao Central was well respected by the government and people of Brazil. Miss Wisp could be his ticket into the market there. She needed his funding and he needed that foothold; this would be a win-win situation for both the Ellenbelt Foundation and Brasil Orfanato Cristao Central. He had set up a 9AM meeting with Dr. Logan which would be just prior to the 10AM meeting with the board and Miss Wisp.

Bob Logan was anxious to be a member of the Ellenbelt Foundation Board of Directors. He felt obligated to provide his latest abortion techniques not only to clinics in the Inland Empire of California but the whole world. Mr. Grump's secretary met Bob with a smile and led him to Mr. Grump's office. On entering the room, Bob held out his hand to the tall, gray haired man with the neatly trimmed beard.

Mr. Grump started the conversation, "I am so glad you were able to fit these meetings into your busy schedule, Bob!"

Bob replied, "I couldn't pass up an opportunity to meet the board, but I am a little confused about this additional meeting with you. I thought we had gone through everything last week during our meeting then."

Mr. Grump thought for a moment as he lightly brushed his beard, "As I thought more about Miss Wisp being at the meeting, I wanted to talk a little more with you about the organization she represents. I know you are one who is passionate about your work, which is good, and one who is ready and willing to provide your opinion, which also is good. But with Miss Wisp, we are dealing with a faith based Christian organization so it would be best to keep a low profile and allow us to be diplomatic in our discussion with her. Do you understand what I am saying?"

Bob was a little taken aback, "Do you mean to say that you would like me to remain quiet during this meeting because you think that Brasil Orfanato Cristao Central may not be willing to update their abortion procedures with those of my medical periodicals?"

"Actually, Bob," Mr. Grump continued, "the dispensary of Brasil Orfanato Cristao Central does not perform abortions. It is an entirely Christian organization."

Bob smiled and remarked with a whimsical expression, "In that case, I would recommend that you not waste our time with this meeting. I have dealt with these fanatical Christians myself and they are impossible to deal with."

At this Mr. Grump remarked, "Well, I do not intend to deal with them on this issue. I have worded our contract with them very carefully. I know some lawyers who have worked with these issues before and have ably disguised the full intent of support to be interpreted, shall we say ambiguously. Once we complete the rebuild of the medical facility and supply doctors, such as yourself, who desire to help the people with undesired pregnancies and make our intentions known, Brasil Orfanato Cristao Central will have no recourse but to submit. They surely do not have the funding nor the connections needed to battle us in court. They are on a shoestring budget as it is. Once the people of Brazil experience the benefits of our support of abortions, it may influence the government of Brazil to change their position on this issue. I like win/win situations! Don't you, Bob?"

Bob frowned and remarked, "I don't know that I like getting involved in this under such false pretenses. I do have my integrity to consider, you know."

"False pretenses, indeed!" Mr. Grump shouted. "You really should not be so hypocritical, Bob. When young girls come to one of your clinics for advice on their pregnancy, do your representatives actually tell them that they are carrying a precious baby and your suggestion is to kill that child? I should say not! They would walk right out the door, and you know it. Instead, you fill their heads with what they want to hear: that a baby has not yet been formed and the tissue can easily be removed. Am I overstating the normal procedures of your clinics?"

Bob felt a little flushed as he continued, "Now that you put it that way, I must admit we do act a little on false pretenses ourselves. Regarding Miss Wisp, most Christians are quite naïve when it comes to real world operations, so I doubt she will have any knowledge of your pulling the wool over her eyes. OK, I'll keep my distance and, shall we say, 'a low profile' during the meeting."

Mr. Grump raised his eyebrows and had a grin on his face as he spoke, "Actually Bob, I didn't mean to imply that you should keep your distance at all but just be on your guard. In fact, the meeting should be over about noon and I would suggest you be the one to take her out for lunch. I don't want the Christians on the board to get too chummy with her, and besides, they are much older and may be a little boring for her to spend time with. You on the other hand, being single and more her age and, from what my secretary tells me, quite charming, may be just the one to help convince her to accept our agreement."

Bob frowned a little, "Well, I will do it for the sake of the foundation, but I'm sure it will not be much of a pleasant lunch for me. I have had Christians picketing my clinics on a regular basis, and my charm, as you put it, has not been at its best with them. I'll use some of my acting skills and put on a good show though."

"Great!" Mr. Grump remarked with excitement. "I knew I could count on you!"

The two men shook hands as Bob left to get a cup of coffee before the meeting with the board and Miss Wisp.

CHAPTER 26

The BOARD MEETING

Gretchen arrived early and Mr. Grump greeted her enthusiastically, "I'm so glad you made it here early so we can chat awhile. Please Miss Wisp, step this way into my office."

Gretchen was impressed with the huge office and the many pictures on Mr. Grump's wall of employees of the Ellenbelt Foundation giving aid to people in various places around the world.

Gretchen stated with a smile, "You must be very proud of the work being done by your organization to help so many people."

"Indeed I am!" Mr. Grump spoke with a bit of a chuckle.

Gretchen continued, "In checking information available on your foundation I have seen so much support the Ellenbelt Foundation has provided to many ministries in South America, but I couldn't help notice that there was no mention of support of any organization in Brazil."

Mr. Grump responded, "That is the very reason we are so interested in Brasil Orfanato Cristao Central. Brazil is the largest country in South America, and we realized that we have been very neglectful in helping organizations like yours there. With this meeting, we hope to rectify that situation."

Gretchen responded, "I have also noted that you have many Christians on the board, but not all of the board members are Christians. I did not see much about your background. Are you a Christian, Mr. Grump?"

"Why of course I am!" said Mr. Grump hesitantly. "There is not much information available regarding me because I have only been here for a few months."

Gretchen asked cheerfully, "Can you tell me about your salvation story?"

"Well, young lady," Mr. Grump replied, "I would like to do just that, but it is a rather long story and the meeting will be starting in about 10 minutes. Are there any other questions or concerns you have regarding the Ellenbelt Foundation?"

"Not really," Gretchen said after a moment of silence. "You have already explained why you selected to help Brasil Orfanato Cristao Central, and the help your organization has given to so many other ministries is pretty clear. I would like to know more details of the plans you have in helping our ministry but I expect that will be covered in the meeting with the board."

Mr. Grump answered with a bit of a grin, "Well, that is the plan along with other things that will be discussed. We probably should make our way to the conference room then. We certainly don't want to keep the board waiting, and it will give you time to get your laptop connected and tested with the smartboard."

Gretchen reached for her laptop case and followed Mr. Grump to the conference room. She was glad that there was no one else in the room yet. This would enable her to get all prepared with no other distractions. There were no problems in connecting to the smartboard. Although her presentation notes were clearly printed on some sheets before her, she did not expect to have any reason to use them, other than a few glances to ensure she stayed on track. She had gone over the powerpoint so many times and felt quite confident of her presentation.

Bob Logan and the board members entered the room and were greeting one another as they prepared to sit down. Bob chose to sit at a seat along the wall while Mr. Grump and the other board members sat around the huge rectangular table. Gretchen was seated near Mr. Grump who was at the front of the table. Mr. Grump introduced Miss Wisp to the board members, and after describing the expertise of each, he quickly mentioned Dr. Bob Logan as a new candidate for membership on the board.

Gretchen wasted no time in covering the mission, goals, operations, and successes of Brasil Orfanato Cristao Central. She added a good deal of humor, especially in discussing reactions from some of the children of the many events provided by her organization. It was clear to the board that she had a genuine love for her work there, and the accomplishments of the organization were very impressive, to say the least.

They chuckled at some of her humorous comments, and a few board members were nearly drawn to tears as Gretchen described the needs of many of the children and teens there in Brazil. It was an excellent presentation. Upon asking for questions they may have about the work there in Brazil, several of the board members asked about more details of the demographics of the area and the population of nearby cities. Gretchen thought it strange that this was on their minds, but at the time did not think much more about it. She pretty much covered the material and manpower needs, especially regarding the medical facilities and personnel, so she was not surprised about no questions regarding these. Up to this point Bob Logan was completely silent but could not help himself by asking but one question.

"Miss Wisp, I would like to ask about the number of unplanned pregnancies in the area and what precautions are taken?"

Gretchen chuckled a little and smiled cheerfully as she answered, "Precautions for pregnancies: None! Dr. Logan, families in Brazil are not planned, they just happen, and with each pregnancy there is great joy. Most of the children we have as residents are orphans, not outcasts, as you may imagine."

A little embarrassed, Dr. Logan simply responded, "I see! I'm sorry, Miss Wisp. I did not mean to imply anything about the culture there."

Gretchen had a serious look on her face as she spoke, "Your apology is fully accepted. I understand! This is not the first time a prospective supporter asked such a question."

Mr. Grump gave Bob a stern look and then smiled as he turned to remark to Gretchen, "Well, Miss Wisp, we certainly are impressed with your work in Brazil. Brasil Orfanato Cristao Central is fortunate to have such a worthy organizer and spokesperson as yourself. Now I would like to present to you a little more of the Ellenbelt Foundation than just the little that was placed in the package we sent to you."

Mr. Grump then described some of the support being done by the Ellenbelt Foundation that had not been mentioned in publications available to the public. He also mentioned the possibilities they were looking forward to supporting, in addition to Brasil Orfanato Cristao Central. Gretchen was happy to hear of these plans and was more at ease than she had been after Bob Logan's remarks.

Additional remarks and questions were then made from several of the board members. With each question, Gretchen easily responded, again with a bit of humor and much detail. This pleased the board greatly. Dr. Logan remained silent. With all of this completed, Mr. Grump assured Gretchen that he would be contacting her before the end of the week with the board's decision and the amount of support to Brasil Orfanato Cristao Central that would be granted.

Just before the close of the meeting Gretchen requested the board to pray for her and the work of Brasil Orfanato Cristao Central. Mr. Grump was taken a little aback by this, which did not go unnoticed by Gretchen. He quickly requested Mr. Wells (one of the Christians on the board) to pray on behalf of the board for Miss Wisp and the Brasil Orfanato Cristao Central ministry. After the prayer Mr. Grump thanked Miss Wisp and made a nice closing statement.

As the members were gathering their notes and leaving, Mr. Grump spoke to Gretchen, "Miss Wisp, would you mind having lunch with Dr. Logan? It is planned for him to be overseeing our medical staff and medical procedures. Additional information you can provide to him would be greatly appreciated."

With a chuckle he added, "He also has a much greater idea of the better restaurants in the area."

She agreed and Mr. Grump, in the process of leaving, gave Bob a hopeful look as he winked and shook his hand. Bob and Gretchen were the only two left in the room. Gretchen was having some problems detaching her connection to the smartboard. Bob was thankful for this occurrence which enabled him to come to her rescue.

He smiled as he reached for the release mechanism and thought of something quickly to say to ease her embarrassment, "I don't understand why there is no standard way for these confounded, implacable disconnections to be designed! I must say, Miss Wisp, I am very impressed with your knowledge and expertise in presenting such detailed work of Brasil Orfanato Cristao Central in the short time provided. I'm sure the entire board was as well."

Now Gretchen felt a little embarrassed from her previous remark to Dr. Logan. "Dr. Logan, please forgive me for my presumptuous statement in answering your question earlier. I have had previous experience with those kinds of questions and automatically assumed the worst. Again, please forgive me."

"No apology is necessary, Miss Wisp! I far too often put my foot in my mouth. I should have studied a little more of the culture of Brazil before the meeting. It is just so frustrating here in the US dealing with so many cases of so-called 'unwanted children.' I personally do not like that term and wondered if a similar problem existed there in Brazil."

Gretchen felt a lot more at ease with Bob and asked, "So does your practice involve working with children?"

"Somewhat," Bob responded, "I am an OB-GYN physician so I do provide services in the birth of children." Bob was carefully deceptive but not really lying. Prior to becoming an abortionist, his specialty was obstetrics/gynecology.

Gretchen cheerfully responded, "It must be very rewarding to be part of the miracle of bringing a child into this world! I can see why Mr. Grump is so determined to get you started right up front as a board member. Your expertise will be very much appreciated in providing for the medical needs of the projects supported by this foundation."

"Well," Bob proceeded, "that is exactly what I am hoping, that my guidance to those in the field will help provide for the medical procedures and practices needed. It's your expertise that is really admirable, though! I can tell that you are very passionate about your work. The way you described your organization's advances and the much needed help to complete future plans really caught the attention of the board members, including me. That passion that you present for this work seems to be contagious to all who hear. And the result is more funding, more enthusiasm, and a real desire for those who hear you speak to take a greater part in your operation."

Bob was really sincere about these compliments. Her expressions of humor and her passion for the children touched a part of his heart that had been calloused for so long. His lifelong goal was to make more and more money without much regard to how it was made or who it would benefit outside himself. And here is a beautiful and intelligent young lady with little regard to obtaining money for herself, but rather engulfing herself in providing for the needs of others. And not doing it to obtain something materially in return for herself (which he thought was the practice of most people). To think that she would do this work for little children and the very poor who could in no way repay her was something foreign to Bob's experience. Yet her rewards were not in the tangible but rather in the intangible: love, respect, admiration, and the feeling of really helping someone in need. She was willing, but no, more than willing, glorifying in sacrificing so much for others who have so little. This intrigued Bob and even more intriguing was the fact that he really enjoyed being around this Christian and was interested in all she had to say. He had initially thought that this luncheon would be a dull and wearisome event. It now seemed that it would be an event definitely out of the ordinary for him, fun and exhilarating.

At Bob's remark, Gretchen blushed a little as she smiled at Bob. "Well, I can't really take the credit for what was presented."

Bob looked surprised, "Do you mean to tell me that someone else really put this presentation together?"

"No, of course I did spend much time putting this material together, but it is really the Holy Spirit who enabled me to get it done in a way that was acceptable to you and the board. As it states in Philippians 4:13:

I can do everything through him who gives me strength.

It is Jesus Christ who provides any success in what I do. That is where my passion, my enthusiasm, and my love for these children come from."

Then Gretchen stopped as she mentioned, "Well, what am I saying? You must have that same passion and joy when you help the birth of a child!"

Bob quickly responded, "Actually most of my time these days is spent writing periodicals and methods of operations as well as mentoring doctors on the latest procedures."

Bob was thinking, "Help the birth of a child, far from that! But I must keep up this deception if we are going to get any piece of the action in Brazil! All of this talk with Miss Wisp does make me feel ashamed at what I do and I should not feel that way. I am helping young girls in a wonderful way, or so it seems to me!"

Bob chose a delightful place for lunch and Gretchen loved it. Bob was a perfect gentleman and took her wrap and pulled her chair out for her. He was pouring on the charm which just came natural with this lovely dinner guest. He was careful throughout the luncheon to keep the topic of discussion on her work and the delights of working with children in such a poverty stricken area. Gretchen tried to open a discussion about Bob's work but with each attempt he cleverly steered the discussion back to Brazil. She loved the children at Brasil Orfanato Cristao Central, so it was easy for her to continue on that subject. Her stories were captivating to Bob and for a brief second caused him to feel like forgetting about abortions and running off to Brazil to help with the medical needs of the children there. Quickly though, reality returned as he thought about and identified his standard of living as something he felt he could not give up. So on went the conversation and before either of them realized it, they were the last patrons in the restaurant. Then Bob's pager beeped and indicated a need for him at the clinic.

Bob commented, "No rest for the weary! I'm sorry Miss Wisp. I really must get you back to your car and be on my way. Some of those I am mentoring have a need for my assistance."

Gretchen responded, "Please, Dr. Logan, call me Gretchen. I have no problem with 'Miss Wisp' from the children, but it makes me feel so old coming from an adult."

"On one condition!" Bob then stated, "You must call me Bob! I have no problem with 'Dr. Logan' from my patients, but in the presence of a lovely lady like yourself, I much prefer 'Bob'!"

This remark caused both to chuckle as Bob signed the credit card receipt.

"Well, Bob!" Gretchen emphasized with a cute smile that caused those lovely dimples of hers to beam, "I can just flag a taxi, if need be."

Bob was quick to answer, "Not at all, Gretchen! It really isn't an emergency, so I would be honored to get you back to the Foundation."

CHAPTER 27

The SCHOOL NURSE

While Gretchen was at the board meeting, Kelly-Joy was back in school. With her condition now showing, she was the talk of the school. The sight of her made Tab feel a little nervous. He told some of his friends about the meeting with her parents months ago and that it was all cool. He said to them, "They are all a bunch of goodie-two-shoe Christians. It would be against their religion to press charges against me."

But his friends remarked, each in his own way, that he should not count on that. One of his friends remarked, "They may lead you on to thinking that they won't cause problems for you, but after learning how wealthy your family is, well, they may decide differently. This could cause grief for you and your parents as well!"

This talk made Tab feel very nervous. He thought to himself, "I've got to think of a plan to get out of any possible trouble that may be on the horizon."

Suddenly an idea did come to mind. He had heard a lot of talk about the school nurse, Diane Langly, and her very liberal stand on women's choice. She had been reprimanded by the School Board for taking some girls out of class without their parents' notification and bringing them to an abortion clinic for pregnancy testing. One girl was even given an abortion. She was not fired though, because some of the board members agreed with her actions.

Tab thought, "She might be the very ticket to my freedom. The very ticket indeed!"

During the lunch break, Tab stopped by the nurse's office to see Nurse Langly. She was busy checking student health records when Tab arrived. Tab was standing in front of her desk patiently awaiting her attention.

"Well, hello young man. What can I do for you? Don't tell me you have the stomach flu too! I have had so many cases this week."

Tab reluctantly spoke, "No Ma'am, I am not sick at all, at least not physically."

Nurse Langly replied, "I'm sorry but you are in the wrong department. Your student counselor is the person you should see about any emotional or other problems you may have. Would you like me to call for an appointment for you?"

Tab spoke compassionately, "No, Nurse Langly, you are the only one that can help in this situation!"

The nurse suddenly felt important in the eyes of this teenager which was a novelty in this school setting.

Tab continued, "My name is Tab West. You see I have this friend, Kelly Wisp. She is one of us who are part of the Progressive Youth Club. She confided in me of her predicament. She has found out that she is pregnant, and her parents are very conservative Christians. They refuse to allow her to have an abortion and told her that she must raise the child. She is not sure if she wants an abortion, but she also is concerned about finishing high school. She is very distraught, and I don't know what to say to help her. I thought maybe you could talk to her and help her. She so much needs a woman with your knowledge and experience to help her decide on the right thing to do. Could you at least talk to her? Please, Ma'am!"

Nurse Langly responded, "I'll see what I can do, Tab. Lunch is almost over and you must get to your next class."

Tab answered with enthusiasm, "Yes Ma'am. Whatever you can do I'm sure will be greatly appreciated!"

As Tab ran through the hall, and meeting one of his friends that he had conspired with, he gave him a high-five, and they chuckled as they headed to their class. After Tab left, Nurse Langly felt very excited. She had been waiting for another opportunity to promote the abortion agenda in the school, and this was a perfect situation to get one started, but she knew this time she needed to be careful. This time she had been approached by a student with the subject in mind, but she knew the request needed to come directly from the girl. She quickly jotted the name Kelly Wisp down in her notebook and started the investigation into her family background to verify as much as she could of what she had heard from Tab.

CHAPTER 28

BACK *to* BRAZIL

Morning came with great delight to Gretchen. She hadn't had a chance to tell her mom and dad about the exciting meeting the day before with the board members of the Ellenbelt Foundation. After her morning devotion, she hurried downstairs for breakfast. The aroma of bacon beckoned her to the meal. Janet was just finishing with setting the table as Gretchen arrived. Tom was already at his place looking over his planner for the day's activity. Tom right away noticed the bounce in Gretchen's step and her cheerful smile and commented, "Well, that must have been some meeting yesterday!"

Gretchen was ready to burst as she spoke of the events leading up to the meeting and the response of the board members. She was excited as she mentioned the names of all except Bob Logan which she was saving for last. She talked of Mr. Grump and his enthusiasm at the prospect of supporting Brasil Orfanato Cristao Central as well as comments from other members. Tom was pleased to hear everything Gretchen had mentioned. With a twinkle in her eye she then spoke of Bob Logan and the exceptional luncheon they had and the discussion that took place. She spoke of his charm and humorous expressions. With the mention of Bob Logan's name Tom's whole countenance changed.

He quickly asked, "Gretchen, is this Bob Logan, by chance, a physician at a clinic in Cortez?"

Gretchen was concerned about the way her father had addressed the question.

She responded, "Why yes, he is a physician, and I do believe he did mention a clinic in Cortez. You sound as though you disapprove of him. Do you know Bob?"

Tom carefully answered her, "Well, if it is the same Bob Logan that I have encountered, I would say that you should be careful with this whole involvement with the Ellenbelt Foundation."

Gretchen was taken back, "Why, Daddy, what do you mean? What do you know about Bob?"

Tom answered her directly, "Gretchen, the Bob Logan that I have faced, on more than one occasion, is an abortionist and owns several abortion clinics within the Inland Empire. He was here in Woodridge Falls visiting Dr. Willis when we had a Pro-Life protest rally right outside Dr. Willis' home. He was stopped from harming Jimmy Slivers, and I also met him at the courthouse in San Ricardo. I have been praying for him, but his heart is so calloused."

Gretchen looked shocked, "He told me that he was an OB-GYN physician. It seems unlikely that there would be two doctors with the same name in the same city. What do you think this means? Why would an organization like the Ellenbelt Foundation with such a good record of supporting Christian missions even consider someone like Bob Logan for a board member, unless there were things taking place to change the whole focus of that foundation to one of promoting abortions? I know from my contacts with government officials in Brazil that they have been pressured by companies and governmental officials from the US to promote abortion with legislation, but they have firmly refused to give in. I suspect this Ellenbelt Foundation may be in the process of compromising their past position of supporting ministries that oppose abortions to ones of supporting them. Mr. Grump did mention that he was recently hired as CEO of the foundation. Even though many of the board members did seem to be authentic Christians, Mr. Grump's actions did cause me to believe that he was not. And Bob Logan was to be a new member of the board, and that was his first meeting. This whole thing is starting to really smell. And not a good odor at that. I'm sure thankful that I didn't have to make up my mind right then about what to do. Of course, I would have still done more research on the Ellenbelt Foundation, but now I will be even more fervent to find out exactly where they are headed in their philosophy of support!"

"That's my girl!" shouted Tom.

After some investigation Gretchen discovered that the Bob Logan of the Ellenbelt Foundation was indeed the same Bob Logan that owned several abortion clinics, the most prominent one located in Cortez. She was furious. Surely the Ellenbelt Foundation must have known

Dr. Logan's position on abortion prior to bringing him on the board of directors. Upon contacting some of the government officials of Brazil that she was acquainted with, she also discovered that the Ellenbelt Foundation had also recently been trying to convince the Brazilian government to allow them to provide a training center for the citizens of Brazil and a medical facility which included birth control and abortion services. Now there was no way she would accept any support from that devious and unethical organization.

With that decision made, Gretchen knew she would need to return to Brazil immediately. She had already wasted enough time on this dead-end prospect. As she contacted her office, she also found that there were several issues that had arisen needing her personal attention there. After a few telephone calls her flight ticket was confirmed. The following Monday she would be taking the first flight out.

That morning Mr. Grump called Bob Logan on the telephone and inquired about the luncheon engagement the day before. "Bob, how did the wining and dining go? Do you think she is sold on us?"

Bob replied, "I will say one thing about Miss Wisp, she is sure full of surprises. I never expected to have such a delightful time with such a conservative thinking woman. She seemed very impressed with the meal and we had a very amusing and intelligent conversation. Do you know she was Summa Cum Laude with her Master's degree at Biola University? She sure has a good sense of humor and she is very quick in her thinking."

Mr. Grump was a little annoyed with his answer and said, "I wasn't asking about your opinion of her. I was asking about her opinion of the Ellenbelt Foundation. Did you even talk about that?"

"To tell you the truth," Bob replied, "the subject of the Ellenbelt Foundation never came up. I thought you just wanted me to show her a good time while dining. I sure had a good time! I never really realized the importance of helping others so much. She is so unselfish and has such a heart to give. Amazing woman!"

Mr. Grump couldn't believe how Miss Wisp could whisk Bob into her little world of do-gooders in such a short period of time. "Earth to Bob! She is a Christian! Why are you so infatuated with her? I admit she is very pretty but there are lots of pretty liberal-minded girls around, including my daughter, Priscilla. Get your mind back to business. Did you mention to her that you are an abortionist?"

"Well, not exactly," Bob responded, "I didn't want her to get the wrong impression of me."

At this point Mr. Grump felt a little more compassionate and said almost in a whisper, "Bob, when she hears of what you do for a living, she will not even talk to you. I'm glad you did not mention anything about your work to her. It may have jeopardized this entire opportunity we have to enter Brazil. Now get your head back on straight, and let's get this deal done."

Bob reluctantly replied, "Yes sir. I know you are right. I've got too much on my plate right now to get involved with anyone. If I talk to her again, I will keep the discussion very business-like. Well, I've got to get to the clinic in Cortez. I have several patients scheduled today."

As Bob hung up, Mr. Grump wondered, "Maybe I should have let one of the other board members take her to lunch. But this may turn out well after all, so long as she doesn't find out anything about Bob."

After breakfast Gretchen made a phone call to her associates at the orphanage. After a few more phone calls, she made further arrangements for her return to Brasil Orfanato Cristao Central. She knew her parents and family would be disappointed, but she knew they would understand. She then sent a cordial message to Mr. Grump stating that she appreciated the board of the Ellenbelt Foundation for allowing her presentation, but had decided that the Brasil Orfanato Cristao Central was not interested in any support from the Ellenbelt Foundation.

On getting the message, Mr. Grump was furious. He immediately set up a meeting with the board, excluding Bob Logan. Since Bob was not officially a board member yet, it would be an easy task to remove him as a candidate for the board.

CHAPTER 29

A *Sorrowful* PARTING

The news spread throughout the Wisp family that Gretchen had to return to Brazil. Kelly-Joy was especially disappointed. Gretchen made it a point to spend a little time with Kelly before leaving. After talking to Mary, Gretchen made a reservation at the nicest restaurant in San Ricardo to have dinner with Kelly on Saturday. Gretchen wanted it to be special. Saturday came quickly, and at the restaurant they both were sipping tea as they awaited their order to be brought.

Gretchen was the first to speak. "Kelly, I get the feeling that you and your mother are not getting along very well. Has anything been firmly decided about the baby?"

With that question the cheerful countenance that seemed to radiate from Kelly clouded with a bit of despair as she responded, "Oh Aunt Gretchen, I continually try to please Mom in all I do, but she just can't believe the change that has come over me since Jesus came into my heart. I get the impression that she thinks my conversion was not sincere. She is just expecting at some point to see me return to that horrible person I once was. I know God wants me to obey my parents, so I must do that, but if they decide to force this adoption, it will break my heart. Every time I feel this little guy kick or move within me, my heart just swells with happiness. God has blessed me with this child, so how can I deny him? I know I have sinned, and the Bible repeatedly states that there are consequences to sin. The consequence of keeping this baby and raising him, no matter how hard the world may think it to be, would be so much easier for me than to hand him over to strangers or anyone. I have already told Mom and Dad that I would abide by whatever their decision was, and I must comply with that decision no matter how miserable it will make me feel. I must resolve that I still and will always have the love of Jesus

Christ no matter what trials lay ahead. I must not let the joy of knowing Jesus as my Savior be stolen away by this or any other decision. I MUST not and I WILL not!"

Gretchen responded, "Well, Kelly, I sure applaud you on that note. You know, a lot can happen in two months. We must just take one day at a time and trust in the Lord. Remember Romans 8:28:

And we know that in all things God works for the good of those who love him, who have been called according to his purpose.

Your Aunt Maggie is a very close friend to your mother. I believe Maggie had a deep conversation with your mother at the reunion last week. You should talk to her. She can be a good mentor to you while I am gone. I promise that I will come back home before the birth of your child."

The next day Gretchen packed for her trip back to Brazil. Kelly made a phone call to her Aunt Maggie and asked if she could come and visit over the next weekend. Of course, Maggie was happy to have Kelly-Joy come to visit her and the family. As Kelly hung the phone up, she smiled as she imagined the wonderful time she would have with her aunt, uncle and nephews.

Monday morning came faster than Tom and Janet had hoped. There was so much more they wanted to do with Gretchen, but they understood the need for her to return to Brazil. Tom drove to the Ontario Airport with Janet and Gretchen right beside him in the sedan. Gretchen was sharing more about the children at the orphanage. Her description of each of the orphans and their personalities made Janet want to just jump on the plane with her and adopt one of those delightful angels. But she knew at her age it would be just too much. Janet surely loved hearing the stories and each brought tears to her eyes and to those of Tom as well. At the same time, some of the stories were also so funny that half of those tears were from laughter. Finally the car reached the airport.

As they were getting out of the car, Janet mentioned, "It is too bad the funding from the Ellenbelt Foundation didn't pan out as you had expected."

"Oh don't worry about that Mom," Gretchen interjected, "I'm certain God will provide and really bless me and the orphanage for not accepting anything from that corrupt organization. I just don't believe how gullible I was to not see through the words of that sweet talking abortionist. I may have initially left your phone number as a contact for me. If Mr. Logan calls, just tell him that the message I sent to him and Mr. Grump should clearly provide a full explanation of my reasons for having nothing to do with the Ellenbelt Foundation and that my decision is final."

As they waited for the time Gretchen would need to go through security and to the gate, Tom was reminiscing the last time they were there to pick up Gretchen.

Tom declared, "Should I pick you up and give you one last spin before you leave, my darling daughter?"

"I should say not!" Janet responded. "Thomas Wisp, you have outdone yourself embarrassing me time after time! Anyway this is not a time for rejoicing. Our little girl is leaving us today and I for one am not happy at all about that."

"Well neither am I!" retorted Tom, "But that is all the more reason for the spin. The next time she returns my back may be out or who knows what else."

It was Gretchen who was quick to respond, "I would love that Daddy, but the security line looks really long and I must hurry." With that said, she gave her mom and dad a big hug and a quick kiss and then off she went. The rest of the family had said their goodbyes Sunday after church at Fernview Cottage.

CHAPTER 30

A VISIT *with* AUNT MAGGIE

Early Saturday morning Doug was driving Kelly to Don and Maggie's house for the weekend. On the way Doug was telling Kelly a breath-taking story just as he had done so many times since she was a little girl and just as Tom had done for him and the rest of his siblings. Kelly had seemed a little sad as they left and Doug had hoped his impromptu story would cheer her up a bit, and it certainly did. His story was about a little boy who was the son of a missionary in Egypt. He made his way to the pyramids and found a mysterious way of entering one of the oldest pyramids. In doing so, he came across a long lost set of papyrus documents which told the entire story of Moses. The pharaoh at the time the scrolls were written had removed the story of Moses from the archives of Egypt, but a close Egyptian friend of Moses secretly had the documents describing the entire account of the Prince of Egypt hidden away in the very pyramid in which the pharaoh was to be entombed. When the Muslims heard of this, many tried to capture the boy before he reached his parents but the boy outsmarted the culprits with each attempt. As a result, the documents about the Biblical story of Moses and the Hebrews in Exodus, were released to the entire world which greatly added to the authentication of the Word of God. Kelly was excited throughout the entire story, and had temporarily lost track of time. Before she realized it, they were turning into her aunt's driveway.

"Oh Daddy," she exclaimed, "You always make trips so much fun. No matter how long they are, time just seems to fly!"

"Well, you can thank your Grandaddy for that! I can't outdo him, but I can sure try!"

Don was busy with a task in the basement as Doug and Kelly arrived, but Maggie was out the door in a flash when she saw the car enter the driveway. Maggie hugged her niece after Kelly stepped out of the car and the two walked into the house.

Doug exchanged greetings with Maggie. "Hi Maggie! Where is Don?"

"He's working with the boys on some flies in the basement which he feels confident will help them win the fishing contest at Woodridge Falls," Maggie shouted in a half-hearted laugh.

"I've got to get in on this!" Don replied and off to the basement he went.

"So, Kiddo! How is that little guy doing? And how are you doing? It looked like you were really laughing as you pulled up. What was that all about?" Maggie questioned.

"As you can imagine, the laugh was from one of Daddy's stories. As far as the baby is concerned, he is fine and so am I, praise be to God!" Kelly said with a gleam in her eyes. "Mom was sure surprised when the results of the ultrasound indicated that this little child was a boy, just as I suspected."

"It seems like just yesterday you were a little girl, but now I can talk to you, woman to woman. I know there is a lot of stress between you and your mother. You need to understand that she is just trying to do the right thing. I also know she is struggling about exactly what the right thing to do really is." Maggie replied.

Kelly had a grim look on her face as she said, "Well, it doesn't seem to me that she is struggling with a decision at all. She has her mind made up that this baby has got to go. I keep praying that she will change her mind, but I don't have much hope that will happen."

Maggie again hugged Kelly as she stated, "Well, I know your mother better than anyone and I'm sure her mind is not yet made up. She is constantly looking at the emotional cost of giving the child away compared to the emotional cost of keeping him. She feels that she is really caught between a rock and a hard place. She wants so much for what's best for the child and what's best for you, but what that really is, she is very uncertain. I will be talking to her more. Kelly, you know where I stand on this. Keep the hope! Keep the faith! Whatever happens, know that God has the best in store for you and the child!"

This was very encouraging to Kelly. Kelly always had fun with Uncle Don and the boys, but she never realized before how enjoyable it was to spend some time listening to Aunt Maggie and sharing concerns with her. She suddenly seemed so wise and understanding.

She thought, "If only mother could be like Aunt Maggie, all would be so much better. But I must be grateful because things could be so much worse. I remember my friend Angela whose mother made her get an abortion. I can be grateful, no, I MUST be grateful that she is allowing this delightful baby to live! Thank you, Lord, for that!"

Kelly and her aunt played a few games and had a wonderful morning together. Then her dad, uncle and nephews came noisily up the stairs casting their sets of colorful flies in front of the ladies so they could judge which they thought looked more authentic and the best prospect for catching fish.

The ladies giggled as they stated in unison, "How can we be judges at all since we know nothing about fishing and, thank heavens, nothing about flies?"

The rest of the weekend was active and exciting. Kelly enjoyed Uncle Don's church and the message from the pastor about the story of Esther was well received. Kelly was thinking about Esther's reply as she waited for her dad to pick her up for the trip home,

I and my maids will fast and pray for three days as you, Mordecai, do. When this is done, I will go to the king, even though it is against the law. And if I perish, I perish.

Then Kelly thought, "Well, I shouldn't fast but I can pray and I will do just that for three waking hours for the next three days."

CHAPTER 31

The INQUISITION

A few weeks had passed since Kelly's first visit with her Aunt Maggie. She had been able to visit three more times since then, and each was so encouraging to her.

During this time, Nurse Langly, at the school, had been looking into Kelly's records for information about her family and was pleased to find that Kelly's parents were divorced, especially considering her father was a pastor. She was thinking that perhaps the father was now out of the picture. If this was the case, it might be an easy task to sway the mother to allow the abortion. But her first move was to have a conversation with Kelly. Miss Langly had a lot of experience talking girls into having an abortion, even those who seemed to be very religious.

It was an easy task to convince the principal to let her have a conference with Kelly. After all, it would be in the best interest of the school, considering Kelly's condition, for the nurse to be acquainted with this student in case some issue with the pregnancy should arise while she was in school.

It was the next morning at school during the home room period that Kelly was informed that she needed to immediately report to the school nurse. Her first thought was that perhaps her doctor had contacted the nurse about some concern resulting from tests taken last week at his office. She was very nervous as she entered Nurse Langly's office.

The nurse was the first to speak, "Won't you take a seat, Miss Wisp? I have been expecting you."

Kelly asked, "Did Dr. Flemming contact you with a message for me?"

"No dear!" said Nurse Langly. "Principal Weston just thought it would be a good idea for me to see you and verify your medication as well as talk to you about your prenatal care, just to ensure all was going well with your pregnancy."

Kelly felt very relieved and responded, "Oh, I see."

Kelly then handed the nurse the list of medications she was taking that she had in her backpack.

After looking over the list, Nurse Langly spoke compassionately, "Kelly, I want to help you. What are your plans concerning your condition?"

Kelly questioned carefully, "I assume you mean the baby?"

"Yes, of course." The nurse responded.

Kelly started feeling nervous again, and stated as a matter of fact, "Well, Nurse Langly, my mother is thinking about finding someone to adopt my little boy."

Nurse Langly looked intently at Kelly as she spoke, "Is that really what you want?"

Kelly was not sure how to answer the nurse. She had heard rumors about Nurse Langly that she did not like. She decided not to confide in her but just give her an acceptable answer.

"Why yes. We talked it over and that seemed to be the best solution."

The nurse responded, "Kelly, it seems like a lot for you to go through. There are a lot of difficulties in having a baby delivered at your age. You know, what you are carrying is not really a baby yet. It's just tissue until it is completely formed. There would be no harm done to just have an abortion. It would be easier for all concerned. Even if your mother is not in agreement, we have ways to override that."

At this point Kelly was furious and spoke spontaneously, "Did Tab, I mean Robert West, put you up to this?"

"Why no, child. I don't even know a Robert West." Nurse Langly surprisingly responded.

Kelly then sharply replied, "I believe you are mistaken about what I am carrying! It is not just tissue but a human being created by God himself. It would be committing murder for me to have this baby, yes I said baby, aborted!"

After saying this Kelly was a little more reserved and softly asked, "Miss Langly, may I now get back to my classes?"

The nurse responded, "Yes, you may go, but please think this through very carefully. You have your future to think of. Please come to me if you have any concerns."

At this, Kelly left the office with a relief that the interrogation was over.

Nurse Langly was very disappointed in Kelly. She thought, "Poor child! Her mother must have put a lot of fear into her to be so assertive.

I'm sure all of that talk she expressed was just to hide the depression and fear she has. It will do no good to talk to Kelly's mother who obviously is too religiously fanatical to understand anything about the real world. This task is going to be harder than I thought, but if I can relieve this child of all the suffering she will have to endure, it will be well worth it."

CHAPTER 32

THE PLANNED ABORTION
Part 1

Several weeks seemed to have just whisked by and Mary was finalizing preparations for the adoption. She was reviewing the information of several families hoping to adopt Kelly's child. Kelly's due date was only four weeks away. Mary wanted Kelly to share in the selection, but Kelly was not at all interested. On her way out the door to school Kelly just mentioned that whoever her mother wanted would be fine. Of course Kelly didn't feel that way at all. She didn't want to give her baby away to anyone, but she was committed to doing her parent's bidding.

Kelly did not tell anyone about the horrible meeting with the nurse. She wanted to forget about that whole event. She had just been to Dr. Flemming's office the day before for an ultrasound. All the tests seemed to indicate that her little boy was doing fine. Kelly was hanging onto Jesus' words from Matthew 21:22:

If you believe, you will receive whatever you ask for in prayer.

As she waited on the front porch, she prayed, "Lord, I know it is not good to get everything we ask for. But those things that are good in your eyes, surely you would want to happen. And, Father, what could be better than for a mother to keep and love the child she bore. You know I want to keep this child, but let not my will but your will be done."

Kelly had not been riding the bus since her 6th month of pregnancy. Doug and Mary thought it would just be best if they drove her to school. This morning was Doug's turn to pick up Kelly for school.

As the normal practice, Doug dropped Kelly off at the back entrance to the school. This way, at least she could avoid the glances and looks of surprise or disapproval from the masses of kids entering the main entrance of the high school.

During the past few weeks Nurse Langly was carefully reviewing Kelly's situation and had private meetings with several of the school board members to express her concern about Kelly. In view of the discussion she had with Kelly and the concerns of Robert West, she felt pressured to not be entirely truthful in those private meetings. She painted quite a colorful picture of the little she knew of Mrs. Wisp. In the past, those same board members had heard similar stories about others that were really true, so they were not reluctant in believing all she had told them. Of course, they could not officially approve of anything she was thinking of doing, and she would not even discuss it with them, but they would be understanding. In her mind, it was better to ask forgiveness than permission.

Tab and some of his friends had also been talking to the nurse with more lies about Kelly and her mother. The nurse felt desperate to do something for Kelly's best interest and the interest of pushing the Pro-Choice agenda. At this point she felt helpless though. She decided she would ask for ideas from her friend at the abortion clinic not far from the school.

CHAPTER 33

THE PLANNED ABORTION
Part 2

Butch Atkins had changed a lot the past few months and had been spending a lot of his time during lunch with Kelly. She was thankful for Butch because the guys that may otherwise be making wise cracks about her kept their distance because of him. Because of his past record many of her used-to-be girlfriends kept their distance from Kelly, too. But she thought that was just as well because they, too, were not very friendly since her pregnancy. It didn't bother Butch though. He liked defending her and knew what it was like to be looked down upon. Since the ride in the bus, Kelly had been kind to him like no one else had. Kelly had even convinced him to attend a Baptist church near his home. He really liked the messages taught there and was on the verge of becoming a Christian.

While Butch had changed so much, not so with Tab. He was as troublesome as ever. With the delivery date so close, he was more worried about what he may be responsible for at some point. For weeks he had been talking to his friends, putting together a plan to end his worries.

Tab had seen Kelly being dropped off week after week by her dad or mother at the rear entrance of the school.

After Kelly climbed the stairs to go to her homeroom Tab thought to himself, "This is the day of my salvation. It has been a long several weeks of planning and now was the time to put it into action."

Tab knew that Miss Langly would really need some convincing before taking drastic measures. Tab had heard from friends he had in the school office that Nurse Langly had met with Kelly. He knew that could mean only one thing. She surely had used that opportunity to try to convince Kelly to have an abortion. He could imagine Kelly's reaction to that. So Nurse Langly was already on his side. He was thinking that maybe she just needed a little something to convince her to take action.

231

He said to his three friends who were with him, "Beat me up good! I need black eyes, a bloody nose, and a banged up arm, but don't hit me in the stomach. We've done this to other guys, so you should have no trouble doing it to me. Come on! I mean it!"

At that moment a girl just entered the rear of the hallway and then jumped back around the turn so as not to be seen.

"Are you crazy?" they shouted.

Tab responded, "You heard me. Now do it!"

Tab staggered to Nurse Langly's office with his friends helping him along.

"What happened to you, Tab?" the nurse inquired.

Tab answered, "Never mind that!" as he coughed up some blood. "It's Kelly Wisp I'm worried about!"

Nurse Langly hurried Tab to the infirmary room and set him down to clean his cuts and bruises.

The nurse inquired, "What does Kelly Wisp have to do with this?"

Making himself tear up, Tab responded, "After Kelly's dad dropped her off, he stayed awhile in the back parking lot talking on his cell phone. My friends and I met Kelly at the back door and she looked so worried. Many of us in the Progressive Youth Club have been concerned about her, as I mentioned to you a few months ago. She is so afraid of her parents, especially her dad. When she told me that he was planning on taking her out of school permanently to take care of the baby and maybe get a job, I didn't know what to say. She told her dad about the meeting she had with you and now he is afraid the school may catch on to his forcing her to have this baby. He is concerned about his reputation as a pastor if his daughter has an abortion. She really wants an abortion so she can have a chance at a good future. She told me so! But she won't tell anyone else for fear of what her dad might do. I felt I had to do something. I thought that if I just talked to her dad, man to man, and explained her situation and how she really wanted an abortion, maybe he would reconsider. Boy was I wrong!

When I told him that Kelly wanted an abortion, he told me to mind my own business. As soon as I mentioned to him that I was going to talk to the principal about Kelly, he grabbed me and started beating me up. He said that if I told anyone about this he would make my life miserable. No matter what he does to me, I need to help Kelly. My friends saw from a distance what was happening and came to my rescue, but by that time he had driven away. I just want to do the right thing for Kelly's sake."

Then Tab cried with those artificial tears, "Poor Kelly! I shouldn't have said anything. He mentioned something about pulling her out of school tomorrow! Can he really do that Miss Langly?"

Nurse Langly suddenly stopped her first aid work on Tab. Tab could tell the wheels in her head were turning. He forced back a prideful grin at his fine performance.

Nurse Langly then gritted her teeth as she spoke, "I may lose my job over this or I may be declared a heroine by the School Committee but it must be done!"

"What must be done?" Tab asked, although he had an idea what that may mean.

Then the nurse asked Tab, "Do you really want to help Kelly?"

"Of course! All of us in the Progressive Youth Club would do anything to help her," Tab responded.

"Then we must act quickly. I will need the help of each of you. It will mean missing some of your classes." Nurse Langly whispered.

"Why? What are you going to do?" Tab whispered in reply.

Again the nurse whispered, "I will need to get her to the Bayside Planned Parenthood right away. I've done this before so I know just the right procedure to get her out of here unnoticed."

Tab exclaimed, "It will never work! She confided in us about her fears and desires, but she would never do so for any official of the school. She is too afraid of her dad. Look what he did to me! He sure has a temper! She will defend him of course and deny wanting an abortion. How can you get her out if she won't go?"

Nurse Langly was deep in thought, "Don't you worry your little head about that. I have my ways."

Right away she picked up the telephone to call the clinic.

Kelly was in her homeroom at the beginning of school when the announcement came over the intercom, "Mr. Mackle, this is Nurse Langly. Could you send Kelly Wisp to my office immediately?"

Mr. Mackle replied, "Yes, I'll send her right down." Turning to Kelly he said, "OK, Kelly, you may go and make sure you take your backpack with you since homeroom is almost over."

Kelly was wondering what this was all about. She was hoping it was not an encounter like the last one. Then her thoughts turned to her recent tests with Dr. Flemming, "Oh I hope nothing irregular was found in my blood or urine samples!"

As protocol, the school nurse had been checking with Dr. Flemming's office to keep up to date with Kelly's procedures. She knew when tests were done but, of course, not the outcome. Nurse Langly had sent the boys away after they checked to ensure the hallways were clear.

As Kelly entered her office, Miss Langly looked calm but concerned, "Oh, good morning Kelly. I'm glad you were able to promptly get here."

Kelly cordially responded, "Hi Miss Langly. Is there something wrong? I have a language arts test this morning, so I should get to class soon."

The nurse responded, "Well, I'm afraid you will need to make up that test. I just received a call from Dr. Flemming and he is concerned about the results of some of the tests you took yesterday and asked if I could take you to his office right away. I already called your mother to inform her and she is planning to meet us there. I also called the school office to inform them and your language arts teacher as well. Are you feeling alright today?"

Kelly answered, "Why yes, I feel just fine. The ultrasound showed that the baby was doing very well. I don't understand?"

"Neither do I, Dear, but I'm sure the additional tests he wants you to take are just a precaution. He mentioned that the procedures may be a little uncomfortable so he wanted you to take medication he prescribed to speed up the process. He had the prescription sent to the CVS drugstore down the street and I immediately sent a carrier to retrieve it."

One of Tab's friends just then entered the nurse's office while carrying a package.

"Hi, Nurse Langly. The office sent me down with this package for you."

The nurse responded, "Did they also send the release form to be signed?"

"Oh yes!" he replied as he pulled a folded sheet of paper from his pocket.

Then the nurse sternly told him, "Next time young man, make sure you keep the forms you bring me uncrumpled. Do you understand?"

"Yes Ma'am." he answered, rolling his eyes as he left.

She handed the package to Kelly who opened it and looked at the information on the bottle. The label had Dr. Flemming's name on it as well as hers. It looked similar to other bottles that the doctor prescribed with a medication name she could hardly pronounce. It did say, "A mild pain reliever. Take 1 tablet per day as needed."

Then Miss Langly gave Kelly a paper cup of water and as she pointed to the bottle she said, "Now take the medication so we can be on our way. The faster we get there the faster we can get you back here to your classes."

Kelly took one of the pills from the bottle and drank the water.

The nurse was pleased that everything was going as planned. Kelly had no idea that the package the boy brought in was all staged and the pill was not at all what Kelly thought she was taking. The nurse had full access to labels to place on a bottle and that is just what she did. That bottle came directly from her desk and she had given it earlier to the boy to bring in once Kelly arrived. She could tell that the pill was working very quickly by Kelly's slow movements.

By this time the nurse had filled out the school medication form for Kelly to sign. Of course, it was actually a student departure form, giving the nurse permission to take her to get an abortion and giving a detailed made-up excuse as to why her parents must not be notified of the event.

Kelly was feeling very distraught over all of this and her head felt woozy. She kept wondering what the problem could be since all indications revealed that the baby was fine. She signed the release form without reading it and handed it back to the nurse. Miss Langly took the form and placed it on her desk. She then turned to her computer and pretended to be typing a note.

Then she turned back around to Kelly, "I just sent a message to the office to have someone come down and pick up this release form for the school records. You can leave your backpack and things here. Is there something you need from your backpack before we leave?"

"No," Kelly replied, "I just have my books and things in it."

"Well," Miss Langly said with a sigh, "we can leave out the back door here. I have my car right there and ready to go."

As she closed the car door, Kelly suddenly felt very tired and was asleep soon after she completed buckling her seatbelt.

CHAPTER 34

THE PLANNED ABORTION
Part 3

Butch Atkins heard about Kelly being called to report to Nurse Langly and wondered what was going on. As he turned the corner of the hall towards Nurse Langly's office, he saw her and Kelly leave out the exit near the nurse's office. He entered the office to look out the window to view what was happening. As he entered the office, there was Rick, the friend of Tab who brought the package to the nurse. He noticed that Rick looked suspicious and was hiding a yellow packet.

"What are you doing here, Rick!" he shouted.

Stuttering a little Rick responded, "Oh nothing. I…I needed to pick up one of my homework papers I left here earlier today."

Then Rick started to leave the office with the packet containing Nurse Langly's forms that Kelly signed, but Butch quickly grabbed his hands.

"Let me look at your so called homework papers!" Butch shouted as he pulled the papers from Rick's hands. He noticed Nurse Langly's and Kelly's signature.

"What's going on here and you better spill the beans or I am going to pound you!"

Rick didn't know what to say as fear overtook him. As Butch reviewed the release form, he looked back again at Rick who was still in his grasp.

Then Butch squinted at Rick and said in a deep low voice, "Your papers! Now I know you don't go around carrying school documents without a good reason. You better tell me all that happened here or you are going to need one good plastic surgeon!"

It didn't take any more convincing. Rick told him everything he knew. The rest Butch pieced together.

He thought to himself, "So that's what Nurse Langly is up to. Another abortion! I'm sure she will be taking Kelly to Bayside Planned Parenthood just like the last time."

In her rush to get Kelly out of there, Nurse Langly left Kelly's file on her desktop. Butch looked through the file and found the list of Kelly's family names and phone numbers. He dialed the number for her mother but there was no answer and he did not want to just leave a message. Next he tried her father and the same problem resulted. Then he noticed her grandfather's name, Thomas Wisp. After noting the phone number he made the call.

CHAPTER 35

The RESCUE

After getting the call from Butch Atkins, Tom wasted no time. He scribbled a note to Janet who was out shopping, grabbed his cane and was out the door. As he drove down the hill from Woodridge Falls, he was formulating some kind of plan to stop that abortion. He had been to Bayside Planned Parenthood several times to picket in order to save some babies. This time he would need to do more than just picket the place.

As Tom stepped into the clinic he recognized Miss Langly from Butch's description. She was on a seat across the room, but she obviously did not recognize him. Tom knew that at this time of day there would not be many abortions scheduled and probably only one abortionist on duty. Tom knew the entry procedure to the clinic operating rooms well. A button under the counter of the secretary would be pressed to open the steel security door which would electronically lock once the door was closed.

He knew he would only get one chance at this so he had to get it right the first time. The clinic security guard was talking to one of the nurses with his back to Tom. Tom was not sure how far along the abortion procedure had gone, but judging from the time Butch called, processing time to check her into the clinic and the time it took for him to get there, he was sure the preliminary processes were completed. Also the medication to start the contractions would have been given and contractions would be well on their way. To make the operation legal, the doctor would take great care (since this was a late term abortion) to ensure the head of the baby was the only part still within Kelly's body. Then he could make the incision into the lower back of the head to suck out the brain which would be of great value for research. They called this procedure Partial-Birth Abortion, but to Tom it was pure murder. Talking to the nurses or secretary would do no good, he knew. He had to act and act quickly. The staff were pretty busy, and so they did not notice him moving to a seat near the door leading to the operating rooms.

The security guard was still talking to a nurse when Tom heard a double beep coming from near the door. Tom knew that this was the signal to the secretary to open the door for someone to come out. The door would open and swing to the inside. The door would close quickly so he knew he would not have much time. As the door opened a nurse came out and turned quickly toward the office counter. With great haste Tom thrust his cane at the bottom of the doorframe just before the door closed. In his pocket, his pocket knife was already opened and ready for use. Quickly Tom rushed through the door and as soon as it shut and the deadbolt locked, he slid the blade of the knife to cut across the wires coming from the deadbolt. Tom knew that opening the door was totally dependent on the electronic system for security purposes. There would be no other way to get in.

Just as Tom slipped through the door, the secretary and several others in the room looked and were shocked at what they saw. She screamed for the security guard who was already on his way to the door.

"Open this door!" he demanded.

The secretary pushed the opening button, but to no avail. The sound was heard, but the deadbolt did not budge.

"What is going on!" cried the security guard.

"I don't know!" she replied. "He must have somehow jammed the lock! This has never happened before! I am going to call the police. Can you shoot through the lock to open it?"

"No way, Betty! The steel lock latch goes clear through the steel frame of the door," the guard shouted with panic and disgust.

Everyone was in chaos as the guard shouted for it to be opened. Fortunately, the thick door and poor acoustics of the hall prevented most of his shouts from being heard in the hall where Tom stood. Tom knew that Kelly must be at least partially conscious. They would need her help to push, during the contractions for the baby to emerge. The medication would most likely put her in a state of just doing what she was told. The contractions would be too painful to do otherwise.

As Tom folded his pocket knife back into his pocket, he rushed down the hall looking through the window of each operating room door. The third door was slightly open and he could hear sounds of activity inside. As he looked inside, he saw the doctor with a sharp instrument in his right hand. His other hand was holding the body of the baby up to the neck with the head still within the body of the girl. And that girl was Kelly.

In an instant he thanked God that he was not too late as he rushed to grab the hand of the doctor. Kelly was aware enough to pull her pelvis up from the edge of the birthing table enabling the body of the baby to rest on the mattress of the table. The baby was still in position as the two men wrestled on the floor.

Suddenly the doctor lay limp in the hands of Tom. His head had hit the frame of the birthing table causing him to fall unconscious. Tom quickly checked the doctor's chest for a heartbeat and noticed the bump forming on the side of the doctor's head. It was then he noticed who he was. It was Bob Logan! Tom saw enough action in Vietnam to know the doctor was not in dire need of medical attention, but he knew the baby and Kelly-Joy needed him.

He called to Kelly-Joy, "I'll be right there, Kelly! Don't push right yet! I'm coming!"

Tom's leg had a bad gash through the artery from the doctor's scissors. He quickly pulled his handkerchief from his pocket and tied it around his leg and then grabbed one of the instruments from the nearby tray and slid it under the handkerchief, twisting it to stop the bleeding and then grabbed his second handkerchief from his back pocket and tied it to hold the make-due tourniquet in place.

Then he rushed to place his hands, bloody as they were, under the baby's head which was starting to appear.

"Grandaddy! The baby's coming!" Kelly shouted as she screamed and pushed for the head of the baby to emerge from her body, completing the birth.

"I know!" Tom answered as he helped guide the baby and held him with the umbilical cord dangling. Clamps were there on the table and Tom used them to clamp onto the cord.

By now the security door had been forced open by firemen, and paramedics were there as well as the police. One paramedic started to care for Kelly, another the baby, and a third was checking on the doctor. As the police grabbed Tom to slap handcuffs on him, he fell to the floor unconscious from his own loss of blood.

CHAPTER 36

A VISIT *to the* HOSPITAL

As Tom regained consciousness in the hospital, he shouted in desperation, "Is Kelly-Joy OK! Is the baby OK! Tell me! Tell me!"

A nurse was at his side with a sedative. She had already heard of the amazing drama and knew exactly who Tom was referring to. A police guard was sitting in a chair outside of the room.

She gently said to him, "You can calm down Mr. Wisp. Rest assured the baby and mother are fine! Your wife just left a few minutes ago to check on your granddaughter and will be right back. She had talked with your granddaughter earlier and filled me in on all that happened. You are quite the hero, you know!"

Just then, Tom peered over the nurse's shoulder. Seeing the policeman at his door he whispered with a smile, "Well, I don't think that officer is sitting there waiting to place a gold medal around my neck!"

Then with a serious look on his face he asked, "How is Dr. Logan? Even as I was helping Kelly with the delivery, I was praying for his well being."

The nurse responded, "I'm really not sure. We had enough on our hands getting blood back into your body. Your femoral artery was badly severed. How do you feel, Mr. Wisp?"

"It is well with my soul," Tom responded.

Smiling, she quickly said, "I was referring to your physical condition, not your spiritual well being."

Tom answered, "For an old man just out of a bit of a skirmish, not bad. I can't quite make out your name tag from here."

The nurse answered, "Oh. I should have introduced myself. My name is Millie. Dr. Minkins who led the surgery wanted to know about a previous surgery that caused the scar tissue on your leg. He will be in later to talk to you about your condition.

243

"Well, my dear," Tom responded, "about my leg, I guess you could say that it was an accident, at least I didn't plan it to be that way. But that's a long story and I'm sure you have more patients to attend to, so I don't want to bore you with that. I do want to thank you for taking such good care of me. I would like to take a moment now, though, to pray for you and your work here. You must know how important that work is."

Millie smiled and said, "Well, that would be just fine, Mr. Wisp."

Tom then folded his hands as he praised God and thanked Him for Millie and her work there at the hospital. He also prayed that Dr. Logan's injury would be minor and thanked the Lord for Dr. Minkins and his work. He then gave praise to his Lord and Savior for saving his great-grandson and dear granddaughter.

As he was praying, Janet was suddenly at the door and waited for her husband to finish. She was so relieved to see him awake and the pale coloring removed from his complexion. When Tom had finished, Janet rushed to his side as Millie was leaving.

Tears came to her face. "Oh Tom, you should see little Tommy! Kelly named him after you. Quite appropriate. You are a hero to all of us. What an adorable baby! You saved him! You saved him, Tom! Despite all the trouble from your actions, I am so glad you did what you did. Our first great-grandson. Oh what a joy!"

Now Tom spoke, "But Dear, how is Kelly-Joy? My dear Kelly-Joy! What a horrible ordeal that Miss Langly put our sweet Kelly-Joy and her baby through!"

"I know, Tom." Janet responded. "But Kelly-Joy is doing just fine. The baby is with her right now and what a glow there is about her! Doug and Mary are also here and Don and Maggie are on their way. We have all been praying for you so much. What a scare we had! You lost a lot of blood, you know. How do you feel, my Love?"

Tom smiled as he looked into the eyes of Janet, "Oh Duckie! I feel a little like I have been run over by a Mack truck, but as I just told the nurse, 'It is well with my soul.' In addition to Kelly-Joy and the baby, I have also been praying for Dr. Logan. Do you remember my telling you about the little run in I had with a doctor outside of the premises of Dr. Willis?"

Janet was deep in thought, "Yes Tom, I do remember you mentioning something about that. Isn't he also the same doctor that Gretchen had lunch with? "

"Yes, that very doctor. I did not know that it was him attempting the abortion until he lay there unconscious. I didn't want to harm him!

I just wanted to stop him! Do you know his condition? Is he here at the hospital?"

"I wanted to see him," Janet whispered, "but his parents and his lawyer were there. His lawyer told me to stay away from his client. He told me that when I see him, it will be in court. I don't want to worry you about this, Tom, but the media is really making a big issue about this. One of the nurses, however, confided in me saying that he hasn't yet regained consciousness, but there is good brain activity from the CAT scan."

Tom clenched his teeth as he spoke, "I can just imagine what they are saying! 'Pick up the news! Hear all about it! A lunatic Christian fanatic has just stormed a clinic and attempted to kill a doctor in the middle of an operation, putting the life of his patient at stake as well!' How is that for predicting the mass media?"

"Not exactly, but you're pretty close!" exclaimed Janet.

With a sigh Tom responded, "Well, it doesn't matter, Dear! I would do it all over again to save that child!"

As Janet hugged her beloved husband she whispered, "I know! I wouldn't expect anything less. I wanted to ask you, how did you find out about Kelly being dragged off to Planned Parenthood?"

Tom raised his eyebrows as he spoke, "You're not going to believe this, but it was Butch Atkins that called me to let me know all that was going on."

Janet looked surprised and said, "The school bully! How does he fit into this?"

Tom replied, "I don't know exactly, but just the way he was explaining it all, I was totally convinced he was telling the truth. I don't know how he knew all the details, but I am sure glad he contacted me just in the nick of time."

The guard called to Janet, "I'm sorry but your visiting time is up."

Janet was annoyed at not being able to spend more time with her husband. She finished her conversation with Tom, "Now that you are awake and coherent, I want to go out and tell the rest of the family. They are all anxious to see you. The guard will only let a few of us in at a time. There are also a lot of other people here praying for you. Sam and Pastor Bob are in the chapel here at the hospital leading the group in a vigil for you, Kelly and little Tommy."

"Praise God for them both." Tom said with a smile, "God has surely blessed us with good friends!"

"Indeed, He has!" Janet replied.

CHAPTER 37

A TRIP *Back* HOME

Back when Tom was being admitted into the hospital, Janet had called Gretchen to update her on what had happened. Gretchen was mortified to hear what her mother had known at that time. To her it all sounded like something out of a thriller movie. In her eyes, as well as her mother's, her father was a superhero saving the life of her nephew.

Directly after receiving the call, Gretchen went to work planning her trip to the states. There were several activities planned at Brasil Orfanato Cristao Central that week, so Gretchen called a staff meeting to explain her situation and arrange for divvying up her responsibilities among staff and volunteers. They were all sympathetic and more than willing to take on new roles to help.

A few hours later Gretchen was heading to the airport for the flight to the Ontario Airport in California. She arrived at midnight. She was anxious throughout the eleven hour trip. Janet was there to meet her. As they ran into each other's arms, the tears of each began to flow.

Janet was the first to speak, "Oh, Gretchen, I don't understand why God allowed this horrific thing to happen, but we must continue to trust in Him. He has a reason for this that is beyond us. I'm just so grateful that your dad was able to save Kelly's baby. The rescue was like clockwork that no one could have foreseen. I'm sure the Holy Spirit was guiding him throughout the whole ordeal. I just wish it all could have been accomplished without so much trouble for your dad and all of us."

Gretchen was patiently waiting for an opportunity to speak, "But Mom, they surely can't charge Dad with any crime since he was just saving the life of his great grandchild from a totally illegal operation since neither Kelly nor her parents approved of the abortion."

"Well, Gretchen, that is not how the authorities see it. According to their charges, your father illegally broke into the secure operating area, blocked the door from others entering, and viciously attacked a doctor with intent to kill." Janet spoke with tears streaming down her cheek.

"Oh Mom!" Gretchen whispered, "What really happened? I did not get the whole story from our conversation on the phone. You mentioned that the doctor was injured in the process of the rescue, but it was hard to understand it all through your cracking voice and cries."

"I know, Dear." remarked Janet. "I will tell you the entire story on the way to the hospital. Or would you rather go home first to freshen up?"

"No way, Mom." Gretchen was emphatic. "We need to get right to the hospital!"

When they arrived at the hospital, Janet had finished filling in Gretchen with all the details. As they sat in the parking lot, Janet and Gretchen again hugged.

Gretchen clinched her teeth as she spoke, "To think I actually had lunch with Mr. Logan and initially thought him to be such a fun and delightful character! I'm sure glad I broke off that relationship as soon as I heard of his evil occupation. Mom, let's pray before we go in. This situation is something only God can resolve."

After praying, they entered the hospital. They did not expect to see many people there that late at night and were surprised to see Sam, Pastor Milhorn, and several other friends in the waiting room as they busily talked among themselves. Of course, Doug, Mary, Don and Maggie were also there quietly sitting in a corner together with Ronny & Joshua. As they saw Janet and Gretchen, they were quick to run to them with outstretched arms.

There were hugs and greetings from the family, but Gretchen just wanted to hear how her father, niece, and great-nephew were doing.

Doug was the first to speak, "They are all doing very well! Dad came through the operation with no problems. It will take his leg awhile to heal, but you know that won't keep him down. As I spoke to him, he quickly mentioned, 'Thank the Lord it was my bad leg! I'm already used to using that cane. I guess it will even come in handy more now.' He was more worried about the condition of Dr. Logan. I just found out that they are only keeping Dr. Logan for observation of a concussion. Kelly is overjoyed at little Tommy and is reluctant to let him out of her sight. Tommy will need to stay in the hospital a week or so since his birth is a little premature, but Kelly is expected to be released tomorrow. I suppose Mom told you about the guard outside Dad's room. The press is going wild over this whole ordeal! The police will only let one person in at a time to see Dad."

Gretchen responded, "I suppose Dad is sleeping, but I would at least like to sit there with him awhile. Do you think they will let me do that?"

"I'm not sure." Doug replied. "It is late and they are pretty strict about people seeing him. I will go to the nurse's desk and find out."

He then turned to Mary, "I'll be right back, Dear."

Janet mentioned to Gretchen, "Why don't we go by the maternity ward and look at Tommy and then stop in to see Kelly-Joy. I'm sure she is still awake. I was talking to her on the phone as I waited for your flight to come in. She mentioned that she so much wanted to see you as soon as you arrived."

"By all means, let's do just that!" Gretchen whispered.

CHAPTER 38

AN *Unlikely* RENDEZVOUS

After seeing Tommy and visiting with her niece awhile, Gretchen was able to sit with her dad as she had hoped. He was peacefully sleeping. She scornfully looked at the guard posted at the doorway.

She thought, "If they only understood how really wonderful her father was and the heroic act he performed, they would be praising him with honor rather than having this guard posted here. The world is sure mixed up. Abortion is good in the world's eye and saving the life of a planned aborted baby is horrific. Just like the Israelites in the desert, people in this country have turned so far away from God."

She then silently prayed, "Oh Lord, I love you and trust you with all things, even this sad situation Dad is in. You know he never meant to hurt Dr. Logan; he just wanted to save little Tommy! I give you praise that Kelly, Tommy, Dad and Dr. Logan are all doing well. Everything could have been so much worse than what it is. Lord, is there anything I can do to help Dad? I know the hype of the media is intended to make Dad look like a criminal and maniac and have him locked up for the rest of his life. Whatever happens, I will give you glory and praise. As stated in Psalm 94:22:

"But the Lord has become my fortress, and my God the rock in whom I take refuge."

She then added and prayed aloud, "Lord, please help Dr. Logan be completely healed, spiritually I mean. He so much needs Christ in his life! In Jesus' name, Amen."

A voice from the direction of the doorway awakened her solitude. Bob Logan had just reached the door as Gretchen uttered her last sentence in her request.

"Gretchen, what are you doing here? I thought you were in Brazil!"

It was unmistakably the voice of Bob Logan. Gretchen walked to the doorway with the guard between her and Mr. Logan.

She responded, "The question might be more appropriate – what are you doing here, Mr. Logan?"

Bob was taken back. Then a look of shock came to his face.

Ignoring her question, he whispered, "Oh, are you related to this man?"

Gretchen's face was starting to redden, "This MAN is my father, and the boy you tried to kill is my nephew! It is you that should have a guard at the door, not my dad!"

For a moment Bob seemed not to hear her words and said, "I tried so many times to call you but was just told to talk to Mr. Grump. He didn't understand why you left but just blamed me and…"

Then her words registered and he didn't know what to say.

A long silence prevailed, then he quietly said, "I was just trying to do my job. I had no idea …"

Gretchen broke in, "No idea of what? That the little girl on your abortion cot was my niece! Should that have even mattered? You were in the process of murdering a baby!"

Bob didn't know what to say. In all his years of practice, he never really thought of his work as killing a baby. Oh, he heard the claims from many protesters that abortion is the killing of a child, a baby, and he knew it was a baby, but he had so often reputed it as a mere surgical procedure to remove unwanted growth of cartilage, and in his mind he imagined it to be just that. He had convinced his conscience that his service was for the good of the nation and for the good of the woman who did not want the pregnancy. Deep down, though, he knew it was greed that calloused his heart. With his head down, he walked slowly away as if in a trance.

CHAPTER 39

MEDIA *Hype*

The morning news was out, twisting the truth of the entire event. Good Day America as well as other news reporting agencies presented, as expected, a gross misrepresentation of the truth of Thomas Wisp's intentions and motives in busting through the security of Planned Parenthood and injuring Dr. Logan. In their discussion, they portrayed Thomas Wisp as a fanatic Christian motivated to stop abortions there at the Bayside Planned Parenthood even to the point of attempting to murder Dr. Logan.

Reporters were not permitted to see Tom so they persisted on trying to get an interview from Janet and Kelly. Kelly had just been released from the hospital that morning. A reporter from FAM news, whom Tom had known from interviews about some of the abortion protests he was involved in, was the only one Janet would agree to meet with. His name was Phillip Canten.

Phillip was appreciative of the exclusive interview with Janet and Kelly. He was already acquainted with Janet from previous interviews with Tom. Phillip arranged the meeting at a quiet small banquet room not far from the hospital. Janet and Kelly gave Phillip a full and detailed description of everything that happened. Kelly gave details from all she remembered, although being drugged by Nurse Langly caused gaps in some of the events. Janet filled those gaps in with information that she had received from Tom. She suggested he contact Richard Atkins. She told him that he was the one who called Tom to let him know about the attempt to abort Kelly's baby.

Kelly was very surprised that Butch knew anything about her abduction. She wondered how he could have known. Right then she made up her mind to call Butch as soon as she could to thank him and hear straight from him all that had transpired. Her mother just mentioned that he was the one that called Tom, but nothing was said of how he knew. She knew that there must be a lot more information that Butch could supply.

Phillip was relieved to hear all of this new information. His acquaintance with Tom from abortion protest interviews in the past left him with the impression that Tom was a kind, compassionate, and clear thinking individual. The recent news reports initially surprised him. However, he was totally aware of the tactics of the liberal media so he wasn't too surprised to hear the truth about all that had happened at the Bayside Planned Parenthood and the events leading up to it.

From the beginning Phillip had received permission from Janet and Kelly to record the interview. From that recording he would obtain a complete transcript of the meeting and have it available for Janet. This would prove to be a valuable asset for her to provide to the lawyer who would represent Tom. He discussed with Janet what parts of the interview he would exclude from his report to the news station. He knew too much publicity on the details could actually work against Tom. An element of surprise would be needed for Tom's defense regarding certain details and Phillip was well aware of what details that involved.

In his mind, Phillip was already accumulating information to provide support for Tom from the public. The human interest story was to highlight the aspect of a devoted grandparent attempting to protect his granddaughter and to rescue her baby from the vicious act by the Ontario High School to drug his granddaughter and forcibly cause her to abort her baby. By accusing the school and in order to defend themselves, school officials would openly provide information to show that the abortion attempt was completely planned by Nurse Langly against all school procedures and that no other school official was involved. This should provide a more favorable slant on Tom by the public. Phillip also planned to report on the credibility of Tom regarding the many children Tom had helped as a representative of the California Children's Defense League. Ordinarily such information may not be presented at a court hearing, so submitting this information via the press would definitely prove favorable to Tom's defense. He was quite sure that the FAM News network would want to release this interview during the noon newscast. This was hot news and every media was highlighting what they believed took place.

The result of this interview gave Janet and Kelly hope for what might happen to Tom. But they also knew, despite public opinion, that abortion attacks were a hot topic and the liberal media could put their own slant on anything FAM News may have to report. Also the attempt to change public opinion may be an uphill battle. People already viewed Tom as a lunatic, just as Tom had predicted.

CHAPTER 40

AN *Unexpected* VISITOR

Tom was in the process of being released from the hospital and into the hands of the Ontario police department. Tom was in his hospital room busily reading news articles about himself and the abortion attempt when the guard announced that there was someone to see him. As he looked up, Tom was surprised to see Bob Logan.

Bob had expected Tom to have an expression of anguish or hostility on his approach but was puzzled at his expression of delight. The same smile and gesture he had seen at the protest and the court house.

Tom started the conversation, "Hi Bob! I am quite surprised the guard allowed you to come in. I was glad to hear from my wife that you were also being released. Sorry about the knock on your head. I didn't plan that, you know."

Bob replied, "I'm very curious. How did you get by the security lock on the entrance door to patient rooms and the guard placed outside the entrance?"

Tom just smiled and said, "Oh, I have my cane to thank for that. The same one that protected Jimmy Silvers."

Bob started to respond, "Jimmy who…" and then remarked, "Oh yea, the boy."

Then Bob continued, "I had no idea the child on my table was related to you or Gretchen Wisp."

Tom inquired, "In regard to the child, are you referring to Kelly or Little Tommy?"

Although Bob still had a serious expression, a slight grin appeared. "Both actually, I guess. So that's the child's name then. After you, I surmise?"

Tom responded, tilting his head and squinting an eye, "What you have surmised is quite accurate. You don't suppose it would have been Bob or Logan?"

"Not at all," said Bob scratching his head and then continuing, "this is quite awkward."

"Indeed it is." Tom replied. "Have a seat, Bob."

The two sat in silence for a while not knowing what to say. Then Tom questioned, "How did you know about Kelly being Gretchen's niece?"

Bob gave a sigh and responded, "Oh, Gretchen let me know that, quite sternly, yesterday when I stopped by and you were unconscious. I must say, I was really surprised. She is quite a remarkable lady."

"I must agree. She takes after her mother." Tom replied. Then he mentioned, "My wife went to see how you were doing yesterday, but she was rudely brushed away by your lawyer. I remember him. Bill, I think. I wonder what he thinks of your coming here. He told my wife that the place she will see you is in court at my trial."

Bob grinned as he folded his arms over his chest, "Actually he would probably be quite angry with me, to say the least."

He then continued, "I did want to ask you something."

"Sure, what is it?" said Tom.

Reluctantly, Bob asked, "Don't you think that it might be wrong to ignore the wishes of your granddaughter who apparently wanted to have the abortion?"

Now Tom had a serious look on his face as he responded, "Did you ask her if she wanted the abortion? I was under the impression that part of the admission procedure is for the doctor to make that inquiry personally of the patient."

Bob nervously answered, "Well, yes, that is normally what is done. But Miss Wisp seemed incapable of answering questions, so her nurse answered for her. Sometimes the patients come in like that after taking some sedative to ease the procedure. I'm probably out of my mind for saying this, but sometimes the girls are forced by their parents to have an abortion and are reluctant to say anything. Often parents do know what is best for their children."

"For the record," Tom responded, "neither Kelly nor her parents wanted this abortion. It was the school nurse who deceptively sedated her and got her into the car by telling Kelly that her family doctor had called and wanted to see her in his office about results from a recent test. Kelly had no intention of having an abortion. She had actually been trying to convince her mother to let her keep the baby once it was born. I have one of her letters that she sent me last week. I want you to look at it and see if it sounds like someone wanting an abortion."

Bob opened the letter and scanned through the cheerfully written note. His face dropped into a saddened expression. "I assure you, Mr. Wisp, I had no idea that your granddaughter was so totally opposed to an abortion. I was just doing my job."

With a very serious look on his face Tom inquired, "Would it be OK if I now ask YOU a question?"

Bob replied, "You can ask, but I am not sure if I can give an answer acceptable to you."

Tom looked deeply into Bob's eyes, "Bob, do you really enjoy what you do for a living? Killing the very lives you were trained to save!"

Bob replied, "I…. I don't know. It's what I do."

Now the guard was motioning for Tom to get his stuff together for the move to the jail.

Still looking intently at Bob, Tom said, "Don't answer this question. Just think about it. If you don't like what you do then WHY DO YOU DO IT?"

Another policeman appeared at the doorway just then and handcuffed Tom and led him away.

The question horrified Bob. He thought, "WHY DO I DO IT?" He remembered that his grandmother asked him that same question. He just answered her with the same nonsense regarding his view of the benefits of abortion that he had convinced himself of. She, too, was a Christian and had taken him many times to church in his youth. He was also remembering when he saw Tom at the courthouse and Tom's last comment to him then was, 'God has great plans for you.' He didn't know what that meant and it troubled him. At the time he knew he had heard it before but wasn't sure where. Now he remembered. It was his grandmother who said that to him on his tenth birthday as he was preparing to visit the pastor to help him understand about salvation. She was so wonderful. She was sweet and kind, so much like this Tom Wisp. So much like Gretchen. He never made that visit. His parents told him he was too young to think about salvation. It seemed he was never old enough. Now perhaps he was too old with too many sins! Too many shameful acts. "WHY DO I DO IT?"

CHAPTER 41

A LAWYER *for* TOM

Janet went to the police station to see Tom. They took Tom from his small jail cell to a private room to talk to Janet. A guard was stationed outside the door.

After giving Tom a kiss and holding his hands which were bound by some cold handcuffs, Janet asked, "How are you, Darling?"

As expected, Tom replied, "It is...."

Before finishing, Janet smiled and cut him off with, "Well with your soul. I know! I have something I need to talk to you about."

Tom responded, "I imagine we have a lot of things to talk about, but go ahead."

Janet said, "Tom, I know in the past you always represented yourself in court, but this is a more serious crime that they are trying to pin on you! Shouldn't I talk to Sam about some lawyers who could help with this?"

Then Tom responded, "Yes, Duckie, that is exactly what you need to do! They won't even let me make a phone call here, so I will need to rely on you and Sam. He has seen enough cases in court to know who the best lawyer is for this situation."

Janet smiled as she spoke, "Well, I'm glad we are in agreement on this. I will contact Sam as soon as I leave here."

Janet looked serious as she continued, "I know you are wanting to see Kelly-Joy. She has been looking forward to seeing you too, but the police authorities have been extremely difficult in allowing visitors to see you. The way they were acting, I wasn't sure they were going to let me in. I guess all the publicity that the press has been releasing has really put a lot of pressure on the authorities here. I'm sure you remember Phillip Canten."

Tom squinted as he leaned forward, "Of course I know Phil. What does he have to do with helping me see Kelly-Joy."

259

Janet answered, "Nothing really. I was changing the subject a little. Well I arranged for Phillip to have an exclusive interview with me and Kelly-Joy. After getting the true story of the rescue, he shared with me his plan to put together a documentary on the actual series of events and include some of your work with the CCDL. Since FAM News will be the only station with this exclusive interview, many viewers will be interested to tune in and watch. He is planning to put the high school on the defensive so they would speak out against the actions of Nurse Langly and be willing to testify to the inappropriate actions taken by her. Hopefully this will help your case when it comes to court."

"Good going Phil!" Tom almost shouted.

When Janet left, she wasted no time in seeing Sam. She knew Sam would be having lunch with Roger Miller at the courthouse café. As she entered the café, she saw them sitting at a table near Roger's office. They were both surprised to see her and jumped to their feet as she approached.

Sam spoke first, "Janet, how is Tom doing? I'm sure by now you have talked to him at the police station."

"Yes, Sam, I have, and I'm sure you could guess how he would answer that question."

Both Sam and Roger said with smiles from ear to ear, "It is well with my soul!"

"Quite so," remarked Janet. "I asked him about getting a lawyer and he wanted you to help select one who would best represent him. You know, Tom knows some things about filling that role from the many times he has represented himself in court. But this is far beyond his capability."

Sam had much to say as he answered, "You are right, Janet. Although Tom has had some charges against him regarding his Pro-Choice activities which put him on the courtroom floor in his own defense, they don't compare with an attempted murder charge. This case is a high profile one that many in the state, including the US Congress and Senate, are looking to use to propagate stricter laws against abortion protestors and justify providing more government funding for Planned Parenthood. From my contacts it looks like Governor Blantz is leading this effort. He will have a big role in how far they will go with this charge against Tom."

Sam's last statement really caught Janet's attention. She pondered in her heart what she could do regarding this but said nothing.

Sam continued, "I was just discussing with Roger some possible choices of lawyers for Tom's defense. Of the ones we were discussing, Jason Hilt seems to be the best choice. I have seen him in action in the courtroom on occasion and he was recommended by Jay Shannon who, you know, is the host of "Jay Shannon Live" and a leader in Christian defense cases. I talked to Jay and explained the series of events. Since then he has already started speaking out in defense of Tom on his radio program. Jay is willing and wanting to support Jason or whoever we choose to represent Tom."

Roger commented, "I know Jason pretty well and can personally vouch for his character. He is a member of my church and sure loves the Lord."

Janet was now ready to speak, "He certainly sounds like our man. Sam, could you inquire on his availability and the possibility of his taking the case? If he is interested, could you also arrange for me to have a meeting with him?"

Sam answered, "Of course, Janet. Roger and I are going to do everything we can to help Tom. How is Kelly holding up under all the trauma she underwent? We have been praying for her, Tom, and little Tommy from the first we heard."

Janet quickly gave the men a rundown on Kelly-Joy's condition and that of Tommy.

Then, with tears in her eyes, Janet grasped a hand of both men and whispered, "God bless you both and thank you so much for all that you are doing. You are the best of friends to me and Tom. I don't know what I would do without your support and prayers."

Sam then mentioned, "Speaking of prayers, let's take a few minutes and pray right now."

CHAPTER 42

A CHANGE *in* MR. LOGAN

Gretchen was very upset to hear that Bob Logan had gone to see her dad. She felt the last thing her dad needed was another confrontation with him, so she was on her way to instruct this low life not to bother her father again. A man was hurrying down the hall and flew by Gretchen just as she neared Mr. Logan's room. The man was Bob's lawyer and he quickly slipped into his room. Bob was getting his things together for his release.

The lawyer, Bill Stant, rushed in with a smile on his face. "Bob, the media is really playing right into our hands. I just hope the defense doesn't call for a change in venue. Well, even if they do, this news is so widespread it will still work in our favor. This man is not very wealthy, but you can still sue him for all he has. This guy has a long record of pestering abortion clinics and hounding good doctors like you. The conviction will not be quick, but all the better for your hope to once and for all get legislation in action to make it illegal to protest abortion clinics in any way."

Bob had been doing a lot of thinking and soul searching since his talk with Tom Wisp. He had his mind made up and stated profusely, "Bill, I have decided not to press charges against Tom Wisp! I want this whole matter dropped. The man was just trying to save his great-grandson. I can't fault him for that."

Gretchen was just beginning to turn around in the hall to leave the two in their discussion when she couldn't help hearing what Bob had just said. It stopped her in her tracks.

Bill was livid and shouted, "What in the world are you talking about! Are you crazy? That clonk on your head must have been more serious than I thought! Do you know what you have put me and many others through getting this story out and getting the influence we need started in the various political chambers? The ball is rolling and you must not stop it!"

Bob replied emphatically, "I can and I will! This is not at all right! I'm getting out of this murderous racket!"

Bill clenched his teeth as he spoke, "You are not going through with this! Do you know what this will do to you?"

Suddenly Bill calmed down and said, "Look, Bob, if you don't press charges, it won't change things much. It is not you that is charging Mr. Wisp, but the state of California. You can drop the charges all you want, and they will still put him away. It will just ruin your reputation."

After a moment Bob replied, "It won't affect my reputation. I am a good doctor. I don't need to do any abortions. I can do what I was trained to do, help heal people."

Bill shot back, "Oh! You're Mr. Goodie-Two-Shoes now are you? It is not that easy, Bob! I'm telling you, if you go through with this, I will make sure you never practice in this or any other state again. I've defended you all these years, remember? Defended you against lawsuits from women who have had medical problems because of abortions in your clinics. I know what you might be thinking. Those mistakes were by other doctors, not you. But they were in your employment, so that makes it your responsibility. I saved you many times and you know it. I'm sure I can dig up some of your old patients who would love to get some compensation for their loss. So not only would you lose your license to practice, but you would be bankrupted as well. I remember you telling me stories of how you were so poor growing up. Well, if you go through with this, poverty and misery will be all you will have to look forward to! I don't think you want that, do you?"

Bob frowned at Bill and said, "After all these years, you dare threaten me with extortion?"

Bill didn't answer. He just stormed out of the room. He was so angry he didn't even notice the lady standing in the hallway against the wall.

Gretchen heard it all and just stood there in shock. She remembered the prayer she said for Bob that morning. She felt that it was really half-hearted but God hears even the half-hearted prayers. She knew there was a chapel in the hospital on the floor below so she headed for the elevator. No matter what may come of this, she wanted to thank the Lord for the transformation in Bob's heart. In her heart she wondered, "Would he really stick to his commitment of leaving the abortion industry and not press charges against her father with all that he stood to lose?"

Gretchen slowly walked into the empty hospital chapel. She went to the very front pew of the small room and knelt before the huge cross that stood there. Everything that had happened the past few days weighed heavy on her heart as she wept before her Lord.

She prayed and wept. Drying her tears she noticed a Bible sitting there on the pew next to her. She opened it near the middle. There she noticed some familiar verses highlighted.

Psalm 37:3-7—"Trust in the Lord and do good; dwell in the land and enjoy safe pasture. Delight yourself in the Lord and He will give you the desires of your heart. Commit your ways to the Lord; trust in Him and He will do this: He will make your righteousness shine like the dawn, the justice of your cause like the noonday sun. Be still before the Lord and wait for Him."

She repeated the portion of the verse that stood out to her and, in her own words, said, "He will make the justice of my cause shine like the noonday sun. Be still Oh my heart, before the Lord and wait for Him!"

She was reviewing those same verses several times with such intensity that she didn't notice that someone had also entered and was now sitting in a pew across the aisle a few rows back. As she heard some heavy breathing she looked back and was surprised to see Bob with his head on his folded arms which were over the top of the pew in front of him. His eyes were closed as in prayer. As he opened them and saw Gretchen looking back, he too was surprised.

She whispered, "Bob, did you follow me in here?"

He answered, "No. I didn't know that it was you sitting in the front with your head down. I just needed to come here. I thought….. Well, what's the use! I don't belong here."

As he started to leave, Gretchen called to him, "Bob, wait! I want to talk to you."

Her demeanor seemed changed since their last meeting which surprised him. This drew him to listen to what she had to say. He stood at a distance waiting to hear what was coming.

Gretchen wasn't sure how to start. She whispered, "I'm sorry for the harsh words I spoke to you last night. Not much of a Christian testimony, was it?"

"Don't apologize Gretchen. I deserved every word of it. I went to see your dad this morning and he filled me in on details I was unaware of. His words made me think and realize how wrong I have been about so many things. I'm a fool and a failure. My grandmother and grandfather shared with me so much about Jesus in my youth and they had such high hopes for me. But I hardened my heart and changed. I started to believe that money would solve all of my problems and make me happy. I could have been such a fine doctor. I could have been healing people and finding better procedures for surgeries that improved the lives of others. But no! I chose to seek my fortune at taking the innocent lives of children, of babies! Why am I here now? How can God forgive me? I am in a no win situation here! I know you won't understand this, but no matter what I do, there is no hope for me. My conscience will not let me testify against your dad, yet if I don't, I am ruined! Well, I guess I'm already ruined in God's eyes. I don't know what to do!"

Bob's eyes started to water as he spoke those last words.

All of Gretchen's hatred for Bob melted away like snow on a sunny day as she sympathetically said, "Bob, why do you ask 'How can God forgive you?' It sounds like you are already in the process of repenting of your sins. That's the first step to forgiveness from God and the salvation of your soul. Don't you see? You asked, 'Why am I here now?' The Bible answers that clearly in 2 Corinthians 6:2:

For God says, 'In a favorable time I listened to you, and in a day of salvation I have helped you.'

Behold, now is the favorable time;

Behold now is the day of salvation."

Bob broke in, "But is that really true for me? I have murdered! God's commandment is clear, 'Thou shalt not kill!'"

Gretchen was emphatic now, "Do you think murder is the unpardonable sin? The apostle Paul murdered many Christians either directly or indirectly by imprisoning them in a very hostile prison, old as many of them were. In Acts 22:4 Paul states:

I persecuted the followers of this Way to their death, arresting both men and women.

He considered himself the 'chief of sinners' yet God forgave and saved him. God used him to write most of the books of the New Testament. God can save you now if you just ask Jesus to be your Savior! Just think of what God can do with your life as a Christian doctor! "

Bob whispered, "A Christian doctor! As I said earlier, you don't really understand the position I am in!"

At this Gretchen confessed, "Bob, I do understand. Before I came to the chapel, I was on my way to see you. I did not know about the discussion you had with my dad, but I did hear that you went to see him and I was very angry. I was on my way to tell you to never see him again.

I was just outside your room when I heard shouting. I must admit that I stayed there to listen to see if something was said that I could use against you. I could hardly believe what I heard. I know what you stand to lose. But I also know what you stand to gain right now."

After a long while, Bob said, "So you know! What good is a Christian doctor without a practice? Do you see my dilemma?"

Gretchen was excited as she spoke, "You don't need to practice here in the US. There are many other places that would be joyful to have you as a doctor."

Bob shot back, "Oh really! Like where?"

Gretchen was quick to answer, "How about Brasil Orfanato Cristao Central? We, like so many other foreign Christian facilities, are in dire need of medical people and there are many opportunities for you to practice. Not much pay but God can sure use you there!"

Now Bob was excited, "That never really entered my mind! I could practice in other countries no matter what Bill Stant did to me here. There is hope for me yet! Maybe God can use this broken down doctor!"

Now Bob had hope. Suddenly all of the anxiety and fear was so much lessened.

"Gretchen, you mentioned that repentance was the first step in the process of salvation. What is next in that process? I want what my grandparents have; what you and your dad have! What must I do?"

Gretchen said, "Scripture tells us exactly what needs to be done to be saved and have the assurance of eternal life. Romans 10:9 states:

If you confess with your mouth that Jesus is Lord and believe in your heart that God raised him from the dead, you will be saved. For with the heart one believes and is justified, and with the mouth one confesses and is saved."

At that moment, Bob knelt in front of the huge cross before him and called on Jesus to be his Savior. He repeated his sorrow to the Lord for his many acts of murder. When he confessed his sins, he was doubled up weeping before that cross. But then, instantly Bob felt relief of all of his shame and sorrow. It was like something he had never experienced before. It was not just a feeling, it was a change of heart and attitude. It was wonderful! The tears of sorrow were replaced by tears of joy. And those tears of joy were not just from his eyes but from the depth of his entire being! This was the most important day of his entire life and he knew it. He could feel it! And he embraced it!

CHAPTER 43

A CALL *to the* GOVERNOR

Sam's comment was still buzzing in Janet's mind as she got into her car after leaving Sam and Roger. "Governor Blantz will have a big role in how far they will go with this charge against Tom."

She thought to herself, "It has been a long time since I even spoke to Alan."

She had fond memories of her college days and the courtship she had with Alan.

"I'm sure glad I broke off that engagement. I know it hurt him so but it had to be done. I had thought I could change him. He pretended to be a Christian, but I could see there was no fruit, and you can usually tell the quality of the Christian by the fruit. Look at him now, Janet, on Capitol Hill and one of the biggest proponents of abortion."

She picked up her cellphone and made a call to Alan Blantz's southern California office to make an appointment to meet with him. The secretary wrote down Janet's name and told her that the earliest time of availability was in two weeks. Janet cordially told her that two weeks was not acceptable and hung up. Alan Blantz, on his way to a meeting, stopped by his secretary's desk to pick up some papers she had printed for him. As she handed the papers to him, he noticed the name Janet Wisp on a sticky note on her desk.

"Why is that name there?" he quickly asked.

The secretary answered, "Oh, I meant to throw it away. She just called to ask for a meeting with you, but when I told her there was no immediate availability, she …"

The governor cut her off, "You did WHAT! Get her back on the phone right now and tell her we can meet at 3PM today, and also tell her I would appreciate taking her out for dinner. She is Thomas Wisp's wife for goodness sake, woman!"

His secretary had a blank stare at the mention of Thomas Wisp.

Noticing that stare, the governor went on to say, "You know? The talk of the news! The man who broke through the security of the abortion clinic and attempted to kill the doctor!"

At this her eyebrows were lifted and the blank stare gone indicating her remembrance. Janet was about to start her car for the trip home when she received the call from the governor's secretary. Janet accepted the time for the meeting but declined the invitation to dinner. After hanging up, Janet started imagining how she should approach Alan and what she should say. She hoped the good memories they had together would outweigh her turning him down in his offer of marriage so many years ago.

CHAPTER 44

A *Second* RESCUE

Although Kelly had been released from the hospital, baby Tommy had to stay in the nursery. Kelly was not told how long they expected to keep the baby.

She was on her way to the nursery to see her son when nature called. The restroom in the hall was in use and she really had to go. She noticed a staff restroom just inside the door of the nursery. The nursery door was not quite closed so she entered to use the staff women's restroom within the nursery. There were several stalls and no one else was in there so she selected the last stall to use. A few minutes later two nurses entered the room. They were whispering to each other and Kelly could hear everything they said.

"What are we to do with the Wisp baby?" One of the nurses said to the other.

The other answered, "What do you mean?"

Nurse #1 responded, "I heard some of the doctors talking. You know that baby is a survivor of an attempted abortion. I'm sure you heard that recently the governor just signed a bill presented by the legislature that surviving babies of an abortion are required by all medical facilities to be denied any food or water and left alone to die. You know that new room they added here behind the nursery. That is its purpose. But the Wisp baby is still in the front nursery."

Nurse #2 whispered back, "But we have not been given any instructions to move the baby there. This is a different case since the mother wants that baby. I saw her this morning smiling through the window at him. She was wondering why he had not been given to her to breastfeed. I was there when the doctor told her that, because of the trauma of the abortion technique, he needed to have special medical attention and be fed intravenously."

Nurse #1 was even quieter in her whisper but Kelly could still hear, "I overheard Dr. Jenkins talking to two other doctors and the hospital director about baby Wisp and their intention to have the baby moved to the isolation room sometime today. They were afraid of repercussions from the state if they didn't act in accordance with the new law."

Nurse #2 then said, "But the mother surely would not approve of that!"

Nurse #1 responded, "They discussed that. The director told them that the mother could be told that the baby needed to be moved for special attention and then later tell her that they could just not save him."

Nurse #2 was upset at hearing this and said, "That's not right! I won't allow this on my shift!"

Nurse #1 then whispered, "Calm down, Abby! It probably won't even happen on your shift. They will probably wait until late tonight. That would be my guess."

They were then mumbling to each other such that Kelly couldn't hear, and then they left the room. At the first mention of this Kelly almost gasped but she forced it back to hear all that would be said. Her first instinct was to rush into the nursery and carry her baby out the door. But that would probably not work. She knew she had to do something, but she also knew she would have a better chance if she had help.

As she slightly opened the restroom door and peeked out, she could see that the nurses were at their desks outside the nursery. Kelly then quickly and quietly left the nursery and went around front to check to make sure that Tommy was still there. As she came to the front, she was glad to see Gretchen peering through the window at little Tommy.

With tears in her eyes, Kelly rushed over and grasped Gretchen by the arm. "Aunt Gretchen, I need your help!"

Kelly was shaking as she whispered, "They are planning to put Tommy in the isolation room to die!"

Gretchen hugged Kelly, "Calm down Kelly-Girl. They wouldn't do that! This is a hospital. Tommy is safe here."

Kelly then took her aunt to a nearby empty waiting room and between the sobs poured her heart out telling Gretchen what she had just heard.

Gretchen told her, "I know about that law. My staff and I were discussing it just before I left Brazil. But Tommy has been rescued. This shouldn't apply to him."

Kelly told Gretchen what she heard about the director being afraid of noncompliance.

Then Gretchen whispered, "We have got to get Tommy out of here! We must be calm though. I have an idea. Kelly, you stay in front of the nursery and keep an eye on Tommy. No matter what, don't let them take him away. If they start to, tell them you want to see or hold the baby. Make a scene if you have to. Just don't let them take him away."

Kelly then asked, "Aunt Gretchen, what are you going to do?"

Gretchen then said, "I am going to try to catch a friend to help if I can get him before he leaves."

Gretchen rushed to the elevator. She remembered that before she left the chapel, Bob Logan mentioned that before leaving the hospital he wanted to see a Christian acquaintance of his who was a doctor working in the cardiac ward. He knew he would be there now. In the past, this doctor tried to witness to him several times, but Bob always brushed him off. He wanted to share with him the conversion that he treasured. The cardiac ward is where Gretchen was heading for. She found that it was on the second floor.

As she approached the nurse's desk in the cardiac ward, she inquired to see Dr. Wenton. The nurse mentioned that the doctor was meeting with a friend. She said that they just left for the cafeteria. Gretchen hurried to the cafeteria which she knew was on the same floor. She scanned the room and noticed the two at a table in the corner of the room. They were laughing as she approached them.

As she stood there at the table, Bob slapped Dr. Wenton on the shoulder and said, "This is that wonderful lady I was just telling you about! Gretchen, this is Dr. Wenton. Sit down and I will get you a cup of coffee. I remember that you like lots of cream in your coffee."

Gretchen quickly responded, "Nice to meet you, Dr. Wenton. Thanks but I don't want coffee now. I really just need to talk to you privately about an urgent matter."

Bob responded, "Of course!" He noticed the disturbed look on Gretchen's face and knew it must be something serious. "It's nice talking to you Nick. Let's meet at the handball court next week on your day off. OK?"

The doctor responded, "Sure thing. You better go, the lady looks anxious."

As they left, Gretchen asked Bob, "Is there a private place nearby where we can talk?"

Bob responded, "I have a key to the locker room down the hall. There wouldn't be anyone there this time of day. I have the locker for times when I am called here for consultation on a patient since I'm a sort of expert in OB-GYN. Sometimes being present on these exams calls for a full dress."

Gretchen responded, "That would be perfect."

When the door closed, Gretchen confided the whole problem to him.

Bob looked serious and sad as he spoke, "I'm sorry to say that I had a big part in pushing that bill through. I went before the state congressional committee with all kinds of faulty statistics. The hospital does stand to be in deep trouble if they don't comply with this law. You are right in saying that we must get that baby out of here. I do have my exam robe and badge here in my locker. I will need to try to make this look official so as not to arouse any suspicion."

Gretchen asked, "What is your plan, Bob?"

Bob responded, "There have been times when the hospital called me to release a patient into my care to do an abortion at my clinic. Sometimes it was due to my expertise in that area and specialized equipment I had. I have copies of the needed release form there in my locker. I can write up the form as I would to pick up a patient, but in this case the baby. I will convince them that the hospital director wants me to take the infant to my clinic for termination to comply with the law and relieve them of any possible lawsuit by the parents."

"What if that doesn't work?" asked Gretchen.

Bob then said, "I guess we will then somehow have to take him by force."

Gretchen looked at Bob and said, "Aren't you concerned about what might happen to you because of this?"

Bob raised his eyebrows and answered, "As Bill Stant mentioned, I will already lose my wealth and my practice in the USA. What else have I got to lose? The form would already be signed for an official release if plan A works. If not, I might have to serve some time in prison, but it would be worth it to save that child and try to make up for the trouble I caused your family."

"What can I do?" asked Gretchen.

Bob told her, "Take Kelly to the loading dock in back of the hospital and wait for my ambulance there."

Bob then called one of his ambulance drivers and instructed him to leave the ambulance at the rear of the hospital at the loading dock he normally used, and then take a cab home.

Bob put on his exam robe and started for the nursery. He waited for Gretchen and Kelly to leave as he approached the nursery room. Abby, the nurse that Kelly had heard in the restroom, was checking on some of the babies as Dr. Logan knocked on the door. The nurse came and opened it.

"Dr. Logan," she said in surprise, "I thought you were checked in here. What are you doing dressed like that?"

Bob answered, "I've been released and while I was here, your director, Mr. Jib, had a patient for me to pick up."

He then handed the nurse the form.

Nurse Abby looked over the form and said, "I did hear that Mr. Jib was talking to some of the doctors here about baby Wisp, but no one told me anything about releasing the infant to you. That's not surprising though. I am so often the last to be informed around here."

She noted the director's signature at the bottom that Dr. Logan had forged, next to Dr. Logan's signature and stated, "Well, it looks all in order. You were fortunate to catch Mr. Jib in his office."

Bob nonchalantly said, "Actually he went looking for me. He was a little nervous about putting this new law into action, and since I was here, he thought this would be a way to put the pressure of a possible lawsuit in my hands. He knows I have a very good lawyer to handle such cases."

"I'm sure you do," said the nurse. Then she whispered, "Actually, I am glad you are taking him away. Do you see that room labeled Isolation Room? Well, that is where I would have to be taking that baby in just a little while and just leaving him there to die! I don't know how you do it!"

She then signed the form and gave it back to Bob for his second signature needed at the bottom.

As he was signing the form, he mentioned, "I will have an employee return the nursery crib and IV rack tomorrow." Bob actually intended to do just that since he had several of those in his clinic, due to the requirement before this recent law for him to sustain the life of a baby who survived an abortion. Of course, he never used any, but the cribs and IV stands made for a good display of pretense.

Bob thanked the nurse and then rolled the crib and IV stand out of the room and to the elevator. Within a few minutes he was there on the loading dock where he would have taken other patients whom he picked up from the hospital.

Gretchen and Kelly were already in the ambulance and Gretchen backed it up to the dock. Bob loaded the crib and stand into the back where Kelly was sitting and then hopped in. Little Tommy was very cooperative and slept all the way to Mary's house.

Earlier that morning, Mary had spent hours at the hospital with Kelly and had been ready to take her home, but Kelly told her at that time that she wanted to stay there with the baby a little while longer. With all that Kelly had been through, her mother complied and told her she would pick her up around 3PM. It was getting near that now, so Kelly got on her cell phone and called her mother.

CHAPTER 45

The GETAWAY

At 4PM just before the shift change, the message came down to the nursery station to have Baby Wisp taken to the Isolation Room. On receiving that message, Abby returned a message saying that Dr. Logan had a release form and took the baby over an hour ago. The hospital secretary notified the Chief of Staff of the return message. Dr. Swaunt was frantic and sent a message asking the hospital director to meet with him immediately at the nursery.

As Dr. Swaunt arrived, Abby asked, "Is anything wrong, sir?"

He answered abruptly, "Why wasn't I notified of this? Who gave the authority to have Dr. Logan transfer that baby?"

Abby answered, "Apparently Mr. Jib," as she handed the form to the Chief of Staff.

Then he said, "Well, Wayne should have contacted me before signing this. He should be here any moment."

A few minutes later the director arrived.

He was the first to speak, directing his words to Dr. Swaunt, "What is this all about? I was just about to give the governor a call."

The doctor answered, "Why wasn't I notified that you had Baby Wisp released to Dr. Logan?"

Dr. Swaunt handed the form to Mr. Jib.

Seeing the initial look on the director's face, the doctor was about to say, "Get me the police on the phone." The director, who had been thinking deeply and rubbing his beard, grasped the Chief of Staff's arm and pulled him aside for a private conference before he had a chance to say anything.

Then Mr. Jib said, "Let's not be hasty here, Harry. This may be a blessing in disguise. If I know Bob Logan, he was probably determined

277

to finish the job he started. He doesn't like to have any loose ends in any of his procedures. He knows the Abortion Survivor Act will back him up, and he has been through situations like this much more than we have. Let him take the heat on this. I was in no hurry to initiate this new law in my hospital. Do you want to be the one to tell that mother that we were not able to save the child? She might find some way of getting information on the baby's stats and open up an investigation."

Dr. Swaunt responded, "But he forged your name. We can't let him get away with this! This baby is our responsibility."

Then Mr. Jib answered sternly, "Look Harry, this is my call! The form is legit. I will just take it to my office and stamp my signature on the bottom of the form signifying the completed release to make it official."

The two walked over to Nurse Abby, and Mr. Jib said, "We have this all cleared up. I did sign this for Dr. Logan. I just forgot to notify Dr. Swaunt. You can go about your duties."

The nurse looked a little confused, but then went about her duties as instructed.

. . . . . .

Mary was running late and it was almost 3PM. She was getting ready to leave for the hospital when she received Kelly's call.

"Hi Kelly, I am going out the door, and will be there soon."

Kelly replied, "Mom, stay there. I am on my way home with Tommy. I know you may have a lot of questions, but please wait until I get there. It is a long story and I will be there soon."

Mary was quick to ask, "Before you hang up, who is taking you home?"

Kelly knew if she mentioned that it was Dr. Logan, she would freak out, so she just said that she was with Aunt Gretchen and that was sufficient to ease her mother's mind.

Mary did freak out a little when she saw the ambulance pull up. She ran out of the house to the driveway and yelled, "What is going on here? And what is Dr. Logan doing bringing you home in the ambulance? I want some answers right now!"

It was Gretchen who spoke, "Mary, everything is alright. Just wait until we get inside and I will explain everything."

Mary gave the doctor a nasty look and was hesitant to let him in the house, but she could see that both Gretchen and Kelly fully approved of him. Stunned, she opened the door for all to enter.

Gretchen was very articulate in describing all the events that led to the second rescue of the baby and Mary was even more stunned than she was at the first sight of Dr. Logan.

Gretchen also told Mary of Dr. Logan's conversion, but Mary was still a little confused and asked, "So you just walked out with the baby and no questions asked?"

Then Bob answered, "The form was quite legitimate, except for forging the director's signature. I have had patients from the hospital released to me before, just not one so young. There was really no alternative. The child would have been moved to the isolation room and that would be the end of little Tommy. It would have taken a while for the death to occur, but they have their ways of speeding that up. They would also have ways of preventing relatives from seeing the child and would have fabricated the occurrence of complications leading to the death of the child."

Mary was still unsure of all this and said, "I haven't heard anything about an Abortion Survivor Law."

Bob noticed Mary's computer on her desk in the room which was up and running.

He then asked, "Do you mind if I use your computer for a moment?"

As she gestured her approval, he sat at the desk and within moments had a display of the State Legislature Abortion Survivor Bill (HR456).

After reading it, Mary gasped, "That is horrific! How could they pass such a law?"

Gretchen responded, "Mary, this is California. The most liberal state in the country!"

Mary never expected she would ever be thankful to the man that nearly killed her grandson, but with grateful tears in her eyes she hugged the doctor. By this time Tommy awoke. They had him bundled in blankets just before leaving the hospital, and now Tommy was kicking about.

Bob mentioned, "I'll go to the clinic to get some heat lamps, IV fluid and other supplies. I won't be going to the Ontario clinic because the officials will be expecting me to be there with the child. I'll go to my San Ricardo clinic."

Mary asked, "But won't they come here and get the baby and arrest us all?"

Bob answered, "You needn't worry about that. I'm sure they think I just took the baby to my clinic to complete the requirements of the law. Before Jesus got ahold of me, I probably would have done just that.

Knowing Mr. Jib, the hospital director, he may be quite glad to be relieved of the situation he was in with this baby."

Bob then thought of his conversation that morning with Bill Stant.

He spoke again and said, "To be on the safe side, I think we should move Tommy to my grandparent's summer home near Big Bear in the San Bernardino Mountains. There would be no way to trace the baby there. There is plenty of room for Gretchen, Kelly, and anyone else in the family who might want to stay there. Does that sound like a good plan to all of you?"

Hesitantly, they all agreed. While on the computer, Bob typed up the address and directions to his grandparent's summer home and printed the page for Mary's information.

He then gave them a key and said, "If I'm not back by 6PM, head on up there. I am going to call my grandparents on my way to the clinic. They will be so happy to hear that I have finally accepted Jesus as my Savior and be glad to have you all stay there at my request."

Mary raised her eyebrows as she said, "This sounds like something out of a movie. I can't believe we are all doing this!"

After Bob left, Kelly asked her mother, "Do you know where Dad is? I tried to call him on the way here but he didn't pick up."

Mary answered, "I believe he is at the police station to see your grandfather. He probably had his phone taken away before entering the prison area."

Then Kelly said, "Well, I hope we can get good reception up there in the mountains. I know he would really want to know what has happened."

Mary then said, almost in a whisper, "He may want to know, but I'm sure he will have a hard time believing it."

CHAPTER 46

A TRIP *to see the* GOVERNOR

At about the time that the second rescue of Tommy was in process, Janet was at the governor's office meeting with Alan Blantz. Alan's office was huge. The enormous glass window behind his desk gave a picturesque view of the valley below.

As Janet entered, Alan stood with a smile on his face and arms outreached, "Janet, it is so good to see you, even under these circumstances."

This statement made Janet feel a little uneasy. After a short hug, Alan suggested they move to his sitting area which consisted of two luxurious arm chairs, a small couch, and a coffee table. Just before sitting, Alan buzzed his secretary to bring in two cups of coffee. One cup, the way she knew he liked it, and the other with just a touch of cream and two lumps of sugar.

Before he finished, he looked at Janet and said, "Is that the way you still take it?"

Janet was surprised he remembered and said, "Quite so, thank you."

Then Alan said, "Janet, you look as dashing as ever. We sure had some good times together. It is good to remember the pleasant times of the past when the present seems so full of trouble."

Janet nonchalantly then spoke, "Oh! Are these troubling times for you, Alan?"

Alan then stiffened a little, "No, of course not. I was referring to the little skirmish your man seems to have gotten into."

"Do you really have all the facts, Alan?" Janet wanted to put Alan on the defensive.

Alan answered, "Well, it's been the hottest topic on the station news since it happened."

Then Janet mentioned, "Did you happen to see the midday news report on the FAM news channel?"

"No. I don't usually tune to that substandard station." Alan was a little annoyed at her remark.

Then she suggested, "Well, you have a fine TV monitor right there on the wall. You could tap into that station right now and get the full scoop."

"Full scoop?" Alan questioned.

Janet answered, "Yes, it is an exclusive interview with my granddaughter and myself."

Alan seemed charmed, "Really, Janet. You in front of a camera? On TV? Quite unlike you."

Alan then buzzed his secretary and asked her to tune in the recording of the noonday news program from the FAM news station.

After a few minutes the monitor on the wall displayed the broadcast of the entire newscast. As Alan watched it, he felt disturbed that his staff did not see this and contact him about the facts being presented. Knowing Janet the way he did, he knew there was no disputing the facts of the presentation.

After the newscast Alan remarked, "I'm really impressed. You were both very articulate."

Janet responded, "You see, Alan, Tom is not a fanatic lunatic. He was just rescuing my granddaughter and great-grandson."

"But Janet," he replied, "he still broke the law! We can't have the public thinking that it is acceptable for someone to illegally barge into a clinic and physically attack a doctor in the middle of an operation. Just think how this might have turned out. Dr. Logan and your granddaughter could have been seriously injured in that skirmish. It was a dangerous situation."

Janet leaned forward and looked intently into Alan's eyes, "Alan, you and Tom were good friends. You know Tom! Couldn't you do something to help him?"

Alan responded, "No Janet, I don't know Tom. I knew him as a friend in high school, but I don't know him now. He changed so much from the war. I couldn't even get him to have a beer with me when he returned from Vietnam. He had become a fanatical Christian and had changed from all of his good liberal views. I don't know if I could help him even if I wanted to. Crimes involving an abortion clinic have recently been under the jurisdiction of the federal government. Tom has committed a federal offense and his case will be handled not by just any prosecuting attorney but by James Dickerson, the federal US Attorney."

Janet quietly spoke, "I know of your liberal views regarding abortion, but, you see, this isn't just a case of stopping an abortion. As you heard from the broadcast, it was an illegal abortion involving the drugging and abduction of a high school student."

Alan responded, "I see that now, Janet. But two wrongs don't make a right. It was horribly wrong for that nurse to do what she did, but it was also wrong for Tom to do what he did. I will personally make sure that this nurse is punished to the max of the law but there is nothing I can do for Tom."

Upon leaving, Janet gave a sigh and thought, "Oh well. I tried."

She then went to see Tom again and was relieved to see Doug there. He had just finished talking to Tom and motioned that she should go in and visit before they take Tom back to the cell. After her visit with Tom and filling him in on Sam's suggestion for a lawyer, she wanted to spend some time talking with Doug.

Just then, on her way to see Doug, Janet received a call from Gretchen. She gasped at the first mention of the hospital's intention and was then speechless as Gretchen went on to explain all that had happened.

After the explanation, Gretchen was concerned that Janet gave no response and shouted, "Mom! Are you there?"

"Oh, I'm here. This is all just so unbelievable! What is the address? Doug is right here and I will be seeing him soon. After dropping off my car to his place, we will be on our way there. I will try to explain all that you said to him, but I'm sure he will be as confused and confounded as I am."

CHAPTER 47

KELLY *Makes* A CALL

Bob called his grandparents, and just as he expected, they were more than happy to have Mary and her clan at their summer home. They had been following the news on FAM and on Jay Shannon's program and were excited to hear the baby was safe and sound there in the mountains.

That evening Mary and Gretchen cooked a fine meal for everyone. Doug and Janet arrived after dinner and all had a wonderful time together. Bob mentioned to Kelly that since little Tommy was close to full term, in a couple of days he could be in a normal crib with no need of heat lamps or an IV. She was happy to hear that.

Later that evening, Kelly called Butch Atkins. She wanted to thank him for saving Tommy's life, and she also was so curious as to how he knew so much about what had happened with her at the school.

As he answered the phone, she said, "Hi Butch! This is Kelly."

"I could tell it was you from your voice." Butch replied, "How are you doing?"

Kelly replied, "Quite well. My grandfather would answer such a question with 'It is well with my soul.'"

Thinking of all that Mr. Wisp had done during the rescue, Butch said, "Man, your grandfather is amazing!"

Kelly smiled and said, "Yes, he is indeed pretty amazing. I wanted to thank you for all that you did. You saved my baby's life! My grandfather just mentioned that you called and told him I was being taken by force to the abortion clinic. How did you know so much? How did you find my grandfather's number? There is so much I don't know since I was so drowsy when leaving the school."

Well, Butch spent more than an hour filling Kelly in on all of the details.

Kelly responded, "Wow! Nurse Langly surely went through a lot of planning to have my baby aborted. What in the world was her motive? Why would she do such a thing?"

Butch explained, "I can imagine exactly what she hoped to gain. It is no secret that she feels that all girls in your situation should definitely have an abortion, and she felt justified in doing what she did to you due to Tab's convincing lies. I'm sure she felt that if she could pull this off, it would elevate her in the school superintendent's eyes and put her in a position to be able to pursue more devious plots, taking girls to abortion clinics without the parents' knowledge."

He then told her, "I was at school today and heard that Tab was called to the office. I made up an excuse to leave my class and went down to investigate. When Nurse Langly came out of the principal's office she really looked downtrodden! Word has it that Nurse Langly was fired and criminal charges have been filed against her. Tab has been suspended from school for his part in all that happened. As far as I'm concerned, I say 'Good riddance!' to the both of them."

"My grandmother went to see the governor," interjected Kelly, "but unfortunately nothing really came of it. She knew him decades ago. He had also been a friend of Grandaddy, but the governor told her there was nothing he could do for him. I am so worried about Grandaddy! He is in prison right now awaiting a trial. The judge has refused to grant bail according to his lawyer. It is all so unfair!"

Butch was very sympathetic in his comments. He felt so helpless.

Then Butch mentioned to her, trying to cheer her up, "Oh yea, that lawyer is a fast worker. He called me today to set up a meeting with him. He wants to hear everything I know about the case. I am not going to hold anything back! I want to help your grandfather any way I can. Once everything is out in the open, I'm sure there will be an acquittal of every charge!"

"I sure hope so!" Kelly responded with tears in her eyes.

Then Butch said, "Your grandfather is a hero, and if it was up to me, there would be a ticket parade as he leaves the courthouse a free and courageous man."

Kelly was touched by his comments and said, "I sure appreciate all you have done and your desire to help Grandaddy."

Then shyly she remarked, "And I consider you my hero in sticking up for me and especially in saving my baby! I don't know how I can repay you."

Butch with great care added, "Well, maybe when this is all over, we can go out for a movie or something. I would really like that, Kelly."

Kelly sighed as she said, "I would really like that too, Butch."

She finished the conversation by just saying, "When this is all over…"

CHAPTER 48

PREPARATION *for the* TRIAL

The next few weeks dragged on. The Logan home in the mountains was a central hub for the whole Wisp family. The focus of the media was on Thomas Wisp as the estimated trial date was drawing near. Bob Logan and members of the Wisp family refused all invitations as guests on talk shows and interviews to prevent anything that may be discussed from being dismissed rather than being used as evidence in court to support Tom. The complete truth needed to be brought up in court in order for Tom to even have a chance of an acquittal.

Jason Hilt was compiling all his data from many meetings and interviews. His meeting with Richard Atkins was especially informative. He was able to obtain the names of all three boys involved with the abduction of Kelly. He had a host of those whom he would have the court issue a subpoena to. For weeks he had been visiting Tom to have him rehearse all that happened over and over, in case the prosecution called him to the stand. Any deviation in his testimony could cause the prosecutor in some way to imply that something was being hidden or falsified.

With this case having such high visibility with the public, it was time consuming accepting a jury that was approved by both sides. The defense and offense had used up all of the challenges allotted to them. Finally a jury was chosen and a court date set.

Not much had been mentioned about Baby Wisp. It had been assumed that the baby was no longer alive and that the Abortion Survivor Act had been carried out.

Bob Logan had originally planned to direct the police department to have his charges against Thomas Wisp dropped, but Jason suggested that Bob not drop the charges to keep Bob's lawyer, Bill Stant, uncertain concerning what his actions would be regarding Tom. Bill, knowing Bob as he did, would probably feel certain that Bob would not jeopardize his wealth and career, especially since the federal US Attorney had also pressed charges against Tom.

That was indeed Bill's suspicion. A few days after the incident that Bob and Bill had at the hospital, Bill had contacted Bob. He was relieved to find out that the charges against Tom Wisp were not dropped. He calmly discussed the importance of Bob supporting the prosecution. Bob did not lie to his lawyer but felt it was important to be a little deceptive in their discussing the case. He pretended to be a little indecisive as they talked. He knew that Bill would be one of the members of the prosecution team as they tried this case. He also knew it would be important for that team of lawyers to be completely surprised in court to find him supporting Tom rather than speaking out against him.

Bob expected that he would lose all of his wealth and his practice, but as Gretchen reminded him, he could still practice in other countries and that was sufficient for him. It was clear that the prosecution felt confident of a guilty charge from the jury of all the charges, including breaking an entrance into a privately guarded area and attempted murder.

Jay Shannon and many other pro-life advocates had been broadcasting discussions in support of Thomas Wisp. At the same time, other liberal media organizations had been broadcasting discussions quite the opposite.

No matter what the outcome of the case, Tom, Jason and Bob all agreed that the focus must be on the horrific act of partial birth abortion. Across the nation people would be fully informed first-hand of what entailed such a gross and inhumane procedure. They were sure that even the hardest of hearts would cringe with disgust upon being informed at what took place in a partial birth abortion. Using a pair of surgical scissors, a specially designed manikin, and a specially designed baby doll, Bob himself would demonstrate in great detail the horrific act of such an abortion. During the demonstration he would also have a recorded ultrasound display of an actual partial birth abortion that had been saved from one that he performed several months prior. This would be projected on the wall showing what would be seen on the ultrasound if this was a real abortion. The ultrasound would coincide with each of the steps that he would be doing during the demonstration. He could also pause the recording during periods when he would be explaining the step in detail.

Bob was sickened at the number of these procedures he had actually done. It would be easier for him to allow someone else to demonstrate what took place, but he felt he had to do the demonstration himself. He had committed those sins and before the public eye, his confession and sorrow must be displayed for the reality of what they were. The demonstration must prove that the act of a partial birth abortion is nothing less than the inhumane and horrific murder of an innocent little baby.

The prosecution pushed for the trial to be a public one, enabling reporters to be admitted. They wanted the world to witness the proof presented against this radical Christian man who had the audacity of charging through a locked medical facility and attacking a doctor in the middle of a surgical procedure with an intent to kill. Their hope was for a maximum sentencing. This would show the world that more laws are needed to protect abortion clinics and more government funding is needed to carry on this important work and to keep the staff safe from such lunatics. So, on went the preparations. Both sides with their own agendas.

CHAPTER 49

BABY TOMMY *is* SAFE

Three months after Tom had been imprisoned, the trial date was getting close. It was just two weeks away. Doug, Mary, Gretchen, Kelly, and little Tommy enjoyed the seclusion of the Logan summer home. After the first day there, Mary was given an immediate leave of absence from her work. Doug only went down the mountain for his prison worship and Bible Study meetings. Most of his work he was able to do right there.

Little Tommy was a real delight and joy to everyone in the house. With all that had happened to Kelly, Mary could not bring herself to insist on putting the child up for adoption. She was also getting quite attached to her grandson, being around him 24/7. They were all still concerned that the law remained which stated that an abortion survivor must be put to death.

Jason Hilt was also investigating every aspect of the Abortion Survivor Act. Deep within the content of the law, he found this wording: *"The survivor of an abortion, having no birth certificate, is to be transmitted to the duly established room for isolation and left unattended for termination as per described within the contents of this bill."*

Excited upon this discovery, he rushed to the mountain getaway to relieve Kelly and her family of any anxiety they may have regarding the future of Baby Tommy since he knew they were all in great distress about this matter.

As Jason came to the door, Doug was there to welcome him in, "Well, with that wide smile on your face I presume you have brought good news about Dad."

Jason said, "I did visit your dad this morning, but I have something else I want to share with your whole family. And yes, it is good news indeed."

As Jason was finding a seat, Doug went about the house, beckoning the rest of the family to come down to the living room. Of course, they all came, excited to hear whatever good news Jason could provide.

Jason showed the specific area in the bill that he highlighted to Doug who read it out loud.

Mary was the first to speak, "Jason, exactly what does this all mean for Tommy?"

Jason smiled again and said, "I'm sure this puts Tommy in the clear. As you all know, Bob had already issued his birth certificate that Kelly signed. I have your copy here to present to you, Kelly. Bob had it registered at the town hall, where they applied the certification stamp and had it filed. The comment in the bill that Doug just read clearly states that if the baby was certified with a birth certificate, the requirement that he be 'terminated' does not apply.

The entire family cheered and shouted for joy. Mary, Kelly, and Gretchen all had tears running down their cheeks in delight. Mary and Doug actually hugged on hearing this fantastic news. It was an impulsive move for Mary to run into Doug's arms. After the hug she felt a little embarrassed and walked away to the kitchen. Doug wanted to follow her but knew it best to sit tight and be patient. Kelly ran to the make-due nursery to wake Tommy up and bring him down to join in the celebration. He didn't even cry when she brought him into the room full of jubilation. He actually grinned and cooed awhile.

CHAPTER 50

THE TRIAL
Part 1

There was much publicity surrounding the trial of Thomas Wisp. Both the defense and prosecution had many listed to serve as witnesses. The courtroom was packed as the judge called the meeting to order.

After the usual opening formalities, the federal US Attorney James Dickerson walked and paused in front of the jurors for his opening statement. His message to the jurors was long and drawn out. Basically, he mentioned that he intended to prove beyond a reasonable doubt that the defendant, Thomas Wisp, performed a premeditated act of forcefully entering a federally guarded surgical area with the intention of killing Dr. Logan who was in the middle of a delicate abortion procedure. In his statement he declared that Thomas Wisp has for decades held a festering grudge against doctors performing abortions and a number of times had been imprisoned for criminal acts against such doctors. Also, according to the opening statement, in the hometown of the defendant, he viciously and physically attacked Dr. Logan as an outlet of his anger months prior to this final murderous plan.

As Jason Hilt approached the railing in front of the jurors, it seemed from the cold look on the faces of those jurors that between the opening statement of the prosecution and what they had been exposed to by the many broadcasts of the media, it was going to be a difficult task to defend Tom.

Jason's opening statement was brief and to the point. He claimed that Tom was just performing the heroic act of rescuing his granddaughter and preventing the murderous act of abortion of her son that neither she nor anyone else in her family wanted. He did not mention the horror of the partial birth abortion procedure which, he was sure, few, if any, of the jurors were familiar with. He was saving that message for the actual demonstration that he hoped would be taking place.

Following the opening statements, the prosecution called one witness after the other of those who were in the clinic at the time of the crime. They all testified concerning their knowledge of what took place. Many expressed the fear they experienced from the defendant's actions and how helpless they felt not being able to stop him with the security door rendered inoperable. The secretary of the clinic went through the step by step process of getting through to the surgical area. She mentioned that he would have needed to know this process and also know in advance that cutting the wire from the deadbolt would electrically lock the door.

Mr. Dickerson then asked, "So, is it your opinion that the defendant must have been planning this crime for some time?"

Jason stood up and shouted, "Objection! The prosecutor is leading the witness!"

The judge called out, "Sustained," but the jurors had already understood the intent.

Next, the federal guard who was at the abortion clinic and initiated the attempt to get back into the surgical area of the clinic after the door had been electrically jammed, took the stand and gave his testimony. Jason had not much to question during the cross-examination.

The prosecution called Diane Langly to the stand and she testified that Kelly wanted the abortion but was afraid of her father who was opposed to the abortion because of the damage it would do to his reputation as a pastor. She told of how badly Robert West had been beaten by Kelly Wisp's father, Doug Wisp. She admitted going against the school's normal procedure for moving a child from the school premises but felt compelled to do so because the father was going to take her out of the school, and so the girl would be forced to keep the unwanted child. With Miss Wisp out of school, there would be nothing she could do to help her. Her interest was solely in helping Miss Wisp out of the horrible situation she was in.

Jason cross-examined her, but she was as cool as a cucumber in her lies. He reminded her that perjury was a criminal offense, but that did not budge her testimony.

The defense then called Kelly to the stand, and in her testimony, she explained that it was her desire to keep the child and that she didn't want an abortion. She expressed that her father was a wonderful dad and would in no way force her to keep the baby if she didn't want to, but in fact, she did want to keep the child. She then went on to explain all that happened and the cruel actions of Nurse Langly in drugging her. Of course, because she was drugged, she could not remember anything after the nurse telling her that her doctor wanted her to go to his office to review problems he found in her last exam. She said that there was no discussion of abortion. She said that she thought the nurse was going to take her to see Dr. Flemming, but instead Nurse Langly took her to Planned Parenthood.

The prosecution cross-examined her and asked, "Is it true that your mother insisted that you put the child up for adoption and that you resented her decision?"

Kelly tried to answer by saying that she had hoped her mother would change her mind and that she didn't necessarily resent it. But when she tried to say these things, Mr. Dickerson shouted, "Just answer the question, yes or no!"

Kelly whispered, "Yes."

Then the prosecutor mentioned, "Now Miss Wisp, in your testimony you stated that you saw your grandfather as he, in your words, 'rescued you and your baby'. Did you see him grab for the doctor's scissors and pull him down?"

Kelly was starting to say that her grandfather just wanted to stop the abortion when he grabbed...

But again came the demand, "Just answer the question 'yes' or 'no', Miss Wisp!"

Again she answered with tears in her eyes, "Yes."

The crowd in the room gasped. Kelly had imagined her testimony would help her grandfather, but it seemed to her that it just made things worse.

As Mr. Dickerson shouted, "No further questioning!" Kelly left the stand in tears.

Next the prosecution called Robert West to take the stand.

Kelly noticed that for him, Tab was unusually dressed in a nice suit with a neatly trimmed haircut. With the questioning of the prosecution, Tab backed up the lies Miss Langly stated and added that Kelly said that if she had to give the baby up for adoption like her mother wanted, she would rather go through an abortion. His testimony was very convincing when he said he saw her father in his car near the rear entrance to the school that morning, and he tried to help her father see Kelly's side of the situation but was told to mind his own business. And then when he persisted, he said that Mr. Wisp got out of his car and beat him up very badly. When his friends from the school door saw this and ran to help him, Mr. Wisp quickly drove away leaving him gasping and bleeding on the ground. He said it was then that his friends helped him into the school and to the nurse's office.

Jason cross-examined Tab with many questions but he couldn't get him to break. He stuck to every lie. Inwardly, Tab was congratulating himself on such a good performance.

One by one the prosecution called to the stand Tab's three friends, Rick Abbott, Jake Andrews and Andy Baker. They reaffirmed Tab's story. Again, Jason cross-examined them, but they stuck to the story. After the last of Tab's friends left the witness stand, Jason called Mr. Wisp, Kelly's dad to the stand.

Jason questioned him, and he stated the truth of what happened after he dropped Kelly off. He said that he just dropped Kelly off and after she entered the school, drove away. He also testified that Kelly really wanted to keep the baby but was completely compliant with her mother's desire to have the baby adopted. Jason also questioned Doug about his dad, Thomas Wisp. Doug mentioned that, sure his dad had been arrested for protesting at abortion clinics and such, but they were all misdemeanors and that his dad had no desire to hurt anyone. That was just not him! He described Tom perfectly as the man people loved, because of his caring for others and his mild manner and demeanor.

After cross-examining Doug, Mr. Dickerson handed a set of documents listing Tom's arrests and times of imprisonment. As the judge looked over the charges and accusations, he realized that all of those charges would have resulted in no arrests and no time in prison except for the fact that they involved abortion clinics. The judge then handed them to the bailiff to be taken to the jurors for their review.

It was looking very bad for Tom. The accusation of Kelly wanting or not wanting an abortion was just her and her dad's word against the testimony of Diane Langly, Tab, Rick, and the other two boys. The fact that Kelly testified that she resented her mother wanting to have the baby adopted seemed to have verified Tab's statement that she would rather have the baby aborted if she couldn't keep it. Also, the jury would likely believe that Kelly's dad would not want her to have an abortion for his reputation's sake. It was on Jason's shoulders to prove that Tom's intent was not to harm Dr. Logan, but only to save the baby.

Bob Logan was anxious to take the stand. He thought, "If I could just get up there and testify now, those jurors would go into the jury room with a different view of Tom and this whole case."

But he also knew that Jason was a good lawyer and would wait for the right time. The day was done and the judge adjourned the court until the next day at 9AM. The news reporters were gathering their notes as Kelly ran to her grandaddy for a hug with tears in her eyes. Janet was there too, giving Tom a hug. Then the guards pulled Tom away as the two ladies were still clinging to him.

Tom whispered to his darlings, "Don't worry! It is well with my soul! It's also well with my defense! You will see!"

Then down the hall he went, a guard on each arm.

CHAPTER 51

THE TRIAL
Part 2

The next day dawned with a bright and sunny morning. After yesterday's testimonies the prosecution felt pretty confident the jurors were leaning towards a verdict of guilty on all charges. Most of the witnesses that they planned to present had already taken the stand and it looked like the defense was running out of witnesses to testify on behalf of Thomas Wisp, or were they?

Once the judge called the court to order, Jason called Richard Atkins to the stand. Jason asked him what really happened at the school after Doug Wisp dropped his daughter Kelly off at the rear entrance. Butch was very articulate in describing all that happened, based on what Rick Abbott had told him. His testimony confirmed that Tab had staged the entire beating to coax Nurse Langly into taking Kelly to the Abortion Clinic. He told how he found Thomas Wisp's phone number and gave him a call.

As he completed his testimony, Jason walked to his desk and picked up the Student Departure Form that Butch had given him the day of their meeting. Then Jason approached the judge's desk and said, "I am presenting Exhibit #1. This is the falsified Student Departure Form that Diane Langly filled out to have Rick Abbott take to the office. Richard Atkins intercepted and obtained the falsified form. I am also presenting Exhibit #2. This is the bottle of pills that Miss Langly told Kelly was a mild pain reliever that, according to her, Dr. Flemming had sent. Though the label describes the pills as a mild pain reliever, you will see from the attached papers that the lab tests indicate that the pills are actually a very strong sedative." These exhibits were then taken to the jury for examination.

Jason introduced the exhibits to confirm Butch's and Kelly's testimony as the truth. James Dickerson then called Miss Langly back to the witness stand.

He then obtained the bottle from the jury and handed it to her and asked, "Miss Langly, do you recognize this bottle?"

Nurse Langly looked at the label with Dr. Flemming's name and Kelly's name on it and said, "I have never seen this bottle in my life. Apparently, at some point, young Richard Atkins must have gone to my office and taken a bottle and label to falsify that information. The school has had problems in the past with this young man stealing. I'm sure he has ways of getting those sedatives. His record stands for itself."

Jason knew it was no use cross-examining her for she would just lie. Next, the prosecution called the school principal, Ellen Weston to the stand. After being sworn in she sat down in the witness stand.

James Dickerson said to her, "Mrs. Weston, please tell us your occupation."

Mrs. Weston replied, "I am the principal at Ontario High School."

"Are you familiar with Richard Atkins?"

She replied, "Yes. He is one of the students there."

James then asked her, "In the two years that he has attended the school there, has he been sent to your office with behavior problems?"

She reluctantly answered, "Yes, he had but …" she wanted to complete the sentence by saying that recently he had changed to be a very honest and good student, but James Dickerson quickly shouted, "Just answer the question 'yes or no', Mrs. Weston!"

She whispered, "Yes."

James Dickerson then produced a document and stated, "I would like to submit Exhibit #3 for the prosecution. This is a document subpoenaed from the Ontario High School files listing the many offenses by young Richard Atkins including lying, cheating, fighting, harassing students, and even threatening teachers."

Then the prosecution stated, "That is all," and then asked her to step down. But Jason stood up and stated, "Your Honor I would like to cross-examine the witness."

The judge gave a gesture of approval and Jason approached the witness stand.

He then asked, "Mrs. Weston, in recent months have you seen a change in the attitude and work of Mr. Atkins?"

She was thankful for the question and had quite a bit to say about Butch's improvements and the model student he had become. But the jury would have a good look at Exhibit #3 which would put a dark shadow over Butch's testimony.

Jason had also been to Ontario High School and subpoenaed documents himself.

He asked Mrs. Weston, "Has Miss Langly ever previously taken girls from the school to an abortion clinic without parental permission?"

She answered, "Yes."

Jason then asked her to expand on the cases. Mrs. Weston mentioned the several cases in which Miss Langly had done just that, and that one girl was even given an abortion. This shocked the jury. Jason then produced Exhibit #4 for the defense, which he explained, contained information of not only the cases described by Mrs. Weston but also complaints of parents and students alike that Miss Langly pushed abortion propaganda excessively.

With Mrs. Weston still on the stand, Jason asked, "Mrs. Weston, do you recall having Richard West, Rick Abbott, Jake Andrews, or Andy Baker in your office for any offense?"

She answered affirmative with details nearly as bad as what was mentioned about Butch. Jason produced Exhibit #5 for the defense which documented what Mrs. Weston had said and more.

Then Jason called Abby Whitman to the stand. She was the student that had witnessed the entire staging of Tab's beating. Jason asked her to tell what she saw on the day in question. Her testimony also backed up what Butch had testified with information from Rick Abbott.

After dismissing her, Jason called Rick Abbott back to the stand. He told Rick that he was still under oath. Rick was very nervous after hearing Abby's testimony. He knew her credibility was beyond reproach. After thinking about the warning given to him of possible perjury charges and after seeing the look on Butch's face, he decided to come clean and told the truth about the staging. He also told what he knew (which was a lot) of Nurse Langly's scheme to drug Kelly for the purpose of taking her to the abortion clinic.

After this there were several individuals, one by one, whom Jason brought to the stand to testify of Tom's good character and his integrity. James Dickerson initially, with the first testimony, stood up and shouted, "Objection, the testimony is irrelevant!" but the judge overruled the objection and the testimonies continued.

Suddenly a diplomatic security guard entered the courtroom and whispered a message to Jason and handed him a note. As he read it his eyes widened and he nodded his head in approval at the guard who then left the room.

To the surprise of all in the court, Jason stood and asked the Honorable Sukhan Chao-wen to take the stand. Everyone looked around the room to look for the renowned President of Taiwan. She had captured the hearts of many Americans as she had been touring the United States. Her love for people, humor and charisma were so alluring to so many, especially the media.

Suddenly the courtroom doors opened and President Sukhan Chao-wen entered with her aura of charm and eloquence. Security guards followed her in and stood at the corner of the room as the celebrity first approached the judge. She nodded her head to him as an expression of honor and then stood in front of the jury and similarly nodded to them before taking her seat on the witness stand. This expression of humility was warmly felt throughout the courtroom. She was smiling at Tom with a gleam in her eyes as Jason approached her.

He then asked, "President Chao-wen, please express to the courtroom your acquaintance with the defendant?"

Before responding, she scanned all those seated in front of her with her delightful smile which rested again on Tom.

"During the Vietnam War, the honorable defendant, Thomas Wisp, single-handedly saved my life and the life of my entire village from an assault of the Viet Cong during the infamous Tet advance."

On hearing this, Tom struggled to associate the name with any of the children he knew from that village. That smile and those dimples of hers did seem so familiar though.

She went on to say that her birth name was Kim Nguyen but was changed to Sukhan Chao-wen by her adopted parents who rescued her and brought her to Taiwan after her parents were killed by the North Vietnamese shortly after the United States recalled their forces.

With tears in his eyes, Tom wanted to jump from his seat and run to the stand for a huge hug and twirl her around like days of old.

The President went on to describe Tom's heroic actions and the events that saved her village. The audience was spellbound with her story.

She told of Tom's wonderful love for her and the children of her village. She also spoke of many other good attributes she saw in Tom Wisp during his many trips to her village. With that said, she took from her pouch a bright star emblem in a golden casing. She held the honorable award up for all to see.

Then she said, "This, my good American friends, is the medal my brave and good friend, Tom Wisp, left behind. It is the Congressional Medal of Honor awarded to him for his heroic actions. I see now that his heroism has not left him after all of these years!"

At this point, many of those present, including some of the jurors, were in tears.

Both the defense and prosecution were speechless as she then got up from the stand and walked over to Tom and presented him, warmly, with the award. Both Tom and President Chao-wen had tears in their eyes as they hugged for a long time.

The news reporters were busy snapping pictures, one after another, each certain theirs would be the one to make the front page.

President Chao-wen then whispered in Tom's ear, "Whiskers, no matter what happens here, we will have a long talk, even if it means prolonging my stay in this country. I secretly witnessed you tossing that award into the pond. After you left my country, I trudged through that swampy pond for hours to find your award and it is my joy to present it to you now!"

Then, after handing him the award within the gold casing, she left the courtroom with her security guards close behind.

James Dickerson would have thought this to be a low-handed ploy of sentimentality by the defense except on seeing the initial expression of shock on the faces of both Jason and Tom, he was convinced otherwise. Besides, his contacts would have informed him if there had been any previous contact between President Chao-wen and the defense attorney.

It was now shortly after noon and the judge looked at this amazing series of events as a good time for a recess. Once the judge announced the recess, all of Tom's family members rushed to surround him with hugs, laughter and joy.

CHAPTER 52

THE TRIAL
Part 3

After the recess, the courtroom was again full as the bailiff announced the entrance of the judge who called the court to order. The prosecution then called Thomas Wisp to take the stand. Jason had his Bible on the table in front of Tom. On his way to the witness stand, Tom picked up the Bible.

As he stood in front to take the oath, the prosecution asked, "What is that in your hand?"

To this Tom replied, "I know they don't use the Bible anymore in the oath to be taken, but I would like to carry on that tradition and take the oath with one hand on the Bible, if it pleases the court."

James responded, just a little embarrassed, "Do what you may, and get on with the oath."

After repeating the "I do" as a response to the oath, Tom sat in the witness seat.

James asked him many "yes" or "no" questions about his feelings about abortion and abortionists. Some of the questions Tom affirmed, others he answered "No."

Tom was then asked on the specified date, "Did you indeed break into the guarded entry to the surgical rooms of the Bayside Planned Parenthood?"

To this Tom answered 'Yes'.

The next question to Tom was, "Did you approach Dr. Logan with the intent to kill him?"

Tom replied with the answer, "No, I was just trying to prevent the death of my great grandson."

James Dickerson again asked Tom if he hated abortion and Tom responded by saying yes.

He followed this by asking Tom, "Do you hate doctors who perform abortions?"

And Tom replied, "No, I do not."

James continued, "How can you hate the procedure of abortion and yet not hate those who indeed commit that action?"

Tom responded, "The Bible tells us to hate the sin, not the sinner."

James realized that he was not going to get the kind of rise in emotion from the defendant as he had hoped, so he told Tom that he may be excused. James Dickerson was now anxious to place Bob Logan on the stand to offset the testimony of President Chao-wen. From his conferences with Bill Stant, he was sure Bob would be the one to put an end to any doubt the jury might have of the defendant's guilt.

He, therefore, stood and stated, "The prosecution would now like to call Dr. Robert Logan to the witness stand."

Bob took the stand after repeating the witness oath. James asked him to identify himself and his profession so everyone in the courtroom would know who he was. Bob responded with the information requested. The prosecution reminded the court that there had been several witnesses describing the events leading up to the assault on the doctor. James announced that it was his intent for the doctor to start his testimony from that point and describe the horrendous actions of Thomas Wisp as he approached the abortion procedure already in process.

James Dickerson next stated, "Dr. Logan, please describe to the court the events that took place as the defendant entered your operating room with the intent to kill you."

Immediately Jason stood and shouted, "Objection, your honor. The prosecution is again leading the witness!"

The judge ruled, "Objection sustained!"

James then reworded the request, "Please describe the events during and after the defendant entered your operating room."

Bob hesitated and then confidently said, "Before starting I would like to say that the intent of the defendant was not to harm me in any way, but rather just to save the life of his granddaughter's son!"

The prosecution was aghast on hearing that statement.

James immediately responded, "Dr. Logan, how can you possibly make such a statement when your head was crushed by the defendant?"

Before Bob could answer, James interposed, "The prosecution submits Exhibit #6. This is the hospital report of the extent of the concussion that Dr. Logan sustained from the offensive actions of the defendant."

After the exhibit was placed on the judge's desk, Bob was ready to respond.

"I can confidently say that Mr. Wisp had no intention of killing me because there were a number of knives and operation utensils right at my side in full view of the defendant that he could have used to take my life. He also could have finished me off as I fell over, unconscious, if that was his intention. No! His intent, I'm very sure, was just to save the child."

James was very confused at Bob's testimony and looked back at Bill Stant and the rest of the prosecution with a deeply questioning expression. He then asked the judge permission to confer with his team. He then sat in his chair next to Bill as the other prosecution lawyers huddled in to hear.

He whispered to Bill, "What is going on with Dr. Logan? You told me that he was ready to put Mr. Wisp away for a long time. Did you not confer with him and clue him in on what would be asked and his expected responses?"

Bill responded, "Of course I did! He initially spoke of a desire to drop the charges against the defendant but I fully explained how that would be such a detriment to his future. I've known Bob for a very long time. He has always been very concerned about keeping his lucrative business going well and he has previously always adhered to my recommendations. I don't know what has gotten into the man!"

James got up and again approached the witness, "Dr. Logan, did you not file charges against Thomas Wisp of attempted murder at the police station? Those charges that you made is what initiated this whole accusation. Are you trying to make a mockery of this court?"

Bob again spoke confidently, "At the time that charges were made, I was in the hospital and completely unconscious. The charges against the defendant were made by my previous lawyer, Bill Stant, on my behalf. I had thought about dropping the charges, but Bill Stant suggested it would be to my ruin. To answer your second question, it is not my desire to make a mockery of the court but just to present facts that the jury needs, to make a just verdict!"

Then Bob continued, "Now I will answer your first request and describe what took place as Tom entered my operating room."

As he started, recognizing that what Bob would say would place a different color on the defendant, James interrupted, "The prosecution desires to retract the request."

The judge answered, "Approved."

Then James questioned, "Dr. Logan, just answer yes or no. Could such an interruption by the defendant at such a late time in your abortion procedure cause injury to the patient?"

Bob answered, "Yes, but…"

Before he could say more James responded, "Dr. Logan, that answer is sufficient."

Then he said, "This is another yes or no question. Did the defendant indeed knock you to the floor during your operating procedure and cause you to be harmed and rendered unconscious?"

Again Bob answered, "Yes."

Now James just desired to have Bob out of that witness stand before more damage could be done to the prosecution. So he quickly responded, "That will be all, Dr. Logan, you may be excused."

But at this Jason jumped to his feet and exclaimed, "Your honor, please. May I cross-examine the witness?"

Before the judge could answer, James shouted, "Objection! The witness was called by the prosecution and is not subject to such a cross-examination."

Then the judge called both the prosecution and defense to approach the bench.

The judge then asked Mr. Hilt what his intentions were in questioning the witness. Jason told the judge that he intended to present a reenactment of the event which would enlighten the jury on exactly what took place.

Right away, James shouted, "Objection! This trial has already gone on longer than anyone expected. I don't see any value added with such a demonstration."

The judge smiled to himself at the notion of some entertainment in the court as well as additional information to the charge. So he responded, "Objection overruled! Counselor, you may proceed."

Jason then approached Dr. Logan and said, "Dr. Logan, please tell the court all that happened, to your recollection, from the point when you were interrupted by the defendant during the abortion procedure to your state of unconsciousness."

Bob always had a great memory for detail and described clearly what happened after Tom grabbed his arm to his last remembrance of seeing the edge of the lab table just before his head struck its corner.

In describing the events he added, "Thomas Wisp did not pull my hand, which held the scissors, toward me, but rather away from me. In the process it caused the instrument to end up in his own leg, causing a much more serious injury to him than what was done to me."

Then Jason gave the signal to Sam Diggs, who was now standing near the entrance to the courtroom, to bring in the prepared manikin to be used for the demonstration.

As Sam went for the manikin, Jason asked Bob, "Dr. Logan, I understand you have a prepared demonstration for the court. What exactly is the purpose of this demo?"

To this Bob replied, "I wish to show the jury and the court why an honorable man like Thomas Wisp would go to the extreme measures that he underwent to stop such a barbaric procedure."

Again, the prosecution interjected, "Objection!"

Immediately the judge shouted, "Overruled!"

Suddenly the courtroom doors opened and Sam entered pushing the manikin, which was set onto a birthing chair with the upper extremities of the body covered. Behind him was Roger Miller pushing in a lab cart that had on its surface a series of surgical instruments covered with a small sheet. A shelf under the top of the cart contained a small ultrasound system and, next to it, a small vacuum unit. These items were set in front of the jury box and in plain sight of the entire court. A movie camera was set to display the procedure, and a projector was arranged to provide a showing of the camera's output. Another projector was set up to display the ultrasound terminal on a screen.

In the corner of the courtroom was a stool that the bailiff used to sit on between his duties. Bob asked to use the stool and upon approval, set it next to the lab cart and in front of the birthing chair. Sam and Roger set the camera to capture the area of Bob's hands. The camera was connected to a projector which provided a display on the white walls just above and to the side of the judge for all to see. The ultrasound display projector was also set up with a large screen.

Dr. Logan pulled a lab coat from the bottom shelf of the cart and put it on. He then pulled the hose of the ultrasound and grabbing the probe, rubbed it across the lower abdomen of the manikin. Then he made the maneuvers with his hands throughout the entire explanation which were respective to the recorded ultrasound display.

As he did this, he explained, "At the start of the partial birth abortion procedure, I will have to reach inside the uterus with a set of forceps to try to find a foot and at the same time move the ultrasound probe for a display of the position of forceps and the child. The feet will be located at the top of the baby's body which is the normal birthing position. The baby will have to be moved to a breech position for the procedure to accommodate legal requirements."

He then physically simulated this procedure with his hands reaching between the legs of the manikin and into the body with the forceps. The ultrasound recording displayed the forceps and the baby's response.

He continued, "During this time, the child is fighting for his life, kicking away the forceps. At the same time, with the fingers of my other hand, I will manually work on moving the body of the baby to a breech position. As you can see on the ultrasound, he is instinctively struggling to prevent the breech position."

Tears formed in the corners of Bob's eyes as he continued, "Once in the breech position, after several attempts, the forceps grab a foot. Grabbing the forceps tightly, I then can pull the foot out of the female's body. The force of doing this causes the child to agonize in the split position."

The ultrasound display gave a graphic view of the baby's maneuvers to get away from the forceps. The courtroom was captivated. As Bob pulled the leg of the baby doll with the forceps from inside the body of the manikin a few women rushed out of the courtroom covering their eyes due to the sight of the ultrasound showing graphically the pain of the tremoring baby.

Choking a little, the doctor continued, "The second foot is probed the same way and pulled out. The baby is at this point trembling with fear and pain. Even through the forceps I am able to feel the trembling."

With shaking hands, Bob pulled the second leg of the doll for the jurors and all in the court to see from the display of the camera. The shaking of his hands simulated the trembling of the baby but Bob's hands were not shaking for that purpose. This description too was clear on the ultrasound display for all to see.

Again he spoke, "With the feet kicking, they are then held tightly to pull the body out to the neck, as the girl pushes. For this procedure to be legal, the head must remain within the body."

From inside the manikin and between its legs Bob pulled on the feet of the doll. The doll was now held in place with only the head still within the manikin.

Bob's shaking subsided a little as he reached for the surgical scissors on the lab table.

He continued, "From the feet, I slide my hands to the chest of the infant for stability."

The people in the court did not believe what they were seeing.

They all thought, "Could this really be true! How could anyone do such a barbaric and insane thing?!"

The projector from the camera clearly showed Bob's hand sliding from beneath the doll to the upper abdomen.

Bob then said, "Now the child's feet will be kicking in pain like a windmill, almost as though he knows what is going to happen."

Bob pushed a button and the doll's legs kicked back and forth.

"I can't hear a cry at this point. The baby has no air, but I can feel the cry through his bones and through his flesh."

And now sweat poured from Bob's forehead, tears from his eyes, and drips from his nose. Bob knew he had to maintain control at least until the end of the demonstration. Gretchen watched in agony, not only from the horror of the procedure, but even more so from the hurt she knew was agonizing Bob's heart. He had actually done this procedure many times, she knew, from one of their discussions at the mountain hideout. Prior to this he had ignored those silent screams. He had ignored the kicking of the legs as a sign of pain and horror for the infant. Though he would normally hum his way through the procedure, he could no longer do so. He had to cry his way through it. But he had to get through it. Not only for the sake of the world to see the insanity of it all, but for closure for himself in full repentance of his sin.

Within himself Bob was calling out to God. "Lord, I know you have forgiven me, please help me forgive myself!"

Bob continued, "With this pair of uniquely shaped, very sharp scissors I need to just make a small deep incision, about an inch long at the backside of the head near its base. As the scissors first touch the skin for the incision into the baby's head, the infant would jerk away trying to get away from the deadly instrument."

At this point, Bob simulated with the doll what he had just explained. "Holding him firmly, I must make the thrust through the lower part of the skull to the base of the brain. This gray matter is removed by the vacuum and carefully saved. It is then sold to researchers which brings in huge revenues."

Forcefully Bob thrust the scissors, and in doing so, many of those watching turned their heads away in disgust. Even the judge looked a little squeamish at that sight.

Bob then removed the scissors and quickly grabbed the specially adapted nozzle of the vacuum hose to push it into the incision. As he turned on the vacuum, the head of the doll within the manikin collapsed as Bob pushed another button on the doll which caused the legs to drop lifeless in his hand. Bob then pulled the doll from the manikin and held it up for all to see. With the doll still in his hand, he walked over to stand in front of the jury.

His eyes were still watery as he shouted, "If anyone is to be charged with attempted murder…, No! Aggravated and premeditated murder itself, it should be me! I am the guilty one! Thomas Wisp is a hero, just as President Chao-wen announced him to be. Thomas Wisp enabled the last baby that I would ever attempt to murder, to be saved, thus saving my conscience from yet another killing."

He then looked into the eyes of the jury and stated, "If you wish to make a guilty judgment, make it against me, not this fine gentleman, Thomas Wisp!"

Turning around, Bob slowly walked to his seat next to Gretchen, who stood to hug him before they both sat down. The courtroom was quiet and motionless, still in shock from what was just presented.

The judge then quietly said, "Does the prosecution or defense have any other witnesses to call?"

Feeling defeated and a little embarrassed, James stood and said, "No, your Honor."

Jason did the same.

The judge peered at James, who was still standing, and said, "The prosecution may now present its closing statement."

James almost felt like raising his hands and just giving up. But he had his reputation to uphold, and his position required him to do what he could for a conviction. James stepped to the front of the jurors and paused to eye each one. After a short pause he presented his closing statements, commenting that this was a clear case of the defendant, Thomas Wisp, deliberately breaking through the guarded and restricted area of the Bayside Planned Parenthood. And then, in the process of stopping the surgical procedure, he rushed in to murder Dr. Logan which, in doing so, also endangered the life of the patient, his own granddaughter. He also mentioned in the closing statement that it was Thomas Wisp's fanatical objection to abortion that initiated his actions in perpetrating this crime.

At James' conclusion, Jason stood and approached the juror box for his closing statement. He gave a short summary of the deceptive and illegal method used in taking Kelly Wisp to the abortion clinic. He then reminded the jurors that, if it was the defendant's intention to kill the doctor, he could easily have done so after the doctor became unconscious from the fall.

As far as breaking into the restricted area, Jason stated to the jurors, "Ask yourself, 'If I had a baby or grandchild that I knew was in the process of being murdered, as described in Dr. Logan's demonstration, would I not do whatever was necessary to break into the room to save that dear infant?'"

He went on to say, "If there was a fire and a baby was trapped inside the burning building, and a man stepped forward and ran into the building to save that infant, he would most definitely be hailed a hero. Yes, he may be 'breaking and entering' into that building in doing so, but there would be no charge against him. I say to you, there is not much difference in what Thomas Wisp did to save that dear baby."

Just then, the courtroom doors opened and Kelly (who had stepped out for a minute), came through those doors carrying little Tommy. Jason then asked Kelly to come to him.

He took the baby and leaned over the juror box for all to see and stated, "This is the dear baby that Thomas Wisp saved. This innocent baby would have been murdered, as you saw being demonstrated, if action was not taken by the defendant."

In closing he stated, "I have a poem to recite, written a year ago by Thomas Wisp, the defendant. It is called 'I Heard a Baby',

"I heard a baby giggle today;
    He moved in such a cheerful way
I laughed so hard my stomach ached
    And Oh the joyful sound he made.
A gift from God, Oh, what a gift!
    None other could give me such a lift.
I heard a baby scream today,
    A silent scream, or so they say.
I cried so hard my stomach ached;
    And Oh the painful sound he made.
If only his mother could have seen him before
    They took the blade and cut and tore.
She would have held him in her arms
    And soothed him with all her charm.
Now I know he's in Jesus' care.

I know someday that I'll be there.
And there will be babies all around,
Each with a little grin; each with a little crown
And Jesus and I will take their hands
And try to help them understand.
Until that day I'll pray and cry
And bow my head and wonder why
The guilty live and the innocent die.
I bow my head and pray;
Again I bow and pray.
Another day I pray
And cry!"

There were not many dry eyes in the courtroom.

Jason concluded by saying, "So what say you, jury of the court? Is Thomas Wisp a criminal or a hero?"

At this, the judge called the court to recess as the jury was escorted by the bailiff to the jury room for a verdict to be decided.

CHAPTER 53

The VERDICT

With recess called, reporters rushed from the room in an attempt to be the first to release a description to the public of what took place. As Phillip Canten approached Tom who was surrounded by family members, Sam stepped up to him and handed him a stick drive of Bob Logan's demonstration.

He smiled at Sam and said, "Is this what I think it is?"

Sam answered, "You wouldn't turn down another exclusive, would you? This is a video of the whole procedure that was done before our eyes."

To that Phil responded, "Not a chance! Thanks Sam. With the publicity this case is getting, the network will clear some of what is scheduled and beg me to get a prelude together for this to be used for the next news slot." After a few moments of thought, he then added, "Once my network broadcasts this, I will hand it off to other stations so that more people will see the horrors of abortion."

Jason was discussing predictions of the verdict with Tom and his family. He stated, "I'm not sure what the outcome will be. If it is not an acquittal, the judge will be determining the sentence. We just need to hope and trust in the Lord."

Tom then responded, "Well, whatever the verdict and judgment, we can rely on God's promise of Romans 8:28:

And we know that in all things God works for the good of those who love him, who have been called according to his purpose.

With this said, they all shouted, "Amen!"

The jurors were only in deliberation for a half-hour before reaching a verdict. As they marched into the courtroom and into the jury box, the judge once again called the court to order, hammering his gavel to its base.

All were anticipating what the verdict and sentence would be.

The judge announced, "Has the jury reached a verdict?"

The foreman of the jury stood up and announced, "Yes Judge, we have. We find the defendant guilty of 'trespassing into a federally guarded area.' To all other charges, we find the defendant innocent!"

Cheers were sounded from all over the courtroom. The judge hesitated, and then with the pounding of his gavel, he again called the court to order.

It was his decision to provide a sentence to the verdict given.

After a long look into the eyes of Thomas Wisp, the judge announced, "Will the defendant please stand for the sentencing?"

As Thomas stood, the judge stated, "In light of the fact that the trespassing charge is the lesser of the original 'forceful entrance into a federally guarded area' charge, I am inclined to be lenient in my sentencing. The trespassing charge, in this case, I view as a misdemeanor. Thomas Wisp, I sentence you to a total of 120 hours of community service to be completed within one year of this date."

The judge then shouted, "Court adjourned!"

Again, the reporters raced from the courtroom excited and surprised by the verdict and sentencing of Thomas Wisp. There was much celebrating as people surrounded Tom to offer congratulations. There were some, of course, like Miss Langly and Tab West, who were disgruntled by the outcome, but they were certainly the minority.

Handcuffs were removed from Tom's wrists, and Tom was then escorted from the courtroom to the police car. The guards were taking him back to the police station for him to change from his orange prison suit to his own clothes and receive his personal items.

Janet and Doug planned to pick Tom up at the police station as the rest of the family left to go to Fernview Cottage for a grand celebration.

CHAPTER 54

The RETURN TO FERNVIEW COTTAGE

The whole Wisp family, except for Janet, Doug and Tom, were already at Fernview Cottage when Bob Logan arrived. He would be honored as much as Tom himself for his role in freeing Tom and putting a real spotlight on the horrors of abortion. They all rushed at Bob with handshakes and hugs. Maggie and Mary had worked together to make one of Tom's favorite desserts, chocolate cake with chocolate frosting. Ronny and Joshua were in the kitchen happily licking the spoons and scraping the bowls used in the cake and frosting. As they came out and hugged Bob, a bit of chocolate frosting lingered on his cheek.

Gretchen pointed to his cheek, smiled and said, "The boys sure made a mess of you!"

Bob took his finger and, after swiping the chocolate from his cheek, placed it in his mouth with glee and said, "Now that's what I call a tasteful welcome!"

This caused all to burst out in laughter. Gretchen had the TV set to record the afternoon FAM News report. Sometime after the rest of the family arrived, she planned to have a showing for everyone to see except the boys. She thought it might be a little too graphic for them to watch.

Maggie looked at Ronny and Joshua and said, "You boys need to go to the bathroom and clean up a bit. Then I want you both to clean up the mess you made in the kitchen."

Ronny responded, "Yes ma'am." And motioned for his brother to follow him.

Kelly smiled as she thought how polite the boys were. She was hoping Little Tommy would grow up to be just as sweet as her two nephews. Suddenly she heard Tommy give his wakeup call from her bedroom down

319

the hall. She announced to the group, "Well, I had better go and tend to that little angel of mine."

As Maggie and Mary went back to the kitchen, Don said, "I think I'll retire to the den and review the rest of the newspaper I was reading this morning."

He surmised that Gretchen and Bob might want to be alone.

Gretchen was glad that the family left and asked Bob, "Would you like to come and sit on the deck? It sure is a beautiful day."

Bob returned, "Yes! I would enjoy that very much."

They sat together on the swing and Bob started the conversation, "How long will you be staying? I know you must really be missed at the orphanage."

Gretchen smiled in a whimsical way and said, "Trying to get rid of me, huh?"

Bob raised his eyebrows and quickly responded, "Absolutely not! I was just wondering how much time I would be able to spend with you here. You know there might be a lot we need to discuss, that is, if you still think I might have an opportunity to work there at Brasil Orfanato Cristao Central."

Gretchen then questioned him, hoping for some enlightenment. "So it's just the job you are interested in?"

Bob then looked at her very seriously and said, "I hope you realize that it is you that I am interested in. I've been thinking of you from the first moment I saw you. That first conversation we had at lunch was, to me, so exciting. I have never felt that way about anyone before. I know it was the Holy Spirit that beckoned me to be saved, but I don't know if I really would have gone through with calling out to Jesus, if you had not been there to encourage me. You bring out the best in me. I know I am just a new Christian and have so much to learn about God's Word, but I know you can help me with that too."

Then Gretchen became very serious as she spoke, "Bob, what you did for Dad was remarkable, and saving my nephew was nothing short of a miracle by God. I know God is going to use you in a mighty way. And I want you to know that the feelings I have for you are more than just gratitude for these marvelous things. When we were in the hospital chapel, I was so afraid you were going to walk out of there and miss the opportunity, not only for salvation, but for us. You see, that luncheon we had was a first experience of, what you might say, romance for me too. Of course, when I found out about you and then later learned of your part in what happened to Kelly, I pushed all the infatuation to the back burner and replaced it with hatred. But when I heard your discussion with Mr. Stant, I had hope! That is why I went to the chapel. And then when I saw you in the chapel, I couldn't believe what was happening. While talking with you, God turned all that hatred for you into joy. I know you are a changed man. Today proved it, but I already knew it. I would love for you to come to Brasil Orfanato Cristao Central. The staff would love to have you, and the children will be delighted. We need you! I need you!"

Hearing this, Bob wanted so much to kiss her. But he didn't want to be presumptuous either, so he wrapped his arms around her for a hug. Gretchen had so much joy and happiness in her heart she couldn't help herself but to give him a delightful kiss.

Then Bob spoke, "Gretchen, I don't care how much money I will lose or what may happen to my reputation here in the States! I am so glad things turned out the way they did! That term 'Born Again' is an understatement for me! I feel like I have really been reborn into a wonderful life beyond my imagination. I hate that person I used to be. Now I have true fulfillment. Having the Lord and having you! God is good! So very good!"

After another hug, Bob spoke again, "You know, your dad was the first to try to knock some sense into me physically months ago. It was here in Woodridge Falls. His group was doing an abortion protest in front of the house of an associate of mine where I was staying. I was livid and got out of my car to attempt to kick down a sign in front of a little boy. Before I knew what was happening, I was on the ground, thanks to your dad's cane. Then a little later at the San Bernardino Courthouse, I was dining with Bill Stant when your dad approached my table. He said that he was praying for me. He then said something to me that I will never forget. He said, 'God has great plans for you, Bob.'

I remember thinking that I heard those words before, but where? Where? Now I remember. It was my grandmother who said that to me when I was only ten. She had been taking me to church and I had just memorized John 3:16:

For God so loved the world that he gave his one and only son that whoever believes in him shall not perish but have eternal life.

When your dad first mentioned those words about God having plans for me, I thought that God didn't exist and if he did exist, he would in no way want to have any good plans for me, let alone great plans for me. Now I know. God really does have great plans for me and it all begins with you and Brasil Orfanato Cristao Central."

CHAPTER 55

The MOURNING DOVES

When Tom entered the door he shouted, "Praise the Lord! Now where is my benefactor?"

Bob and Gretchen could hear him, all the way from the back deck and came in to greet him. As Bob was shaking his hand, Tom whispered in his ear, "I heard all about your salvation. God is good, Bob!"

Everyone in the house came running to see Tom, Janet and Doug.

After the excitement of everyone being together died down, Joshua shouted, "Can we have some of that cake now?"

Everyone laughed, and Maggie smiled at him and said, "It is Grandy's cake! So you will have to ask him."

He looked at Tom and said, "Grandy, please!"

Tom replied, "Of course, but I get the first piece and it better be a big one. They didn't give me any cake in prison."

That evening Gretchen and Bob were sitting on the love seat, Tom and Janet on one couch and Don and Maggie on the other. The boys were sitting on bean bags on the floor. Kelly was sitting on the big easy chair with Tommy in her arms. Mary was sitting in the second easy chair and Doug was sitting on a hard chair that he brought from the dining room. Doug was looking intently at Mary. It had been a long time since the family was all together, and he felt awkward not having Mary sitting in a seat next to him. All were quiet, even the boys, when Doug spoke, "Mary, it is a delightful evening. Could we go for a nice walk?"

Doug didn't know it, of course, but Mary and Maggie had been talking about him when they were making the cake and later when they went to the kitchen for cleanup. Maggie had been telling her how much Doug seemed to enjoy the prison ministry. She also told her that Doug had seemed to change so much for the better. Mary listened to all she said and in her heart agreed. Doug had been right about wanting to keep Tommy. He had been right about so many things.

After a short pause Mary answered Doug, "Yes, Dear. It will be nice to get some of this wonderful, mountain fresh air!"

Doug was surprised. She hadn't called him that in a long time. As they walked out the door, they strolled down the path towards a nearby open field. Tom got up and stood by the doorway watching them. Soon Janet walked over to stand by him. They had their arms around each other as they watched the two walk through the soft blowing weeds that reached to their knees. After a few minutes Kelly walked over to watch as well. Suddenly, as Doug and Mary hugged each other and embraced in a kiss, in amazement to all who watched, a small flock of mourning doves burst forth from in front of them. They were so absorbed in their embrace that they did not even notice.

Tears were flowing down the cheeks of Tom, Janet and Kelly as Tom whispered, "It's a miracle! The mourning doves have returned, just as I predicted! Right Kelly-Joy?"

As she tightly grasped Tom's arm, she whispered, "You're right, Grandaddy! I never expected Little Tommy to be the one to bring my dad and mom back together. Isn't it wonderful! There is magic here in the mountains just as we suspected. And that magic is the magic that is everywhere: God's love!"

. . . . . .

It was all a delightful memory now to old Tom. The years had been good. In looking back at the amazing events that transpired during those years and the results seen today, Tom reflected on God's word from Jeremiah 29:11:

"For I know the plans I have for you," declares the Lord, *"plans to prosper you and not to harm you, plans to give you hope and a future."*

That hope and a future were not just for the born, but for the unborn as well. As his wobbly legs carried him to the Grandstand of Washington Park, he would have little to say but much to thank God for!

APPENDIX

Thomas (Tommy) Atkins – *Tom and Janet Wisp's great-grandson*

Kelly-Joy Wisp – *Tom and Janet Wisp's granddaughter*

Mary Wisp – *Tom and Janet Wisp's daughter-in-law, Doug's wife*

Gretchen Wisp – *Tom and Janet Wisp's daughter*

Don Wisp – *Tom and Janet Wisp's youngest son*

Maggie Wisp – *Don's wife*

Ronny & Joshua – *Don and Maggie's children*

Joe Turner – *A close friend of Gretchen Wisp*

Doug Wisp – *Tom and Janet's oldest son*

Bob Logan – *Cortez Abortionist*

Dr. Willis – *Abortionist that lives in Woodridge Falls*

Tim Weber – *Tommy Atkins' pastor*

Jim Willis – *Woodridge Falls abortionist*

Mr. Walker – *Kelly's bus driver*

Jimmy Silvers – *Abortion survivor*

Maggie Barns – *Protestor against abortion*

Reggie McCoy – *Handicapped boy*

Betty McCoy – *Reggie's mother*

Judge Crawford – *Reggie's Judge*

Mrs. Parks – *Reggie's case worker*

Sam Diggs – *Bailiff and Tom's friend*

Roger Miller – *Coffee shop owner*

Billy, Andy, Jack – *CSB boys*

Bob Milhorn – *Pastor of Woodridge Falls Community Church*

John Lewis – *Police captain, a Godly man*

Sergeant Hogan – *Police riot squad leader*

Aunt Milly – *Police Chief's aunt*

Alan Blantz – *Governor of CA*

Mrs. Cross – *Janet's school teacher (when she was small)*

Butch (Richard) Atkins – *class bully*

Jennifer Wilson – *freshman at Kelly's school*

Mr. Walker – *School Bus Driver*

John Cast – *County Road Crew Foreman*

Dr. Flemming – *Kelly's Physician*

Tab (Robert) West – *The baby's father*

Rick Abbott – *one of Tab's friend*

Jake Andrews – *one of Tab's friend*

Andy Baker – *one of Tab's friend*

Tony & Joan West – *Tab's parents*

Gerry Woods – *a boy from Kelly's school*

Linda Colt – *Kelly's friend*

Mona Trift – *New Life Pregnancy Center director*

John Cast – *Woodridge Falls Civil Engineer*

Major Steven Canter – *Tom Wisp's Commanding Officer*

Greg Larison – *Missionary to Viet Nam*

Chi Nguyen – *Vietnamese Officer (friend of Tom Wisp)*

Kep Nguyen – *Chi Nguyen's wife*

Kim Nguyen – *Chi Nguyen's daughter; Sukhan Chao-wen, President of Taiwan*

Chem Lee – *Vietnam Village leader and church leader*

Sal Nguyen – *Kim's cousin*

Chim Lolw – *One of Kim's friends*

Mr. Wells – *One of the board members of the Ellenbelt Foundation*

Mr. Grump – *Chairman of the Board and CEO of the Ellenbelt Foundation*

Pricilla Grump – *Mr. Grump's daughter*

Diane Langly – *School Nurse*

Principal Drake – *Kelly's school principal*

Dr. Minkins – *Tom Wisp's surgeon*

Nurse Millie – *Tom Wisp's nurse*

Mr. Mackle – *Kelly's home room teacher*

Phillip Canten – *FAM news reporter*

Bill Stant – *Bob Logan's lawyer*

Jason Hilt – *Tom's lawyer*

Jay Shannon – *Radio show host and Christian defense lawyer*

Dr. Wenton – *A friend of Bob Logan*

Mr. Wayne Jib – *Hospital Director*

Dr. Harry Swaunt – *Hospital Chief of Staff*

James Dickerson – *the federal US Attorney*

Ellen Weston – *Ontario High School Principal*

Bill Purgoe – *Mary's friend at work*

Made in United States
North Haven, CT
03 June 2023